MAINTAINING NONUNION STATUS

MAINTAINING

NONUNION STATUS

Cornelius Quinn

Thomas Hill

James L. Nichols

CBI Publishing Company, Inc.
51 Sleeper Street
Boston, Massachusetts 02210

Text Designer: Donna Miner
Compositor: Haddon Craftsmen
Cover Designer: Mary Aufmuth

Library of Congress Cataloging in Publication Data

Quinn, Cornelius.
  Maintaining nonunion status.

  1. Trade-unions—United States—Recognition.
I. Hill, Thomas (Thomas W.) II. Nichols,
James L. III. Title.
HD6490.R4Q56 658.3'153 82–1130
ISBN 0–8436–0870–5   AACR2

Printing (last digit): 9 8 7 6 5 4 3 2 1
Printed in the United States of America

CONTENTS

Chapter 13. Union Campaign from Management's Side: A Positive Approach to a Negative Problem 185

APPENDIXES

A A Guidebook for Union Organizers   231

Preface

Nonunion status doesn't come about by luck; it depends on sound management practices and good relationships among management, the organization, and the employees. Once that relationship is broken, it can be far more difficult to recoup than to have prevented it from happening in the first place.

You should be assured that your managers are aware of the importance of your present nonunion status. You also want to know that you are doing everything you can to ensure against unionization.

This guide deals with the policies, practices, and procedures that create and maintain a positive and union-free environment in your organization. We will discuss:

- Current trends in unionization efforts

- The real cost of having a union

- How company policy affects unionization

- Maintaining open lines of communication

- Increasing the effectiveness of present policies and practices

- Recognizing hidden signs of union activity

- Responding to the union organizing campaign

- Winning elections

The guide includes:

1. Current trends in unionization
   - White-collar and blue-collar workers
   - Have unions changed or have employees?

2. Why employees unionize
   - Why would your employees join a union?
   - The high cost of having a union
   - What unions can and cannot do for employees

3. The union contract
   - The costly economic and noneconomic demands
   - Promotion, layoff, seniority, and overtime
   - The grievance procedure

4. How to use proven practices, policies, and procedures to stay nonunion
   - Establishing sound employee policies
   - Motivating employees toward organization objectives
   - Developing employee understanding
   - The role of the first-line supervisor
   - Using constructive versus destructive discipline
   - Controlling absenteeism and turnover

5. Current legal issues and labor practices
   - Knowing the legal do's and don'ts

- Avoiding unfair labor practices
- Keeping supervisors informed

6. What to do during a union campaign
   - What you can do, must do, and cannot do
   - Your rights and obligations as management
   - Using a Management Action Program
   - Specific steps to take

7. Effective day-to-day operations to stay nonunion

ACKNOWLEDGMENTS

This book is the result of the authors' day-to-day experiences in labor relations over the past twenty years. We would like to thank our many client companies for providing the knowledge on which this book is based. We would particularly like to express our gratitude to Russ Ikerd and the *Detroit News* for their permission to reprint "The Union Diary." Also to Robert Bales, Vice-President of Personnel, Coors Container Company, for his help on the Grievance Procedure chapter. Finally, to Professor Dean Baker, School of Journalism, University of Michigan, who was instrumental in the preparation and editing of this book.

PART ONE

WORKERS, UNIONS, and MANAGEMENT

Chapter One

Introduction

If you have opened this book expecting us to tell you why unions are bad, evil, and out to destroy America—forget it! And if you expected us to discuss how to make your people feel they don't need a union because you love them so much (spell that P-A-T-E-R-N-A-L-I-S-M), you won't find *that* approach in this book. We are not going to talk about the "good guys" and the "bad guys" either. That's a discussion about people, and while we're certainly not ignoring people in this book, we want to start by examining *organizations* and what they do or don't do for people. Unions, of course, are organizations. Before we can look at the necessary steps in maintaining a union-free operation, we have to understand unions *as* organizations.

GOALS OF UNIONS

To understand whether any organization is good or bad, it is necessary to look at its goals—what it offers its members and potential members. *Unions have two primary goals:*

1. *More Money.* Isn't this goal left-wing, radical, socialist, pinko, un-American? Or is the goal of more money all that bad? Do you personally feel you are overpaid? If you were offered a $3000 increase, or if the president of your company said, "I want to give you a raise in appreciation of your contribution to our company," would you turn it down? The union's first goal of more money is a good goal. Are unions therefore *good?*

2. *Job Security.* Unions protect older employees from unfair and arbitrary treatment. Therefore aren't unions *good?*

To see what this second goal means, let's look at the case of Al Palmer. Al was a nursing assistant in a large hospital where he went to work in 1946 after receiving medical training in the army. Seventeen years later, he was a permanent employee in the third-floor surgical department, where he gave general nursing care to postsurgical patients. He also accompanied doctors on their rounds, changed dressings, took blood pressures, kept his own charts, and became a well-respected member of the nursing staff.

A new floor supervisor, Sister Mary, took an instant dislike to Al. She contended that he was not an R.N. and how dare he go on rounds with doctors, take blood pressures, and sign charts! Sister Mary took away Al's responsibilities and reassigned him to cleaning up the kitchen, making beds, administering enemas, and other menial tasks. Al's requests for an explanation were ignored. Finally, when Al felt there was no other choice, he quit—losing not only his job, but his pension as well. Seventeen years of Al's life went down the drain—and why? Because he had no one to represent him, no power—and Sister Mary didn't even realize that she had taken anything away from him.

Let's take a look at another aspect of job security. An automotive supplier in Michigan employing 200 workers was faced with a severe layoff when car sales dropped in a recession. The manager of manufacturing called the supervisors together and told them to prepare layoff lists for their departments and shifts. The general guideline he gave them was to respect seniority, but to retain employees who were qualified.

In the assembly area, 48 employees were laid off, based on LIFO (last-in, first-out). However, in the shipping department, the supervisor laid off two employees with three years of service, but kept one employee with six month's seniority "because he's so sharp, knows the parts numbers by heart, and is terrific at paper work" (which made it easier for the supervisor to do *his* work).

In the wire department, ten people were released, five on seniority and five because "it's a good time to get rid of the deadwood." One of the women with low seniority was kept on. She was dating the maintenance foreman. The maintenance foreman had mentioned to the general foreman that he hoped Sally would not be laid off because her ex-husband wasn't paying any support, and she really needed the job.

That is not only unfair treatment, but favoritism. Unions protect employees from unfair treatment and favoritism. Therefore, aren't unions *good?*

What do all employed people want today? They want to participate in decisions that affect their working lives:

- Health and safety

- Equal pay

- Environment

- Opportunity for advancement

- Training

- Fair evaluation

- Quick resolution of disputes

Unions *force* a company to meet the basic job security needs of all workers—*plus* more money. It's important to understand that unions have a *good product* to sell and do a good job of selling. Unions have won approximately 50 percent of the elections conducted by the National Labor Relations Board (NLRB). Any company would like to have a record of closing a sale with every other potential customer.

We've examined the two fundamental union goals, and they are good goals. They are not only union goals, however, they are *people goals.* Our point is that organizations end up with unions if they are insensitive to legitimate concerns of *people.* Unions are *caused*—caused by issues that will be discussed in this book.

GOALS OF MANAGEMENT

We've established the goals of the union; let's look at the goals of management. What is the purpose of your organization? The answer is: *to be successful.* Specifically, management has two goals:

1. *Quality Product/Service.*   Management becomes successful by making a quality product or providing a quality service, *on time.* Your customers would like to receive products or services as scheduled.

2. *Lowest Cost.*   Management's goal is to operate at the lowest possible cost. By lowest cost we do not mean the lowest wages and fringes management can get away with. Companies with low wages and poor benefits have high turnover and untrained workers. Paying competitive wages and providing competitive benefits to attract and keep good employees are in the long-range interest of any organization. By lowest cost, we mean efficiency—not having two people on a one-man machine, reducing excessive overtime, and not having workers say, "I don't have to do that; it's not in my job description."

RESOLVING THE CONFLICT OF GOALS

As the union reaches its goal of more money for less work—more holidays, longer vactions, more wash-up time, longer coffee breaks, and so on—company costs go up. As the union reaches its goal of job security —promotions based on seniority, grievances filed over discipline, arbitrators reinstating terminated people—quality and quantity of products and services go down. Note the basic conflicts between goals as depicted in

Figure 1-1. In this book, we describe ways to recognize these potential conflicts and methods to deal with them before they get out of hand.

UNION GOALS

More Money
Less Work
More Benefits
More Grievances

COMPANY GOALS

Quality
Quantity
Efficiently
Profit

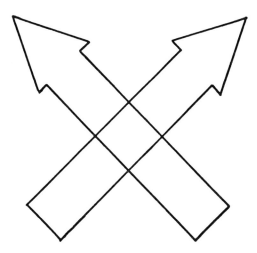

Unions didn't invent the goals of fair pay, good benefits, or job security. Unions were formed because companies didn't meet the legitimate needs of people voluntarily. People then turned to the unions out of frustration.

We were asked once in a seminar: "What does a union say to people when trying to get them to join? How does a union get people interested?" Ninety percent of the time, the union doesn't find the employees; the employees seek out the union. In the first meetings, the union organizer says very little. He does what management has failed to do: *listen.* When he does react, he has two ready phrases, no matter what issues employees raise.

EMPLOYEE: We haven't had a raise in eighteen months.

ORGANIZER: Oh, my God!

EMPLOYEE: We got a raise, but the company said they had to follow the presidential guidelines, even though other companies ignore them.

ORGANIZER: Oh, my God!

EMPLOYEE: We haven't had an increase in vacations in four years.

ORGANIZER: Oh, my God!

EMPLOYEE: They used to provide us with free coffee, but one of the beancounters said coffee is too expensive and they took away the coffee.

ORGANIZER: They didn't!

EMPLOYEE: We used to be able to take our vacations the last two weeks in December, but somebody said that wasn't efficient, and they took it away.

ORGANIZER: They didn't!

If the issue raised particularly frustrates employees, the two phrases are combined:

EMPLOYEE: The new plant manager announced that this year the traditional Christmas turkey is out.

ORGANIZER: Oh, my God! He didn't!

Understanding why employees sometimes feel compelled to turn to a union instead of bringing their problems to management is an important first step toward keeping unions out of an organization. Our goals in this book are relatively simple. We want to help identify what people want and need from work, and how management can provide it voluntarily. More importantly, how to communicate to workers what has been done and why. If the union arrives on the scene claiming, "We will get *this* for you; we will get *that* for you," employees can legitimately respond, "We already have that, and we don't even have to pay dues."

Chapter Two

The Changing Union, The Changing Worker

Historically, a basic conflict developed between unions and management that can be described as the "United Kingdom Trade Union Relationship." From union beginnings in the United Kingdom and the United States, the concept has been: "Us versus Them." This approach has been nurtured by the behavior of both unions and management for so long that the concept is largely unquestioned.

However, many organizations are striving to develop a Japanese or Scandinavian labor relations philosophy of cooperation between labor and management. Although this is an excellent goal, we are not convinced it will work in America for two reasons:

1. The long "Us versus Them" pattern

2. The dramatic rise in costs for management when the union reaches its goal of more money for less work.

Changes in business, for example, mergers and business closings, and changes in unions (mergers and decline in memberships), have largely been due to the inability of management and unions to resolve conflict equitably. There has been a dramatic drop in union membership in the percentage of work force organized. The United Mine Workers, a classic example, had over a million and a half members in 1945, but today has fewer than 400,000 as a result of automation, movement of companies to the union-free mines in the West, and the development of alternate energy sources.

Many industries have had to automate to meet foreign competition. The automotive, steel, machine-tool, and electronic industries, all heavily unionized, have been unable to move as rapidly as necessary because of restrictive union contracts. As a result, entire plants have been closed permanently. Industries are being tested on whether inherent conflict between unions and management in North America can be resolved successfully. Unfortunately, the success rate has been low.

The first contracts provided for orderly resolution of grievances, just cause for discipline and layoff, and recall and promotion provisions based on seniority. However, in following contracts, restrictive and often nonproductive provisions are added, for example, crew sizes, exhaustive bumping, retraining, tight jurisdictional lines on work to be performed, and long and often unnecessary tasks in apprentice trades. These restrictions often make unionized plants noncompetitive, and operations are moved to the less-unionized South in the United States or foreign competition forces American companies out of business.

THE CHANGING UNION IMAGE

The trade union movement has seen the percentage of membership in the work force drop over 15 percent in the last thirty years. There has been ample reason for change—and for changing the union image. Many people have a mental image of a union organizer as a six-foot-two, overweight guy with a sloping forehead, wearing a shiny suit, and saying "dese," "dem," and "dose." He's a basic Cro-Magnon man (and if he's wearing white socks, he's obviously a Teamster). Forget that image. The new generation of trade union leaders are often college graduates with extensive research departments at their disposal. Unions are also hiring minorities and females as full-time organizers. The days when the leaders threw union literature out of Lincoln Continentals or Cadillacs are gone.

Perhaps the best example of new organizing efforts is the case of North and South Carolina, the least unionized states, with less than 5 percent of the potential members organized. In an eighteen-month period at the end of the 1970s, the Teamsters won over twenty elections, including some in large organizations, such as the Miller Brewery and PPG. Their organizational drives were directed and conducted by a union organizer typical of the new wave—a young woman from New York with an undergraduate degree from the Cornell School of Labor and Industrial Relations and an MBA from the London School of Economics. This organizer has been able to identify with and organize three groups: young workers, women, and blacks.

The American Federation of State, County, and Municipal Employees (AFSCME) is sponsoring very effective television commercials: "The union that works for you." The United Food and Commercial Workers, a merger of the Retail Clerks Union and the Meat Cutters, is doing an excellent job of image-building by sponsoring athletic events and presenting a television series on John F. Kennedy's *Profiles in Courage.*

The union flyers depicted are examples of literature used today to hit issues important to workers. Figure 2-1 zeros in on inflation. Figures 2-2 and 2-3 are aimed at two crucial aspects of job security: merit pay plans and disciplinary procedures. (We will discuss pay and disciplinary policies in detail in later chapters).

Mergers are taking place in the trade union movement as rapidly as they are in industry, and for the same reason: efficient use of capital. Numbers mean more money, and money means power. The merger of District 50 of the Mineworkers with the Steelworkers; of the Lithographers, Pressmen, and Bookbinders into the Graphic Arts International Union; and the talks going on in the electrical industry to merge the IBEW, the IUE, and the UE are a few examples. We project a continuing merger of unions in the 1980s. Perhaps by the end of this decade, only thirty international unions will be functioning in the United States, down from over 150.

The change in leadership is strikingly illustrated by the succession of Lane Kirkland to the post of president of the AFL-CIO, held so long by the late George Meany. Meany, who made immense contributions to unionized workers, viewed gaining additional wages and benefits for his members as the primary union function. Meany did not greatly concern himself with organizing. Kirkland sees the major thrust as organizing the unorganized, with increased funding of the Industrial Union Department (IUD), the

Figure 2-1

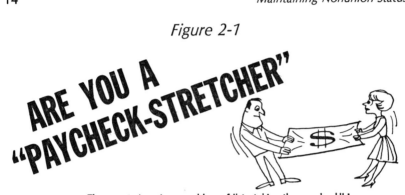

The great American problem of "stretching the paycheck" is known to nearly every wage and salary earner—especially if they don't yet receive <u>union</u> wages and salaries.

Union paychecks stretch farther because they are bigger—<u>actual</u> <u>statistics</u> <u>prove</u> <u>it</u>!

Look at your paycheck—then look at your needs, today <u>and</u> <u>for</u> <u>the</u> <u>future</u>! If more money today and for your future needs, concerns you enough to <u>do something about it</u>—then <u>unionism</u> is <u>your</u> <u>answer</u>.

OD A-32

Figure 2-2

How do you Rate yourself?

	SUPERIOR	SATISFACTORY	UNSATISFACTORY
QUALITY OF WORK	✓		
QUANTITY OF WORK		✓	
JOB KNOWLEDGE	✓		
RESOURCEFULNESS	✓		
VERSATILITY		✓	
DEPENDABILITY	✓		
ATTITUDE	✓		
PROMOTIONS	?	?	?
WAGE INCREASES	?	?	?

Does the boss agree?

The only chance you will ever have to rate yourself and make it count is with a union contract. Without a union contract, when the boss disagrees–that's it brother, you've had it.

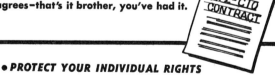

- **PROTECT YOUR INDIVIDUAL RIGHTS**
- **IMPROVE YOUR STATUS**

THROUGH COLLECTIVE BARGAINING

O.D. A-35

Figure 2-3

organizing arm of the AFL-CIO. The United Auto Workers and the Teamsters likewise have beefed up organizing staffs. AFSCME, the most rapidly growing of American unions—1000 new members a week for the past fifteen years—for the first time will be organizing nonpublic employees, primarily in banking and insurance, where unions have had little success.

The UAW, Teamsters, and Steelworkers are also organizing white-collar employees.

What do these dramatic changes in unions mean to American management? Simply that continuing the tactics of the past forty years will not keep out unions. The progressive company today must run on a pro-employee, pro-company record, and not on an anti-union attack. Whether companies will have a union representing their employees or will continue a union-free status depends on their records. We have only to look at the records of union-free companies like IBM, Eastman Kodak, and Standard Oil of Kentucky to understand that providing fair compensation and fair fringe benefits and job security on a voluntary basis is the "secret."

THE CHANGING WORKER

One reason for the union's new approach in organizing is the changing worker. As the workers' view of themselves changes, their view of what the job must provide has also changed.

The educational system has radically changed in the last thirty years. Older workers learned the multiplication tables by rote and repetitive exercises. Miss Grundy, in the third grade, stood at the blackboard and went, "Whack, whack, whack." The class in unison responded with, "2 $\times$ 2 is 4, 2 $\times$ 3 is 6, 2 $\times$ 4 is 8," and they never forgot that 7 $\times$ 8 is 56. Teachers we've talked to in the past ten years tell us that their major competition is television. Today students are not required to learn by drill; the television generation refuses to participate in repetitive exercises. Kids today declare that school is boring. They won't spend two or three hours trying to memorize a passage from Shakespeare, the Declaration of Independence, or the Gettysburg Address. Those of you who deal with younger workers often hear: "This job is boring. This job is dull. Why do we have to do this?" Television, besides offering passive entertainment, without requiring much taxing of the viewer's brain, also raises expectations—especially among the young. Television viewers receive entertainment with fore-and-aft commercials that urge everyone to live the good life and be happy by buying products that will make hair soft, armpits sweet, teeth white, and everything smelling lemon-fresh. The marketing people have just done too good a job—everybody wants to live that good life, particularly the younger worker. When does he want a car, a house, nice vacations, good times? *Now.* Many supervisors know all too well that young employees want better paying jobs, but don't want to learn the necessary skills to get those jobs.

Another basic change that management must learn to deal with is women in the work force. Formerly, a majority of women workers felt they were working on a temporary basis, earning money to pay off bills, get a down payment on a house, or to put Billy through college. Today, the vast majority of women workers expect to remain in the work force permanently, as attested in studies by the University of Michigan's Institute for Social Research. Their statistical data indicate that as recently as 1968, less than 50 percent of women workers viewed themselves as in the work force on a permanent basis. By 1978, those statistics had changed dramatically; a large majority of the women in the work force stated: "I shall be working on a permanent basis all of my adult life, even if I am going to drop out for several years to have children or to raise a family."

RECOMMENDATION TO MANAGEMENT

This change poses a number of new problems for management. Women are legally guaranteed equal pay for equal work and equal opportunities, but this does not give job security. What is the greatest job security anybody can have? The greatest security that workers can have is a skill that is readily saleable in the marketplace, and women are demanding training to qualify for skilled positions which in many companies have been men's jobs.

Historically, companies that employed 70 percent or more females had little or no problem with unions. It was particularly difficult for unions to run successful organizing drives in such companies. However, with the vast majority of women workers today working on a permanent basis, those factors that appeal to male workers—job security and opportunity to improve technical skills—will become of primary importance to women. Failure of management to respond will make the situation ripe for union activity. Many supervisors believe the myth that women can't master skills necessary to perform craft jobs, that the work is physically too hard or too complicated, or that women don't care for or want certain jobs. Remember Rosie the Riveter during World War II? Women, in fact, were successfully performing all types of jobs—from building ships to driving dynamite trucks to flying airplanes.

Management must respond by opening up not only jobs in low-level supervision, but also career opportunities that result in women rising to senior positions in management. We don't suggest that all women want to be toolmakers or electricians or pipefitters, or that all supervisors or managers should be women. We recommend that companies establish a policy that spells out procedures to promote opportunities for better paying, more skilled jobs for women, and that supervisors will promote and implement the policies. Resistance by supervisors to promotion of women is a luxury that management simply cannot afford in the 1980s.

In conclusion, workers know what they want from their organizations. Management must deal with workers on the basis of facts rather than myths. Progressive companies *communicate* to their employees their status in regard to pay and benefits. In addition, the company makes a commitment to meet the total job security of the workers. Management must develop a credible record to run on if they are to win a union election.

Chapter Three

Management: Union Contract or Union-Free

Supervisors in union-free companies sometimes think a union would not affect day-to-day operations or one-to-one dealings with employees. In our experience, the most emotional distress in a union shop is not suffered by senior or middle management, but by first-line supervisors who must interact with union officers and stewards, day to day, hour by hour. Too many times, supervisors in union-free companies feel that if a union organized the company and achieved economic gains for employees, supervisors would also benefit. Supervisors either say it's a battle between senior management and the employees and they are neutral, or sometimes actively encourage employees to vote for a union.

Supervisors who feel this way dramatically increase the union's odds for success in an election. Supervisors need to know what they'll be up against if they supervise a union shop. In this chapter, we want to give supervisors a feel for what happens day to day, once the labor agreement is signed.

PROMOTION

The language included in the contract on promotion will be similar to the following:

> In the event there is a job opening, the company will post all open jobs for a minimum of five days. Employees eligible to bid and interested in a position will sign the job bid sheet. Openings will be filled on the following basis:
>
> 1.   Qualifications
> 2.   Ability
> 3.   Education
> 4.   Performance
>
> Where the above factors are equal, seniority will be the determining factor.

Supervisors must administer the labor contract, and are forced to make a number of decisions daily. One basic decision is who is going to be promoted. When an opening arises and two employees bid, the supervisor has to administer the contract—and cannot add to or delete any of the agreed language. The following case illustrates the problems of supervisors.

Bill Smith has been with the company three years. His record as a material handler has been excellent. Bill is cooperative, energetic, and always willing to try new means and methods. He has also worked as a replacement in other areas. He's attending community college at night, taking classes in mechanics, shop math, and other job-related courses. His current supervisor says Bill is an outstanding employee, and he'll be happy to recommend Bill for promotion.

Fred "Eight-Ball" Jones has been around the company eight years— literally. He's been in four different departments; the longest any supervisor could tolerate him is about two years. Eight-Ball, so-called by everybody because of his eight-year record, has been a material handler and a driver, and he worked the second shift where he had problems staying awake. Eight-Ball has an average-or-below work performance and a what-are-you-going-to-do-for-me-next attitude. He's also crazy about motorcy·cles. Weekends, he's at the dirt bike races, and he's generally operating at the plant at about half-speed on Mondays. He also loves duck hunting and bowling. For the former, he takes six or seven days off in October, and for the latter he always devotes Thursday nights. Friday's are, unfortunately, also not one of Eight-Ball's better days. When he's in, usually a little bit hung over, he manages to recover by the time he receives his paycheck. Eight-Ball is also interested in a college education; he is going to community college at night, and he's majoring in taxidermy.

You, as supervisor, have to interview Mr. Jones to find out whether or not he is eligible under the terms of the union contract for a trial period. The conversation between Eight-Ball *(8-B)* and the supervisor *(S)* will go something like this:

8-B: Hello there, Bill. What the hell is happening today? I see you got an opening.

S: That's right, Fred. We have an opening here for a set-up operator.

8-B: Yeah. I see that set-up job. Well, I'll tell ya. That's what I always wanted to do.

S: It is?

8-B: Oh yeah. I been here eight years and I've been in four departments. I've been a material handler and a fork-lift driver. One time I ran production. Didn't come out the best in the world there because the foreman didn't like me. But set-up I know I can handle.

S: Well Fred, that's interesting. In this job, we need dedicated people who can work well with other people because you're going to be setting up equipment for three to five machines and working with six or seven different people.

8-B; I'm glad you said that because if there's one thing I can do it's get along with other people. For example, I bowl two nights a week, and I'm captain on both bowling teams. They really like me. And the guys in the department, they really like me. My foreman told me that anything he can do to help me get over here to work as a set-up operator, he'll be glad to do.

S: Oh. You mean your supervisor would recommend you to this department?

8-B: He said any recommendation he could give me to get in another department, he'd be glad to.

S: I see. Does that mean you're not going to have any openings there?

8-B: I don't know. You'd have to talk to him.

S: Well, I would like to look at your total record. You've been here eight years. You mentioned bowling quite a bit, and I notice that the day after bowling your attendance is not too good and that you've made a number of errors around those times.

8-B: That's been totally blown out of proportion. Occasionally, after bowling when I get a good series, I stop with the guys for a few beers and once in a while when I'm here the next day, I don't feel the best in the world, but I'm generally here and do a good job.

S: Well, I notice that Mondays are not your best days either.

8-B: Well, Mondays . . . I have this motorcycle that I race on weekends. Occasionally I fall off and once in a while on Mondays I have a few aches and pains, but generally I'm okay on Mondays.

S: Well, this set-up job means it's absolutely essential that you be here every single day to set-up for the other people.

8-B: I'm here all the time just about except in the fall. I save my sick days for the fall. I do a lot of duck hunting.

S: I notice that your attendance in the fall is not too good either.

8-B: Well, when I go duck hunting, it's no fun to go just Saturday and Sunday, so I save my sick days and vacation days and go out on Monday. Duck hunting—that's my number one hobby.

S: Well, I notice one of the other people who's bid on the job is going to community college, taking classes that are job-related.

8-B: That's interesting you mention it, because I'm going to community college. I'm taking taxidermy.

S: Taxidermy isn't too job-related, Fred. You see, what we're looking for here is someone who can demonstrate by his qualifications and performance that he's really going to do a good job in set-up, and I'm just not sure that you're going to be able to handle this.

8-B: I'm sure I can.

S: Well, Fred, I'm afraid we're going to have to give the job to Bill Smith, based on his previous experience and record here.

8-B: Smith's only been here three years. I've been here eight years. That ain't fair.

S: Well Fred, there's nothing that guarantees you a job here, and particularly a promotion. We have to look at all the candidates and determine who's going to be the best one.

8-B: We've got a union here **now**, Bill. You can't get by with that stuff. I'm gonna see my **union** steward.

S: Well, if you feel that it's necessary, we could have your steward come.

8-B: Fine. He'll be in to see you in the next five minutes.

Eight-Ball tells his union steward his side of the story: he's been denied a promotion though he has eight year's seniority, and the supervisor has decided to give the job to "a more qualified" junior employee with three years of service. The union steward *(U.S.)* responds, "Oh, my God!" and now protects the worker's "rights" that the supervisor (S) has violated.

U.S.: Hello, Bill. I understand you've made another mistake.

S: Well, I certainly wouldn't say that.

U.S.:   I just saw Eight-Ball and he said he bid on a job. He's got eight years of service and you've decided to give it to an employee with three.

S: Yes, that's correct. We looked at the qualifications of both Eight-Ball Jones and Bill Smith. And, Bill Smith, even though he's been here three years, has a better record and he's better qualified. He can do a better job.

U.S.:   Let's deal with the facts. We have a labor contract. Let's look at what your company signed, because you're not going to add to the contract. That's not your job, is it?

S: No. I have no desire to add to the contract. But it is my job to interpret the contract.

U.S.:   Fine. Let's look at the facts. The contract calls for seniority. Who wins on seniority?

S: No. The contract does not call for seniority. The contract calls for someone to be qualified.

U.S.:   But you do see the word "seniority" in the contract?

S: Well, yes, but only after all other factors.

U.S.:   Well, let's look at the factors. The contract says qualifications and abilities. What's the difference between qualifications and ability?

S: What do you mean, the difference?

U.S.:   I don't know. That's your job.

S: Well, qualifications obviously relate to whether or not the person can perform the job in a quality manner.

U.S.:   I don't understand that.

S: Well, that means can he perform the job to an excellent degree.

U.S.:   Isn't that ability?

S: No. Ability is different. While there isn't a whole lot of difference between qualifications and ability, they both relate to how well an employee is going to do on a job. And that's *my* judgment. I have the right to judge who has the qualifications or ability.

U.S.:   Your opinion and 35¢ will get you on a bus in Philadelphia. You must be able to prove, not project the future. You're not a mind reader.

S: I never said I was!

U.S.:   I've made a note that you don't know the difference between qualifications and ability. Let's move on to performance. What does that mean?

S: Performance means whether he can perform the job.

U.S.:   You're not going to be able to figure that out unless you give him a trial period, are you?

S: I can determine based on what they've done in the past. A man has to run on his record, doesn't he?

U.S.:   Performance means what he's going to do in the future, not what he's done in the past.

S: No. Performance means what he is currently doing.

U.S.:   No. That's past performance. If that's what the company meant to say, they would have said past performance in the contract. Performance means what's going to happen in the future. They both have the education. Isn't that right?

S: Well, Bill Smith's education is related to the job. Eight-Ball's is related to duck hunting.

U.S.:   The contract doesn't say related to the job. You're trying to add to the contract again.

S: I don't think so.

U.S.: We're not interested in what you think. We're interested in what the contract says. The last thing in the contract is seniority. Eight-Ball does have eight years. Bill Smith has got three years. You can't understand that?

S: Well, Eight-Ball does have eight years. There's no question about it.

U.S.: Let me summarize your position on this job. You admit you don't know the difference between qualifications and abilities. You're confused about performance. You're talking about past performance, when it's performance now. Education. You're talking about something being job-related which is adding to the contract, and you admit Eight-Ball wins on seniority. You're in a lot of trouble.

S: Well, I don't think Eight-Ball can do as good a job and I'll bet you don't think so either. If you were me, you wouldn't give him the job.

U.S.: I'm not you. I'm here to protect my workers. Let's give him a thirty-day trial period or I'm going to file a grievance.

S: Well, well, I'm not sure . . .

U.S.: How about a fourteen-day trial period?

S: Well, I guess I don't have any choice. But I'm going to keep my eye on Eight-Ball during his trial period.

U.S.: I also want you to know that I'm going to be checking on him daily to make sure he's getting the proper training and you're not out to hang him.

S: That's okay with me.

U.S.: I also want you to know this. I've got nine more grievances that I haven't filed in your department, and I'll have my eye on you.

The preceding dialogue exemplifies one of the most critical aspects of the supervisory-union relationship in a union shop. The supervisor tried to exercise proper supervisory and managerial judgment, but the union saw only the bypassing of a senior employee for a junior employee. The goals of the union and the supervisor clash head on in such instances. The union aims to protect all workers, including the most marginal; the supervisor tries to run his department efficiently and productively. Such day-to-day conflicts face supervisors wherever there's a union. And as for that fourteen-day trial period, employees like Eight-Ball show up on time every day, bound through the job with enthusiasm, and try to meet requirements. Starting with the fifteenth day, with the job sewed up permanently, they fall back into the late-show, early-leave, goof-off patterns. The supervisor tries to deal with marginal employees—and the union is right back in his office, alleging abuse and discrimination.

Advice to Union-Free Management

Management places itself in the position of promoting marginal employees by failure to move early and rapidly to terminate them. Marginal employees in union-free shops, particularly on one-step, line-of-progression jobs, are often disqualified because they have not been satisfactory workers, not because of lack of ability, qualifications, or education. Management should not deny people wage increases as discipline.

RESTRICTIONS IN LABOR CONTRACTS

Management—supervisors particularly—face some restrictions under a union contract.

Layoff and Recall

> The company recognizes that in the event of a reduction in work force, seniority shall be the determining factor, providing the employee is qualified to perform the job to which he bids after a reasonable break-in period.

Any progressive company would recognize security rights in reducing force, if employees can perform without productivity loss and in a reasonable period. In many union shops, employees do not replace the least senior worker in the classification to which they're bumping; they replace senior employees in the classification, triggering a series of bumps throughout the operation. Union-free companies *should* have a policy guaranteeing seniority as the determining factor in layoffs, by classification or job group rather than by a plant-wide seniority, particularly for short-term or temporary layoffs.

Job Assignments

> Employees shall not be required to work outside of their primary job classifications without their permission on short-term assignments.

This single sentence, common in many labor contracts, can cause much grief for a supervisor, day by day. If there is no work for employees to do in union-free shops, the supervisor assigns other available work. Unions have a problem with flexibility. "One man, one job" is the union's position. Unions can build walls around job classifications. Supervisors are likely to be told by employees: "It's not in my job description. I don't have to do that work if I don't want to." This drastically reduces supervisors' flexibility to move people when work schedules, job orders, production problems, and equipment breakdowns necessitate.

Limits on the flexibility of management to assign work are one of the largest hidden costs of unionization. When a contract states that working outside an employee's department constitutes reassignment, the issue gets further complicated. One of the worst examples of loss of flexibility in assigning work is the unionized construction industry. In the past few years union-free contractors did more than half the construction work in the United States. Many union-free contractors are paying union scale and union fringes, and sometimes above scale. The union-free contractor has the flexibility to work people across job jurisdictional lines. For example, it's not necessary to have an operating engineer to start a three-horse motor five times a day.

We encountered another example in a hospital where the Steelworkers represented employees. The contract not only stipulated that employees would not be assigned work outside their own job descriptions, but also that working outside of one's department constituted a transfer. The contract language was originally applied to a 6000-person steel mill, with 600 or 700 people in a single department. In a hospital, a department may be as small as two or three people, and it is not uncommon to move an orderly from a patient-care floor to the emergency room to help with victims of an automobile accident, or because of an absent employee. Under the terms of this contract, the hospital was not allowed to move people from one work location to another without prior notice and the employee's permission. Frequently an employee would refuse to help out in another area of the hospital, reducing efficiency and creating health hazards. Any organization that has committed itself by contract to the "one man, one job" concept will require additional workers, creating higher costs for the organization.

Rights of Union Officers: Super Seniority

Most union contracts include a section granting union officers and stewards number one seniority in such areas as layoffs, recall, job bids, shift preferences, and vacations. Many times, the company must call in a union steward to "guarantee the rights of the workers" if any overtime is worked.

Voluntary Overtime

More and more, union contracts provide that employees have the right to refuse to work overtime. Voluntary overtime is a sensitive issue in union-free shops. A policy on overtime should be clearly spelled out. We will discuss overtime policy in a later chapter.

Supervisors Working

All bargaining unit work must be performed by members of the bargaining unit.

Sometimes subtitled "A Training Program for Supervisors," this article gives the union clout in whipping supervisors into line. Unions don't really care whether the supervisor helps occasionally and pitches in because of shortage of help, and this doesn't really bother the average employee. Many times, employees appreciate a little bit of help from the supervisor. The union doesn't generally jump up and down when a supervisor works. *But,* if the supervisor has been enforcing such rules as no-smoking or leaving the work area, or for some other reason has gotten the union down on him—as in the promotion case cited earlier—the union will use this contract language to harass the supervisor. Every time the supervisor picks up a piece of tubing, he's doing material handler's work; or one portion of a subassembly, and he's doing inspection work; or if he moves a lift truck, the union says he's doing bargaining unit work. The supervisor's job becomes more and more complicated, and to buy peace, he surrenders some of *his* rights and goes along with the union.

Subcontracting

> There will be no subcontracting without prior notice to the union, and there will be no subcontracting without the approval of the union while members are on layoff.

Whether the company should "make or buy" a product or portion of the product is the guts of managerial decision making. Under a contract providing for union control over the decision, the union is usually very tough about allowing any subcontracting.

Joint Committees

Union-management committees of some type are included in most labor contracts—joint committees on facilities, health, welfare, recreation—and most common of all, the joint committee on safety.

Abuse of the safety committee function is frequent. For example, in a union-organized tool repair business, a second-shift union steward with a drinking problem had a habit of leaving work for lunch about 8:30 at night and extending his "lunch" until near quitting time. The company documented the case, issued warnings, and suspended the steward twice, and when nothing worked, finally fired him.

The union was not in a position to file a grievance, for the company had taken all the right actions, and the union knew they couldn't win in arbitration. A month after the steward was terminated, the union filed forty-four safety violations, threatened to bring in OSHA, and threatened to call a safety strike, legal under this contract. The union was adamant in the position that terrible conditions and numerous safety violations that could cause serious physical injuries and in some cases threaten workers' lives existed.

The company met with the union to see if the complaints could be resolved. Finally, a remark was dropped in the corridor that a resolution probably could be found if only good old Harry were somehow reemployed. The general manager, who had a huge backlog of work—the union was well aware of this—said: "I can't take a strike. We've got a lot of work orders." He knew taking Harry back would mean that Harry would not only behave as he had, but that it was likely to be worse. But the general manager said: "Well, there's no way that I can go to my customers and tell them that I can't repair their equipment and get it back in the time I promised. If it means that we've got to bring Harry back, then I guess we'll bring him back."

At a meeting with the union, the company stated that the discharge of the second-shift steward had been rescinded, and he was on the job again. The safety problems quickly disappeared. This is clearly a case where the union used alleged safety grievances as a way to protect one of its own.

HIDDEN COST OF UNIONS

The typical articles in a union contract that we've described are referred to as "noneconomic articles." However, they represent a direct financial cost to the company, demonstrated in the following conservative estimate of the cost of a union's noneconomic demands.

1. Office, department, or plant of 300 employees.

2. Average wage: $200.00 per week or $5.00 per hour.

3.   Time span: two-year contract.

Two contract negotiations:

240 hrs. × 3 union stewards = 720 hrs. × $5.00 =	$3,600.00
720 hrs. lost in direct labor × $5.00 =	$3,600.00
Time lost in grievance procedure:	
6 stewards half time = 6180 hrs. × $5.00 =	30,900.00
Direct labor hours lost	30,900.00
Arbitration cost (8 × $900.00)	7,200.00
Management time (total) 3 full time	45,000.00
Estimated lost productivity due to transfers, promotion, retraining and grievance procedures:	
10% efficiency loss	300,000.00
TOTAL	$421,200.00

   This is a *conservative estimate* of the costs of noneconomic articles. Three union people negotiating for 240 hours is really not exorbitant. Many times, union committees are larger, and negotiations take excessive amounts of time. Negotiations taking five weeks for a cost of $3600 and six stewards—or one for every fifty workers—is minimal. To have four arbitration cases a year over a two-year period with a new contract is low —and you can't arbitrate today for $900, not including management time involved and the preparation and presentation of the case. Three full-time management labor relations people for a unionized plant of 300 workers is normal.

   The major cost lies in the estimate's last item, which is unfortunately reflected in the bottom line of the Profit and Loss Statement. Ten percent lost productivity is relatively conservative, considering the number of companies who claim that inefficiency due to the labor contract, particularly on job assignments, is running 20 to 30 percent.

   A figure not included in the estimate that should be considered is the amount of supervisory time in a typical union shop that is spent directly dealing with the union. It's time over and above time spent in daily contact with employees in a union-free shop. Approximately two hours per day of a supervisor's time is spent directly on nonproductive union problems: investigating grievances, checking with personnel, checking with the general foreman, checking with industrial relations before giving answers, building a case, investigating and documenting disciplinary problems, meeting with management before meeting with the union, and meetings with stewards.

Our goal is to demonstrate to first-line supervisors the critical issue of dealing with the union on a day-to-day, repetitive basis. To convince supervisors of the necessity of maintaining a union-free status, the easiest way we can think of would be to let them supervise in one of the Detroit automotive plants for six weeks. The problems of supervisors—the hassles, the discipline and performance issues—would shake up the average union-free supervisor so much that they would no longer have to be motivated to treat their employees fairly and sensitively to avoid unionization.

Unions are caused by management's failure in one of two areas: company policies that are outdated, unfair, discriminatory, or simply are not communicated, and second, supervisors who play favorites with employees under their jurisdiction. Let us begin with a discussion of policies.

PART TWO

COMPANY POLICY

Chapter Four

Wages

If an organization wants to remain union-free, management must design policies, practices, and procedures to satisfy employees' needs: fair treatment, economic well-being, and job security. Management of union-free operations all too often design "Catch-22" policies.

AUTOMATIC VERSUS MERIT PAY PROGRESSION

The first, and perhaps the most basic, decision that a union-free operation must make concerns wages, how to pay people. Fundamentally the two ways of paying workers, whether they are hourly, exempt, nonexempt, supervisory, managerial, or technical, are merit pay or automatic progression. The majority of union-free organizations pay on the merit system; the overwhelming majority of unionized companies pay workers covered by labor agreements by automatic progression.

Under either system, management must first determine the value of one job to another, for example, the highest hourly rated job might be experimental tool and die maker, while janitors or sweepers would be lowest. Other jobs are then slotted somewhere in between, based on a variety of formulas. These jobs will fall somewhere between the toolmaker level and the janitor in terms of skill, experience, and job knowledge. In a financial institution or service industry, the lowest-rated job might be file clerk and the highest might be electronics technician. No matter what the system, however, understanding merit versus automatic progression is a must.

In Figure 4-1, assume that ten employees are hired on January 1, 1980. Under the merit system, they all start at $4.00 an hour. One year later, two could be at the top of the range, making $5.00 an hour; two at $4.75; and two still at $4.00 an hour. Progress through the pay range is based on performance within that particular job. Under automatic progres-

Figure 4-1

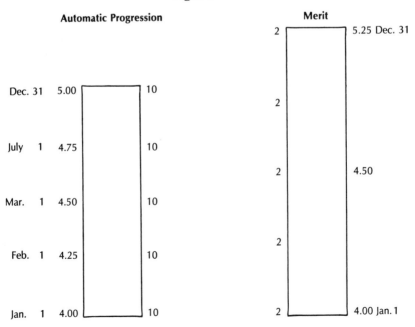

sion, the same ten employees, hired on January 1, at $4.00 an hour, in thirty days could progress to $4.25, in sixty days to $4.50, in six months to $4.75, and at the end of a year to $5.00. Any variety or combination can be used; the length of time between increases can be lengthened or shortened. Under the automatic progression system, the supervisor's decision in evaluating an employee is whether or not the employee will stay on the payroll. It is permissible—and has occurred—for an employee to receive a 25¢ per hour raise and a warning letter of possible termination if poor performance doesn't improve.

Figure 4-2

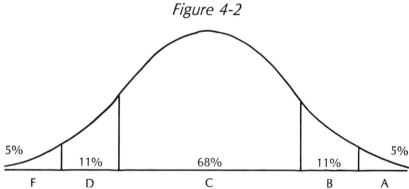

A major problem with merit pay is the bell-shaped curve. Remember when the high school or college instructor graded on the curve? As Figure 4-2 illustrates, the bell-shaped curve can apply whether we're talking about grades, intelligence levels, voting, or church attendance. In terms of employee performance, the curve demonstrates that 5 percent of the typical work force are superstars, A's; that 5 percent are unacceptable, or F's (and should have been discharged); that 11 percent are above average, B's; that 11 percent are below average, D's; and that 68 percent fall into the average, or C, range. If an organization has a merit system, administered fairly and justly, the normal percentage of meritorious workers would be 16 percent. If a company wishes to remain union-free, 50 percent of their workers must be convinced this wage and salary administration plan is fair. It is interesting to note that, as engineers, teachers, university professors, lawyers, and other professionals have unionized, the first issue at the bargaining table has been to eliminate the merit pay system.

The decision to pay merit is normally made in a union-free organization by the president and/or vice-presidents. These individuals have functioned under a merit system and have won, and often develop a Horatio

Alger attitude: "I played the game and won; therefore, anyone can play the game and win." The majority of workers are never going to be vice-presidents, however.

Figure 4-3

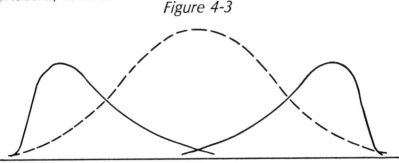

Department I   Department II

The bell-shaped curve applies well to a group of 200 or more, but many organizations apply it to groups of eight to twenty. In Figure 4-3, one curve is skewed to the right and another to the left. In practice, the lowest of the outstanding employees in one department receives no merit pay, whereas the best of the worst in another department can receive large merit increases.

Any organization wishing to maintain union-free status should pay hourly rated and lower level, nonexempt office and clerical jobs on automatic progression.

Merit pay can build marginal workers into the work force, because many supervisors, to avoid discipline, withhold merit increases to motivate marginal employees. This is an exercise in futility.

Several additional problems arise with merit pay for lower-rated jobs. One is that the money involved isn't that substantial, particularly to the marginal workers. Many organizations know that management can be motivated by substantive increases or bonuses, but at the hourly rated level, an employee being evaluated may react as follows: The top merit raise is 50¢ an hour, but the employee who has been late and used all of the sick days provided will receive 40¢ an hour. The employee responds: "You mean, if I come to work on time every day, and don't use all of my sick days, I'm going to receive an additional 10¢? To hell with it! I'd rather be late and use my sick days."

More and more companies are moving to automatic progression because it is administratively consistent, the majority of employees view it as fair—*and it reduces vulnerability to a union.*

Promotions are a great way to recognize and reward performance and meritorious work—and provide additional incentive. Companies with a fair promotion policy and automatic pay progression can defend their practices more effectively during a union campaign.

The worst position a company can be in is claiming to have a merit pay system when, in fact, none exists. Companies claim to have had a merit system for thirty or forty years. However, 95 percent of the people have been paid and moved through ranges strictly on the basis of seniority. The recommendation is to *tell it like it is.*

Supervisors are in a real bind administering a merit pay program. Managers are given a "merit budget" and instructed to give raises fairly. What does the supervisor do if everybody in the department has been performing meritoriously? Game-playing occurs. Some supervisors tell everybody: "I'm not in a position to say some of you are performing better than others, so everybody is going to get a flat 6 or 7 percent raise." Or: "Because you're near the top of the range, and so-and-so is younger, just getting started, and has some heavy house payments, I'm going to give him a 10 percent raise, but you're only going to get 4 percent. It's not because you have done anything wrong—you're doing a good job; it's because those guys upstairs told me I have to do it this way. Don't blame me."

PERFORMANCE EVALUATION

No matter what wage and salary administration plan an organization uses, whether the employee is a janitor, tool and die maker, clerical, draftsman, or engineer, management must evaluate performance prior to paying dollars. Personnel has spent decades designing employee evaluation forms similar to the one in Figure 4-4. In using such forms, what happens between supervisor and personnel? A typical scenario:

Annual appraisal time for two employees, both payroll clerks. Sally Sweets is twenty-nine, has been with the organization seven years, and has received a meritorious pay raise each year. Nellie Nasty has been employed for twenty-three years and has never gotten a merit increase. Nellie can be heard before she is seen in the morning, the employees say she's a complainer, a "moaner and groaner," and most of the employees think her last name fits her exactly. The discussion between the supervisor *(S)* and the personnel representative *(P)* goes as follows:

P: Well, Tom, you know it's time for the annual appraisal for these
     two employees in the Payroll Department.

S: Sally Sweets I don't mind evaluating a bit, but why bother to
     evaluate Nellie Nasty? She's never gotten a merit raise in
     twenty-three years and she sure won't this year.

P: Well, Tom, that's company policy.

S: Well, all right, if we have to, but I want to start the evaluation
     with Sally Sweets. She has a lot more to measure.

P: OK. Here's the form we're going to use. Let's start from the
     bottom up. How does Sally rate on job knowledge?

S: Sally knows the job cold. She studies manuals, she cross-trains,
     she really knows the job inside and out. She doesn't race off and
     jump off the pier before she does anything. She thinks about it.
     She really likes her job. I'd rate her excellent on job knowledge.

P: Loyal and honest?

S: Sally is the most loyal, dedicated employee in my department.
     She loves this organization. As a matter of fact, she wrote the
     company fight song and is the one who leads cheers for the
     president of the company in the cafeteria. Very loyal!

P: Outside activities?

S: Sally is into everything. She's president of her church club, a Girl
     Scout leader, and president of the ski club. As a matter of fact,
     Sally gets a lot of calls here at work about her outside activities
     and she runs a lot of outside material on our mimeograph
     machine, but Sally is literally into everything. Rates excellent
     there.

P: How about promotability?

S: I wanted to talk to you in Personnel about that. She's getting an
     MBA on the tuition reimbursement program, and she's now ready
     to move on as soon as you have an opening in another
     department.

P: Well, won't you be having an opening in this department soon?

S: I don't foresee any openings here.

P: But you would rate her promotable potential?

S: Absolutely! She wants to get ahead.

P: Well, I think we can rate her excellent, but off the record.

S: Off the record? This won't show up?

P: That's right.

S: The truth is, she couldn't administer a two-man rowboat, but she wants to be promoted.

P: The next item here is safety.

S: Sally has never been injured on the job. In fact, she doesn't move fast enough to get hit with anything. Excellent.

P: The next item we have is housekeeping.

S: Well, she won the award in this department last year for having the cleanest work area in the place. You could come through this department any time, look at Sally's work area and not know anybody had worked there. Excellent.

P: Sounds like a terrific employee. How about her personal appearance?

S: She's the neatest employee we have. Always well groomed, well manicured, and her hair is always nicely styled. Also dresses very well.

P: OK. I'll rate her excellent on appearance. How about planning?

S: Sally knows where she's going to be five to fifteen years ahead. She plans everything in great detail before she moves on anything. I would rate her excellent on that.

P: Next, we have ideas, initiative, and ingenuity.

S: Sally is always willing to try new methods.

P: So far, she looks like an outstanding type of employee. Now, cooperation is divided into two parts: cooperation with you and then cooperation with other employees.

S: That's really one of Sally's strong points. She calls me sir, and she's just the most pleasant person I've ever been around. And the other employees love her. She's the one who brings a cake when anyone has a birthday; she counsels the younger girls about problems they're having with their boyfriends. I'd say she spends an hour to two hours a day counseling my junior employees.

P. Boy, that's super! Next, we have attitude.

S Great! She just sparkles daily.

P: How is her attendance?

S: She's always here, always on time, never misses, loves her work.

P: Well, the last two items we have, Tom, are quantity and quality.

S: Got to be honest?

P: Well, it's helpful.

S: Well, she's so busy cooperating and counseling and doing these other things that, in fact, she really doesn't get a whole helluva lot done. But don't mark it poor.

P: Well, no. We in Personnel never like to mark these issues poor. Quantity is not strong?

S: Not really.

P: I know what we can do. We can mark it fairly poor. I'll put it right on the line.

S: That's good. Maybe nobody will notice it.

P: Right. Now, Tom, her quantity may not be too strong, but how about the quality of her work?

S: Well, she tries all these new methods and processes, and really . . . got to be honest?

P: I think you have to.

S: Well, what she does get done probably could be best described as garbage—an awful lot of rework. But she tries.

P: I'll mark that fairly poor as well. Now, she has eleven excellents and only two fairs. So, who is going to get your merit raise?

S: Well, I think that Sally certainly deserves it based on her total performance as a well-rounded individual.

P: Well, Tom, that's terrific. Now, I think we should take a look at Nellie Nasty. Let's pick up with her evaluation.

S: She does nothing but complain, moan, and groan—gripes constantly.

P: OK, Tom, let's start with job knowledge.

S: She only knows her own job; she won't even cross-train, and she doesn't always follow SOP. I'd give her just a fair.

P: A fair. How about loyal and honest?

S: Well, she hates the company and many times she's said: "I'd never work for this company again. Nobody here cares; it's a rotten place to work." She's the one who had one too many at the Christmas party and told the vice-president off. We shouldn't have to put up with this kind of disloyalty. She says: "Twenty-three years; nobody cares."

P: Well, I guess you'd like to . . . that's a poor?

S: Is there a lower rating on the form? I liked hopeless.

P: Well, we took that off the form. How about her outside and civic activities?

S: None. That should be another poor.

P: What about promotability?

S: I asked her one time: "Nellie, you know, you don't act like you wanted a promotion, do you?" She said to me: "Sonny Boy, take a promotion and lose my overtime and get your job? You must think I'm crazy."

P: So you would rank her not interested—poor on that. How about this next item? How is she on housekeeping?

S: Nellie is a mess. Last year, she burned out two machines running them too fast, had papers all over the place. Just an absolute mess.

P: How about her personal appearance?

S: She's grubby. She looks like an unmade bed.

P: I guess we'll just say poor on appearance. How about safety?

S: She's the one who couldn't wait for maintenance to come and move the blocks, so she picked them up and hurt her back—a lost-time accident of three days. Ruined my entire safety program. Less than desirable.

P: How about ideas, initiative, and ingenuity?

S: She's never had any. I asked her about that one day, and she said: "Sonny Boy, what do they pay you for?" Never had an idea all her life.

P: How about cooperation with other people or with you, the supervisor?

S: She says the company must really be hard up to hire a college kid as supervisor, who doesn't know anything about anything. She doesn't like me at all, and with other employees I had another uprising. Remember when Nancy Nice was pregnant, and they had a little going-away party, and they didn't invite Nellie? When they got back, she said: "Welcome back from vacation." She's always complaining that she does all the work and the rest don't do anything. They hate her guts.

P: What's her attitude around the company?

S: She grumps at two levels: hates the company, hates the president.

P: What about her attendance?

S: She's usually here.

P: We'll give her a good. Tom, there's quality and quantity of work. How would you rate her on that?

S: Well, you have to give the devil her due. She really cranks it out. About 160 percent of standards.

P: That's quantity, but how about quality?

S: Any time I check her work, she says: "Why are you checking my work? I never make a mistake." And she *never does* make a mistake. Zero defects.

P: Well, at least she has a few excellents, but she has a lot of poors.

S: Two percent below the average, I think, is sufficient again this year.

P: Sally Sweets, then, will get what kind of merit increase?

S: I think Sally Sweets should get the most, our highest merit increase.

This dialogue, unfortunately, is repeated to some degree in many organizations. Whether an organization uses merit or automatic pay progression, employees are entitled to be judged on a *fair and factual basis.*

What is important to the company about employee performance? Quality and quantity—period. How much they do and how well they do

Figure 4-4

Sally Sweets = X
Nellie Nasty = O

	Excellent	Good	Fair	Poor
Quantity	O			X
Quality	O			X
Attendance	X O			
Attitude	X			O
Cooperation	X			O
Others	X			O
Supervisor	X			O
I, I, I	X			O
Planning	X			O
Appearance	X			O
Housekeeping	X			O
Safety	X			O
Promotability	X			O
Community Activities	X			O
Loyal & Honest	X			O
Job Knowledge	X			O

it. Other criteria may be measured, such as attitude, attendance, cooperation, and initiative, but the employee should be rated satisfactory or unsatisfactory on those. Either employees are at work or they are not. As to safety, how can employees possibly have excellent, good, fair, or poor records? Either they are working safely or they're not. The advice here is that unless action or inaction affect quality and quantity of an individual's work, or other workers, the company should avoid subjective judgments.

For example, if the personnel department hires a new representative, and nine supervisors call and say, "Keep this idiot out of my department; nobody likes him," management must counsel the representative about attitude. A personnel type who can't communicate with supervisors will not be effective in quality and quantity of work.

If an employee is uncooperative on a team job and other employees refuse to work with him, that employee must be counseled to improve cooperation, since this behavior is affecting the quality and quantity of others' work. However, until management can document and prove effect, evaluation should be objective, not subjective. Later in this book, we will provide a form that has worked in both union and union-free shops to keep track on a daily basis of the employees' positive and negative work performance.

Once more: *Quality and quantity of work. Period. Unless some other factor is affecting workers' production, ignore it.*

As an additional note about performance evaluation, consider that the typical supervisor, filling out the forms, uses the report card approach, and generally doesn't like paper work. They can't remember everything that went on for a whole year. They're lucky if they can go back three weeks, six weeks, or, at the outside, twelve weeks on the positive side—but they aren't likely to forget the negative side. Most people can remember the screw-ups and mistakes of ten years ago as though they had happened yesterday. It's amazing how most of us can look back and remember errors, but forget all the good things people have done.

FINAL THOUGHT ON WAGES

What the company has done in the past is history; employees want to know what's been done lately. In a union campaign, the company must run on its recent record. The company must be able to demonstrate to employees that the organization has had concern for them, has been fair in determining wages and in giving appropriate increases to meet their financial needs. However, workers are more concerned about their take-home pay today than what the company has done over the past fifteen years.

Chapter Five

Benefits

HOSPITALIZATION

The benefits companies need to provide for employees—health, welfare, and so on—are becoming a greater and greater part of the compensation package. What employees think and feel about their benefit package is the paramount issue, and supervisors' views and understanding of benefits are even more important. We've asked supervisors if they have a good benefit package. They usually answer yes, but occasionally they'll say it's adequate, and some say it's not too good. They're reflecting their experience with the benefits package.

Supervisors need a basic knowledge of the insurance package. They do not need to become insurance experts, but they should understand the basic provisions. We pose the following questions to test your knowledge.

1. If I worked for you, got seriously ill, and had to be hospitalized, how many days of my hospital stay would your current
   policy cover? 30 60 120 365
   Unlimited (If you're a typical supervisor, you're not too
   sure.)

2. There is a lot of confusion about Major Medical, which most
   organizations have to supplement the basic hospitalization
   insurance. Do you have a Major Medical Program?
   Yes   No

3. If you do have Major Medical, generally it provides so many
   dollars. Does your current Major Medical package provide:
   $10,000   30,000   100,000   250,000
   $1 million   No Limit

4. Many companies have a variety of programs to provide
   employees protection against a long-term illness or some
   major disaster. Are you sure you know your own current
   benefit package?

If supervisors don't know the answers to basic questions, it's guaranteed that employees don't either. People generally find out whether or not
they have a good hospitalization package when they need it. We didn't
ask complex questions: "Do you have radiation therapy?" "Do you have
outpatient diagnostic?" "Do you cover for dialysis?" Most companies fail
to communicate hospitalization coverage adequately, although the company may be spending hundreds of thousands of dollars to provide medical benefits. Supervisors are in an excellent position to communicate company benefit programs. Using an anecdote or an example to explain the
coverage to employees is the best way.

For example, a supervisor in one of our training courses gave the best
possible answer to our question about hospitalization. He said, "I'm not
sure what our package is, but when one of my employee's wife was sick,
had to go to the hospital, was in for about six weeks, and had surgery; the
total bill came to about $22,000; and all he had to pay was $60.00 for
the TV and telephone."

HOLIDAYS

When is the next paid holiday? Do you get the day after Christmas off? Do you get a half-day before Christmas? What about Good Friday? Do you have a floating holiday for your birthday? Other floating holidays? How much vacation do you personally receive: one week?   two weeks? three weeks?   four weeks?   five weeks?

We'll wager you scored well on those questions—and so would your employees. Most employees and supervisors know by day and date every single paid holiday, the number of annual vacation days they are entitled to, and how many days they have used.

The message here is that employees are well aware of their paid time-off benefits. Company managers totally underestimate the importance to employees of paid time off; supervisors usually relate to employees' desires on this issue. The fact is, presidents and vice-presidents love their jobs and look forward to coming to work every day. If they want a day off, they can easily take it. The typical employee, however, doesn't come skipping in to work every day, humming: "Hi, ho, hi, ho, it's off to work we go." Many people come trudging in to work Monday morning saying: "Oh, brother. Another week!" They *do* skip out merrily on Friday, singing: "Hi, ho, hi, ho, it's off to play we go."

Most companies do an outstanding job providing for the long-term benefits that protect employees and their families from financial disaster caused by long periods when they can't work. Unfortunately people generally don't look ahead or even consider the possibility of a long-term illness, and give the company little credit for the coverage. A supervisor must look for ways to sell the benefit package and emphasize the good things the company is doing.

Fast payment of claims is extremely important to employees when medical bills are submitted. Claims should be processed quickly and accurately. Employees legitimately become terribly upset when submitted medical bills get pigeonholed in processing, either at the company benefit office or at the insurance company. This may be due to technical holdups, an improperly submitted bill, or some other minor problem. The employee is then hassled by the hospital, or even worse, by the doctor. Doctors have canceled patients, just sending a letter saying: "You are no longer my patient because I can't wait any longer for your insurance company to pay me."

Hospitals and doctors are not as lenient as they once were, many times turning over bills sixty days overdue to a collection agency. The agency threatens people with lawsuits, makes continuous phone calls, and generally harasses the employee. This creates a major problem for an employee who was told he had good hospitalization coverage. A supervisor who becomes aware that this is beginning to happen should do everything possible to expedite processing of claims. Employees can be turned off on their hospitalization plans, even when the plan is excellent, by failure to communicate the plan and by sloppy and slow administration and payment. The advice to management is to *communicate and expedite.*

Many organizations have salary continuation programs to provide income protection in the event of illness: short-term disability (STD) or long-term disability (LTD) programs. The company should give examples demonstrating the benefits employees have received from these plans.

SICK LEAVE

More and more companies are providing sick leave plans for all employees, and abuse of sick leave is becoming the number one problem in many companies. Unfortunately the company creates the problem by developing a "Catch-22" sick leave policy. Management rewards poor performance, and ignores good performance—or worse, punishes good performance. Sick leave is a classic example. For example, a company provides ten day's sick leave per year. If an employee does not use the sick leave, the "reward" for not missing a day all year is loss of ten paid sick days. On the other hand, a less dedicated employee may use seven or eight sick days, year in and year out. Supervisors feel: "Well, there's nothing we can do about it. The employee is using a benefit provided by the company."

Many employees view sick leave as an "earned" benefit they can take when they want a day off. Company policies that don't reward attendance punish regular attenders by eliminating sick leave at the end of the year. *This is a mistake.*

In an industry where sick leave is common, companies must have it to recruit and retain good employees. If a company has this policy, dropping it may turn employees to a union. Company policy should state the number of sick leave days granted for the year and spell out under what conditions days can be used.

Employees who have not used any or a portion of their days should be paid for the balance of the days not used. This payment has been earned through good performance and regular attendance. In short, it rewards them for good attendance; it is "well" pay rather than sick pay.

Time off with pay should be on an hourly basis of work hours equivalent to five days, for example, forty hours or 37.5 hours, with the employee charged for partial days off in two- or four-hour time blocks. Supervisors should be sensitive to employees' legitimate medical appointments, but also concerned about scheduling needs. Later, in the chapter on discipline, we will discuss supervisory follow-up on employee attendance delinquency.

Life insurance, another benefit most companies provide, is generally group term insurance, many times an amount that is tied in to salary or hourly wage. Group term insurance is inexpensive and a good benefit, but buys little employee loyalty and dedication.

PENSIONS AND PROFIT SHARING

Companies normally provide pension and/or profit-sharing programs. Managers should not overestimate employee gratitude for these, especially if little or no communicating has been done to underline such a program's long-term value, particularly for older employees and those who plan to remain with the company until retirement. As in wage administration, pension programs often reflect senior management's view: "We need pensions and deferred income, and so should everybody." Many employees, especially short-service workers, couldn't care less about pension programs. For example, Mary Jones is nineteen and works as a nurse aide in a hospital. Mary thinks she won't be there in two years, so she'll never collect a pension. What does she really care about?

Explaining the pension program, indeed, may get only a lukewarm response. A hospital nurse with seven year's service, when told that at retirement in the year 2027 she will gain the magnanimous sum of $422 a month, will, if she's a nice person, probably say thanks, but what's really on her mind is inflation.

Figure 5-1

THE PROFIT SHARING MYTH

In talking with some of the employees of Lucas County State Bank, we've found the employees are enamoured with the Bank's "Profit Sharing Plan".

We've been told that an amount equivalent to 15% of the employee's salary is placed into the account for distribution when the employee leaves or retires.

If the employee leaves with less than 3 years of service, they are not entitled to receive any portion of the fund that was placed there for their benefit.

Then a proportionate share can be withdrawn as the years of service increase until you can draw 100% at ten years of service.

Isn't this really a forced savings program designed to enrich the older employee at the expense of the younger?

And since it is designed on salary paid, the Officers of the bank will be eligible for the lion's share of the fund.

A true profit-sharing plan is when a percentage of the profits are divided among the employees quarterly or semi-annually because of profits made during the time.

To those employees who leave with less than five years of service, their withdrawal amounts to so little, that they have been literally cheated out of a 15% salary increase for all the years they have been there.

If it is designed to be a substitute for a pension plan, then shouldn't you have vested rights for all money that has been placed in escrow for you?

With a high turn-over rate of employees, all the present program does is to serve and fatten the accounts of the officers and higher-paid employees of the Bank.

If you should want to leave the labor force temporarily and return at a later time, shouldn't you have the right to pick up the fund at the point you left?

Isn't it fair that you should have maternity leave rights so as to protect your fund and your years of service for vacation and other rights?

Isn't it fair that you should have higher salaries and a meaningful pension plan with vested rights for all years of service?

Now is your opportunity to do something about the unfairness of such a program and gain something for yourself. By signing and returning the card you will be telling us that you believe you are entitled to the full salary rate plus a meaningful pension program covering all years of service. ACT TODAY!

Office & Professional Employees International Union, AFL-CIO

339 HURON ST., TOLEDO, OHIO 43604   419-246-1540

An excellent union flyer (Figure 5-1) makes fun of the "profit-sharing myth." This union position paper demonstrates how vulnerable a company can be with a profit-sharing plan designed by senior management to benefit senior management.

Pension and profit-sharing plans are fine fringe benefits, but too many times management overestimates their impact on employees during union elections. Employees begin to think about retirement at about age 50 and get serious about it three to four years before they retire. With pressure on workers to pay for possessions *now,* talk of twenty-five to thirty years hence has no direct impact. Senior management's desires—tax shelters, deferred income—are not shared by employees making $9000 to $20,000 a year.

Some profit-sharing programs provide payments annually, semiannually, or quarterly. Cash payout, impacting employees *now,* appears far more attractive than retirement income years away.

Profit-sharing incentive programs, however, may raise unmet expectations. Immediate dissatisfaction among hourly employees results when profits dwindle or disappear—possibly triggering a union election. Supervisors, in this connection, underestimate their impact on employees in word and attitude. Supervisors who lead the griping and complaining about wages or pensions stimulate negative feelings among employees. Their continual griping hurts their organizations. If they think the company is cheap or uncaring about workers' long-range interests, they should do the company a favor and quit.

Chapter Six

Job Descriptions and Overtime Policy

PURPOSE AND USE OF JOB DESCRIPTIONS

"Where does it say I'm supposed to do that in my job description?" If supervisors hear that statement very often, industrial anarchy is approaching!

Job descriptions, developed during World War II, are the most misused documents in industry today. The government imposed wage-price freezes and set up a board to hear wage increase requests. Employees could only get additional wages if the board was convinced that their "duties" had expanded, entitling them to more money. Many companies subsequently thought job descriptions were useful, but reached illogical conclusions.

A job description does not tell employees what their jobs are, and certainly doesn't tell supervisors; its only purpose is pay rates. Job descriptions are not standard operating procedures (SOP)—that's "how to do" jobs. Long, detailed job descriptions cause employees to say: "Fine, I'll do that and nothing else."

All companies should have a pay policy on work above or below an employee's classification. Our guidelines would be:

1. Continue higher pay rates if they are required to work in a lower classification temporarily or for short term.

2. Continue higher pay rates if they are required to move from lower- to higher-rated jobs for extended periods.

The company will have flexibility in job-to-job movement.

In companies with long job descriptions, where secretaries from personnel were asked to type letters for marketing, their response indicated this was almost a mortal sin. No job description should exist for personnel, sales, or accounting secretary; a secretary is a secretary. Janitors have also refused to sweep anything not "in my job description;" a tool and die maker has refused to help take tool room inventory; and so on. In a hospital housekeeping department, a custodian, when asked to help clean up surgery between operations, refused because he was only assigned to work on the first floor.

The job description sets a job pay rate, and should only include the highest skill required. A couple of examples:

1. Tool and Die Maker—A journeyman's card or equivalent experience. (To slot the job with that knowledge, use of calipers, screwdrivers, pliers, lathes, and blueprints need not be spelled out.)

2. Fork-lift Driver—Drives fork-lift safely and efficiently. (No need to say "picks up boxes with fork-lift, checks air in tires of fork-lift, and fills out invoice forms.")

Such detailed duties belong in standard operating procedures, describing how to perform a task, and *not* in the job description. Employees often confuse SOP and job description—don't add to the confusion.

A progressive company's position should be that everybody's job is to build a quality product and ship it out the back door, or, in a service organization, to provide quality service. However, two exceptions to requiring employees to do whatever is necessary are: safety and demeaning work. To ask an employee with no knowledge of electricity to run 440 wire is to invite the legitimate response: "I don't know anything about electricity and I could electrocute myself." But it's not a safety issue to ask an electrician to help take inventory. To ask a hospital nurse to clean bedpans for the next thirty days invites the response: "I didn't spend three years of my life acquiring my RN to spend my time cleaning bedpans!" Asking a millwright to cut grass for six months deserves the statement: "I didn't spend 8000 hours of apprenticeship to cut grass." However, companies shouldn't be overwhelmed by the demeaning work issue. The rule prevents supervisors from "getting even" with employees who have displeased them. Unions not only prevent this, but proper rules can deal with it, too. If the supervisor issues a directive that's neither unsafe nor demeaning, the employee should perform the task and file a complaint on completion.

Asking people to work above their job responsibilities without compensation for it, for example, an operator to fill in for an absent set-up person or a material handler to cover inspection work, also creates job assignment dissatisfaction. Supervisors should approve pay for that time— but not for brief periods (half a day or thereabouts), nor for combinations of set-up and material handling or checker and inspection work. The supervisors should explain tactfully that pay is not for how *hard* people work, a general misconception of employees. Companies pay for employees' highest skills, used regularly. Otherwise, employees emptying boxcars would deserve more money than experimental tool and die makers, and hospital orderlies more than neurosurgeons. This must be explained so employees don't feel their work is demeaning—and they are entitled to know how and why they're paid.

Finally, abuse of the job description rationale has often caused overstaffing, particularly in white-collar and clerical areas—another costly mistake.

OVERTIME

Many company overtime policies are unclear, causing shift-to-shift and department-to-department inconsistencies and creating employee resentment. To understand the problem, basic overtime issues having to do with types of overtime must be examined: degree of overtime, timing, and company expectations. For example, is overtime voluntary? Mandatory? Emergency? Excessive? Did employees get notice of upcoming overtime? What are the overtime job assignments?

Overtime issues relate mainly to changing workers, particularly the younger, who feel: "The company hires me for forty hours, but the rest of the time is my own; the company has no right to expect me to work overtime unless I want to." Many workers today are not interested in overtime for reasons previously cited: double incomes, working husbands and wives with home schedules, transportation (for example, car pools), and so on. The supervisor—told by the production manager or department head, "We've got to get this work out. I will approve overtime"—is caught in the middle and has to find volunteers willing to put aside home and personal schedules.

Company policy manuals should communicate overtime policy, specifically, with supervisors given direction on implementation. A simple overtime policy would be: "This organization must be sensitive to the needs of our customers, and because of customer needs, of production schedules, or attendance problems, scheduling may require people to be available for overtime. Availability to work a reasonable amount of overtime is a condition of employment in this company." With this principle established, supervisors may exercise voluntary application. Calling for volunteers, if the entire crew isn't needed and enough people want overtime, avoids problems. If there is a shortage of volunteers, or the entire department is scheduled to work ten hours a day or eight hours on Saturday, overtime is mandatory.

A completely voluntary overtime system puts the supervisor in a bind if he gets only six volunteers, but needs ten. Reluctant to admit he didn't make the quota, lest the production manager conclude he can't motivate his crew, or they are being uncooperative, the supervisor puts pressure on good, cooperative employees, saying: "I'm really in a bind. Can't you do me a favor? I need you to work overtime." He won't ask the griper, who wouldn't help out under any circumstances, so the cooperative employee gets stuck working overtime in summer months and on holiday weekends —that's the reward for being cooperative! Moreover, the supervisor pays a price in asking for a favor; it's likely to come back to haunt him—when the employee asks a favor. If the employee needs to leave early Friday, the supervisor feels obligated to honor the request, and right away the non-volunteers, gripers, and complainers are screaming "favoritism." So the supervisor is right back in the middle again, because of company policies.

When company policy states clearly that a condition of employment is a certain amount of overtime, the supervisor can fill a volunteer quota by telling the needed people: "You are required for overtime work this week."

Emergency Overtime

Emergency overtime needs become self-evident when the unexpected occurs: rush orders; accident victims rushed to a hospital; a particularly heavy workload, a particularly busy day in a bank (like the day after Christmas); work piled up after a long weekend; unanticipated emergency; or a breakdown in equipment. No employee notices should be required, nor should they expect to be released until the crisis passes. Most employees will recognize no-notice, emergency overtime as valid. Pipefitters or millwrights, for example, are unlikely to declare: "I don't feel like staying around until this work is done."

Pre-employment interviews and communication throughout the year should stress occasional emergency overtime requirements.

Excessive Overtime

Organizations should avoid this if possible—or bring in part-time workers. Excessive overtime causes additional problems for both company and workers, especially when it continues for any length of time, and then suddenly stops. With excessive overtime, people get tired, accidents occur, and attendance problems mount (employees take Monday or Tuesday off after working Saturdays or twelve-hour shifts). Also, employees become accustomed to regular, extra income, virtually a new income level, at which they start living. If the overtime ceases, families may see appliances, cars, or furniture repossessed.

Companies may need to consider controlling overtime by requiring only that employees be available for a certain amount. Twenty years ago, as union officers, we spent a lot of time negotiating overtime equalization so that extra money was shared. Today, workers reject overtime because federal income tax would take so much, and they want time off to do their own thing.

Companies may have to weigh modified mandatory overtime, with a maximum and minimum requirement: employees must be available two Saturdays per month, or twenty weeks a year, or 400 hours a year, scheduled during the week, on Saturdays, and so on. Companies are well advised to deal with overtime—a possible trigger for union activity—justly, but firmly.

Many companies have avoided excessive overtime by utilizing part-time workers, but there's a joker in this deck. Part-time workers on regular schedules earn equal votes in union elections, and they have sometimes been prime movers for a union in union-free organizations. For example, hospital and banking part-timers, feeling nobody could speak for them, started the organizing drive.

Part-timers may well solve problems posed by employees' changing needs, however. Many times, child-care responsibilities or lack of time for full-time work make part-time jobs feasible for women. Current attempts to provide jobs for the handicapped, many of whom could *start* working part time, and for unskilled minority youths who could be trained for full-time employment offer promise for companies with continuous process operations.

The NLRB views temporary employees—college students desiring summer work only, or seasonal workers—as not having permanent employee-employer relationships, but if a company hires the same workers year after year, they are considered eligible for equal votes in a union election. So, if part-time or repeatedly rehired temporary workers are the solution to excessive overtime, companies had better develop fringe benefits for them. Two of these are vacations and paid holidays. For example, an employee working two-fifths time, should receive two-fifths pay for normal vacation, based on years of service, and two-fifths pay for holidays. Part-time workers really want the paycheck and time off to spend it, but the law doesn't require that they be included in profit-sharing and pension plans

Chapter Seven

Advancement Opportunity

One benefit most union-free organizations provide is the opportunity to advance, on the basis of talent, skill, ability, job knowledge, and seniority. Most progressive, union-free companies stipulate that, when possible, promotion to supervisory and technical jobs should be within the organization, but too often they don't market the policy very well among employees. Companies should exemplify plant managers' and supervisors' opportunities for advancement by citing cases of vice-presidents, for example, who started in lower-level jobs.

Organizations should also do career planning with employees, projecting their future with the organization. This may include suggesting further education or skill training. Most companies provide tuition reimbursement programs if employees wish to attend technical or secretarial schools or community or four-year colleges. Courses generally need personnel or management approval as job related. These programs are excellent fringe benefits, and generally only require a passing grade for payment.

Employee counseling implies honesty, however, concerning their mobility within the organization; it *should not* lead to false promises. Too many supervisors and managers tell employees: "The company has its eye on you; the future is unlimited if only you had a college degree." Obtaining degree credits at night school is a long, rigorous, time-consuming process not approached lightly and only if one has firm motivation. When, as a way to avoid honest discussion with an employee, college education is suggested and the employee takes on that burden, rankling disappointment may result. Having achieved a four-year degree after six or seven years, when the employee reports, "I'm qualified and ready," all too often the response is: "We don't have an opening. We think you've peaked out."

Even worse than false promises, is a certain kind of supervisors' nasty habit of "sitting on" promotable employees. These are usually good workers with excellent attitudes who could serve the organization well in higher-level jobs, but whose skills the supervisor has utilized in training or some other supervisory duties. Fearing loss of this good employee, the supervisor doesn't make promotion opportunities known. This little game quite often culminates in no-score for the supervisor, who has implied he will "take care of" the employee. Many times, he can't produce—or doesn't even intend to—and he loses a good employee's confidence and respect. This creates a monster from the company's point of view, and, from the union's, an organizer's dream—an extremely dissatisfied, frustrated good worker.

Moral for supervisors: Do not sit on promotable people, even if good workers are lost, requiring training of replacements.

Immediate supervisors are ideal choices to merchandise advancement and tuition reimbursement programs to employees. All too often, employees are unaware of these excellent benefits and how they can be used. Most companies are justly proud of promotion-from-within policies, but it is equally important that first-line supervisors communicate this, because it establishes employee rapport with the supervisor as the source of information about upward mobility and realistic job goals.

JOB POSTING AND BIDDING

A basic issue in any job advancement policies—one requiring a first decision—is whether or not open jobs are going to be posted. Otherwise, employees find out about openings and promotions by word of mouth.

Companies of larger size—200 or more employees—make a serious mistake not posting jobs. Hearing about jobs after they have been filled causes employees to think that the company wouldn't consider giving them a chance at a more interesting or better job.

Some companies don't post jobs because they have to tell what they pay, and they, unfortunately, prefer secret wage scales. The only reason for a secret wage system is shame or failure to justify differences in pay to different types of employees. To have a reasonable job posting system, companies must be willing to cite beginning rates for jobs, or communicate, for example, that a clerical 3 position or an inspector's position at labor grade 7 is open and what the beginning salaries are.

Once available jobs are to be posted, there are two choices:

1. Posting them as they open.

2. Inviting employees who are interested to sign up for jobs they aspire to.

We recommend the second approach for reasons that will become apparent as we outline problems with the first.

Under the first system, job openings are posted in the department first, and then plant-wide (or bank-wide or hospital-wide). Interested employees sign up for screening interviews by the supervisor who selects the one he feels would fill the job best. It sounds all right, doesn't it, but we advise rejecting it, for several reasons.

First, it is the worst time to tell an applicant that he or she isn't qualified for a better position. Employees have often waited six months or several years for a particular job, only to be told that some qualification they didn't know about is required. For example, a machine operator, feeling he is in line for promotion to maintenance electrician because he is qualified and a senior employee, is told he doesn't qualify because he doesn't understand ac/dc theory and needs additional electrical repair training.

Second, employees who are on vacation or sick, even in the hospital, when a vacancy occurs are passed over for a job. They are very unhappy because they felt they were qualified and that the job was one to which they were entitled.

Third, filling the job is delayed because it must remain open for some time—three days, five days, two weeks, or whatever period management needs to inform everybody, and to interview and screen candidates.

The advantages of the second system are:

1. Employees aspiring to a particular job are told the required qualifications before the job opens.

2. They may then get training to qualify under the tuition reimbursement program.

3. It counters employees' suspicions that the company has written a job description to ensure that their candidate receives the job.

The following is an example of a permanent job posting system.

ADVANCEMENT—JOB BIDDING

Selection Procedure:

A. Each employee will be given a Job Preference Card to fill out when employment starts at [name of company]. The purpose of this card is to inform the Company as to what positions the employee desires in the future. An employee may change his card at any time by so notifying his supervisor. This system will ensure that anyone interested will be considered when a job vacancy exists.

B. When the Company determines a position is open, they will rely initially on the Job Preference List. Position opening means a classification as listed in the classification section, excluding any managerial positions such as supervisor or foreman.

C. Temporary position openings will not be posted and will be filled by the Company to ensure the orderly and efficient operation of the plant.

D. Should no qualified applicant have filled out a card for the position, or if all applicants, after being considered, are not qualified, the Company may fill the position from any source.

E. No employee may bid on and accept more than one (1)

lateral transfer or downgrade every one (1) year. There is no limit on the number of times an employee may bid and receive an upper grade classification.

F. The selected applicant will move to the new job when a replacement becomes available.

G. An employee selected to till a vacancy who fails to qualify or disqualifies himself, within a calendar month, will be returned to his former classification and rate of pay.

H. In all cases of selecting an employee for any position, the following factors shall be equally considered:

1. Seniority. Definitions include:

   - *Plant*—Plant seniority shall be the continuous service at [name of company] from date of last hire for full time employment.

   - *Department*—Department seniority shall be the continuous service with a department at [name of company].

   - *Classification*—Classification seniority shall be the continuous service with a department in a classification at [name of company].

   - *Displaced Employee*—An employee who has been displaced from his permanent job classification but continues to work for the company in another job classification shall continue to accumulate seniority in his previous position for a period of time not to exceed six (6) months.

   - *Laid-Off Employee*—An employee who is laid off without pay shall continue to accumulate seniority for a period of time equal to his length of service but not to exceed three (3) months.

- *Conflicts*—In the event that two (2) or more employees begin work with same day and time, the employee originally interviewed first shall be deemed the most senior.

- *Seniority for Part-Time Employees* shall be the time actually worked. Should a part-time employee go on a full-time status he shall be given a credit of seniority from the time he goes on full time.

2. Past experience and ability to perform work.

3. Physical fitness to perform the work without jeopardy to the health and well being of the employee or fellow employees.

4. Productivity and attendance and compliance with company rules.

5. Mechanical comprehension and other skill and ability testing the Company feels is necessary for the job requirement.

Our recommendation is to *out-union the union*—give employees everything a union contract would give them, plus more notice and more flexibility. During layoff and recall, ensure that both are based on seniority, whether by department, classification, or plant-wide. This will depend on the organization's product mix and type of skills. We are not suggesting laying off a machinist with three years' service and keeping a janitor with five years' service. Union-free companies should ensure that employees with seniority can perform and have necessary qualifications for the job they are bumping into.

Rapid union expansion in white-collar, professional, technical, clerical, and public sector areas many times is due to management's short-term policy of layoff without regard to seniority. Destruction of job security at the time of layoff has probably organized as many unions as any other factor. Laying off senior technicians or engineers on a project basis when they could replace junior technicians or engineers on another project, has been the "triggering incident" in unionization. *Management cannot ignore seniority rights and the importance of seniority in basic job retention.*

Final advice: Do not lay off marginal employees; terminate them. Other employees may not cheer loudly, but they will understand termination; they will *not* understand layoff out of seniority lines. Layoff indicates a continuing employee-employment relationship.

FORMAL LAYOFF AND RECALL PROVISIONS

Management should not use layoffs to get rid of the "deadwood." Nor should performance be the primary criterion for layoff. Management makes a serious mistake when facing production problems and looking for cost reduction; supervisors are told that the work force must be reduced. Supervisors, having usually anticipated this, are ready to suggest who should be laid off and use the downturn to get rid of their poor performers —a horrendous mistake. Remember our discussion of subjectivity in merit evaluation, culminating in the strong admonition to respect seniority? The same discussion applies here. *Do not* lay off people on the basis of performance as the primary factor; *do* lay off workers on the basis of seniority within their classification or on a plant-wide basis.

The following discussion focuses mainly on manufacturing organizations, because they more often face periodic downturns in sales, backlog, and volume, requiring a decision as to whether other work can be assigned to employees or a layoff will be necessary. Hospitals, banks, and office and clerical departments, without rapidly fluctuating workloads, face the problem of layoff on a less frequent basis.

Management is responsible for communicating to employees the basis for layoff, how long the layoff may last, and whether or not the layoff is the beginning of a series of crunches employees will have to face.

Figure 7-1 explains how employees will be laid off and their rights to return to work when jobs are available. Note that this requires notice and perhaps time for the employee to decide about returning; employees who have found employment elsewhere want some assurance that another layoff won't occur soon.

Figure 7-1 LAYOFF AND RECALL PROCEDURES

For the purpose of this article the following definitions will be used:

Displaced Employee: An employee who has been displaced from his permanent job classification but continues to work for the Company in another job classification.

Laid-off Employee: An employee who is laid off without pay but continues to accumulate seniority under this article.

Departments:

Assembly	Warehouse
Slitting & Scrolls	Electrical
Press Room	Receiving
Machine Shop	Quality Control
Shipping	Production Control
Packing	

The Company believes in the principle of seniority and to the extent that the Company can maintain the operation efficiently, it will use that principle in a layoff situation. However, those employees we feel have special skills, abilities, or we consider necessary to the operation will be retained.

A.   When an opening occurs in a department, displaced employees from that department within the plant will first be offered reinstatement to their previous department in order of seniority.

B.   Should the Company be unable to fill the open position in this manner, employees on layoff from that department will be offered recall in order of seniority.

C.   Should the Company be unable to fill the open position in this manner, employees on layoff from other departments who have requested transfer to that department will be considered under the conditions as outlined in Selection of Employees Section.

D.   If the Company is unable to fill the open position in the preceding manner, it shall hire applicants from outside the Company.

cont.

E.   Employees will be on the recall list for a period of time equal to their service with the Company, not to exceed two (2) years.

F.   Laid-off employees must accept recall regardless of shift or their previous department or be terminated. If an employee on layoff rejects the recall to a lower department, the employee will not be called again for a lower-paid department unless the employee notifies the Company in writing. If thereafter the employee rejects such recall to a lower-paid department, the employee will be terminated.

G.   Employees on the recall list, when recalled to work, shall be given one (1) day in which to report for work, unless the employee has an excuse acceptable to the Company. Such notice shall be by telephone or certified mail. When the employee receives notice of recall, the employee must notify the Company by 12:00 noon of the next working day following the receipt of such notice of his intention of accepting or rejecting recall or the employee will be terminated. Notice by mail shall be completed by deposit of notice in the United States Post Office, Certified Mail, Return Receipt Requested, directed to the employee at his address shown on the Company records.

H.   In instances in which employees cannot return to work within the required time limit, the next eligible employee may be recalled and may be permitted to work until the senior employee returns. The next eligible employee may reject the temporary recall without losing his or her seniority on the recall list.

I.   Employees shall notify the Company of their proper Post Office address or change of address, or the Company shall be entitled to rely upon the address in their records.

J.   Employees accepting recall will be paid the job rate for the job for which they are recalled.

Chapter Eight

Grievance Procedures, Employee Manual, and Policy on Unions

A typical supervisor, making 200 to 500 decisions daily, is usually right 98 percent of the time, but the other 2 percent of the decisions can create serious problems if an employee feels the company doesn't care or "always backs the supervisor." All organizations have occasions when employees think a supervisor's policy, practice, or action is inappropriate, a policy violation, or unfair. The grievance procedure provides a right to appeal to employees who feel adversely affected by a supervisor's decision.

Most grievance procedures follow these steps:

1. The employee and supervisor discuss the problem, and, it is hoped, resolve it.

2. Lacking resolution, the employee has appeal rights, generally informal, to personnel or a department head, who re-

view the facts with the supervisor, and promptly answer the employee.

3.   If still dissatisfied, employees may take formal steps, perhaps stating their position in writing—possibly assisted by personnel or employee relations. Some companies have an ombudsman to protect employee rights in such circumstances.

Some companies with no formal grievance procedures beyond an "open-door policy" of complaint resolution—meaning any employee may see the plant manager, the vice-president of manufacturing, or the president—create the unfortunate tendency for employees to bypass supervisor and department head. When they go directly to the top, the supervisor feels threatened. People often use the open-door policy to bring baseless charges and complaints against their supervisor to the higher-ups, or they may bring complaints of which the supervisor is unaware. The supervisor finds out for the first time that he has a problem when it's communicated downward to him, and he feels threatened by orders from on-high to "go clean this up."

The ideal policy on grievances is a formal procedure to settle complaints fairly, justly, and equitably for both employee and supervisor. By settling, we do not mean procedures will always uphold either party; we mean management will give the complaint quick attention, formally, in a structured manner, and rapidly communicate an answer to the employee.

Employees in a union-free shop will determine whether or not the grievance procedures are effective. If they perceive the system as fair, not threatening, and representing a real desire to service complaints and give prompt answers, the system will be effective. The last grievance procedure action is particularly critical in a union-free environment, for most union grievance procedures end with an arbitrator's hearing. (We will discuss arbitrators—their means, methods, and processes—as well as rulings and hearings in Chapter 9.)

In union-free organizations, grievance procedure often ends in a review by the chief executive officer or the general manager—who also often end up being hoisted with managements' own petard. If they rule in favor of the employee, the supervisory staff says: "See, they will never back us." If they uphold the supervisor, even if the employee has legitimate complaints, the employees say: "The grievance procedure here has all the validity of the review board at Dachau."

Fairness is the name of the game in complaint/grievance procedure.

FORMAL PROCEDURES

Arbitration is one of the two possible final grievance procedure steps in union-free companies. An example is Figure 8-1, an in-house final-appeal panel of managers and employees; Figure 8-2 is an example of an alternative procedure. Both procedures have been successfully used by progressive, union-free organizations. Appeal as a grievance procedure's final step is essential if companies wish to combat the union effectively on the fundamental job security issue.

EMPLOYEE MANUAL

Union-free companies should communicate in employee manuals company policies on benefits and procedures applying to workers. Without this, workers may believe they are dealing with changing, vestpocket policies which can be applied differently to any situation. The employee manual should read like a union contract. Organizations can have employment contracts without a union.

We advise publishing policies and distributing them *now,* before the union knocks at your door. Smaller organizations can ask trade associations or their Chamber of Commerce for prototype policy manuals.

Some areas that should be covered in the policy manual are: attendance, address change, awards, bereavement, cafeteria, call-in, equal employment opportunity, leaves of absence, lockers, medical, military leave, personal business, personal telephone, plant shutdown, probationary period, report-in pay, rules, safety, seniority, shift preference, uniforms, vacations, wage attachments, workers' compensation, and working hours.

Figure 8-1 PERSONNEL

Company Guide	Original Issue Date 11/18/74	Revision Date 9/5/81

TITLE	APPEAL PROCEDURE
SUBJECT	Coors Container Company encourages its employees to present to higher authority any complaints or injustices that cannot be resolved between the employee and the immediate supervisor.
	Management retains the right to operate in the best interest of the company and for the majority of its employees. The policies under which it operates are written to fulfill that right.
	Retaliatory measures toward an employee for using the appeal procedure are not tolerated. Disciplinary action is administered in such cases.
APPEALS	Employees can appeal the *application* of company personnel policies, *not the policies themselves.*
	Note: When an employee feels a policy is unfair or unreasonable, the situation should be referred to the appropriate EPC Task Force or division head.
	Terminations may be appealed in the same manner as any other disciplinary procedure.
	Probationary employees are not eligible to use the appeal procedure.
COMPANY APPEAL PROCEDURE Step I: Meet with Immediate Supervisor	The first appeal should be to the employee's immediate supervisor. The employee may request that another nonrelated employee be present at the scheduled meeting. The supervisor informs the employee of the decision regarding the dispute within five working days after the meeting.

cont.

TITLE	APPEAL PROCEDURE
Step I: Meet with Immediate Supervisor	If the nature of the appeal is such that the employee does not wish to discuss it with the supervisor, this step is bypassed and the procedure starts with Step II.
Step II: Meet with Department Head	Problems not resolved in Step I are taken to the department head.
	The employee must submit a dated, written request to the department supervisor for a meeting with the supervisor. The supervisor signs and acknowledges receiving the request. The employee, upon receiving the acknowledgment of the meeting request, will forward it, along with a brief handwritten summary of the nature of the appeal or reason for requesting the meeting, to the department head.
	The employee and the department head must meet within seven days from the date the request was received by the supervisor.
	The two parties may conduct a second meeting at the discretion of the department head. That meeting must include the employee's immediate supervisor. The employee may request that another nonrelated employee, a Personnel Representative, or both, be present.
	The department head informs the function head (or the division head if there is no function head) of the decision in writing within seven days of the final meeting.
Step III: Meet with Function Head	If the department head's decision under Step II is not satisfactory to the employee, the employee submits a written request to the department head for a meeting with the

cont.

TITLE	APPEAL PROCEDURE
Step III: Meet with Function Head	function head (in divisions where there is a function head). In divisions where there is no function head, the procedure goes immediately to Step IV. The department head signs and acknowledges receiving the request. The employee, upon receiving the acknowledgment of the meeting request, forwards it, along with a copy of the handwritten summary of the nature of the appeal or reason for requesting the meeting, to the function head. The employee and the function head must meet within seven days from the date the request was received by the department head. The function head informs the employee and the appropriate division head of the decision in writing within seven days of the meeting.
Step IV: Review by Vice-President of Employee Services Division	If the function head's decision under Step III is not satisfactory to the employee, the employee makes a formal request through the Personnel Administrator for a review of the problem by the Vice-President of Employee Services. The Personnel Administrator investigates the case within seven days after receipt of the formal request and presents the facts of the case to the Vice-President of Employee Services. The Vice-President of Employee Services reviews the case and determines whether the employee is appealing the policy or the application of the policy. Application of the policy is appealable; the policy is not.

cont.

TITLE	APPEAL PROCEDURE
Step IV: Review by Vice-President of Employee Services Division	The Vice-President of Employee Services has five days to make a decision and advise the employee of the decision. If the Vice-President decides the case is one of policy application, the Appeal Board meets for a review of the case within ten days (unless delayed further by severe scheduling problems).
Step V: Appeal Board Review	The Board interviews the employee to determine the specific nature of the appeal. The Board may also interview any other personnel they consider necessary to arrive at a just decision. The appealing employee and the supervisor may, at their option, be present during the entire hearing up to the point where the Board begins deliberation on their decision.

The Appeal Board must present a decision to the employee in writing within seven days after all interviews are completed.

The judgment of the Appeal Review Board is determined by a majority vote and is *final.*

Employee Services sends copies of this decision to affected supervisors for corrective action if necessary. Personnel will not make copies public or place them in the employee's personnel file.

A special confidential file of appeal cases is set up in Employee Services for record purposes only.

APPEAL BOARD COMPOSITION	Appeal Boards are composed of the following:
	1. The Vice-President of Employee Services Division.

cont.

TITLE	APPEAL PROCEDURE
APPEAL BOARD COMPOSITION	2. The employee's division head.
	3. & 4. Two other employees chosen by the employee.
	5. Another employee chosen by unanimous consent of the above four members of the Board.
Selection Guidelines	1. Employees may not select a relative for the Appeal Board.
	2. All members should come from the same division.
SOURCE AND INFORMATION	The source of this policy is Personnel Services. All requests for information should be directed to Personnel Services.

Figure 8-2 GRIEVANCE PROCEDURE

As employees of the Company we must rely on your ideas and suggestions for improvement and continuation of successful operation. We are aware that from time to time situations arise where employees have a complaint or misunderstanding with their supervisor concerning Company policies.

We have established a procedure that should resolve problems quickly and on a fair and equitable basis. You should feel free to discuss any concerns you have with your immediate supervisor.

The following procedure shall be used to settle complaints, misunderstandings, and other problems:

The Informal Level

Any complaint must first be taken to the employee's immediate supervisor. The supervisor and the employee will make every effort to resolve the problem.

cont.

The Formal Level

Step One: In the event the employee is not satisfied with the results of the informal conference, he may submit his complaint in writing to his supervisor. The supervisor will reply within seven (7) working days.

Step Two: If the employee is not satisfied with his supervisor's decision, he may request a meeting with the Plant Superintendent, or his designee, within seven (7) working days of receipt of his supervisor's decision. The Plant Superintendent, or his designee, will meet with the employee within seven (7) working days and reply within seven (7) working days.

Step Three: If the employee is not satisfied with the Plant Superintendent's, or his designee's, decision, he may appeal to the General Manager or his designee, within seven (7) days of receiving a reply from the Plant Superintendent, or his designee, and the General Manager, or his designee, will meet with the employee within seven (7) working days of receiving the appeal and the General Manager, or his designee, will reply within seven (7) working days of his decision.

This procedure is designed to maintain cooperation between employee and supervisory personnel. We are certain that the vast majority of problems will be solved at the informal level. If the employee wishes to have other employees involved, to assist him in presenting his case, management will make the necessary arrangements. There will be no negative action against any employee for processing any complaints.

ARBITRATION PROCEDURE

The Company recognizes that job security is a basic need of all employees. Therefore, we have established an arbitration procedure for any permanent employee with one year of service or more who is discharged for reasons he feels are unreasonable and unrelated to his job performance. Any permanent employee with one year of service or more who is discharged may invoke this procedure provided he notifies the General Manager within forty-eight (48) hours of discharge. The General Manager will request an arbitrator be assigned according to the rules of the American Arbitration Association and that the arbitration hearing be conducted under American Arbitration Association rules and regulations. The em-

cont.

ployee shall have the right to have a noninvolved Company employee, such as the Director of Personnel, or any other fellow employee of his choosing, help him prepare his case. The employee shall be able to call other employees to act as witnesses in his behalf, cross-examine witnesses and have access to pertinent data.

The General Manager will appoint a management person to present the Company's case to the arbitrator.

The arbitrator shall be the sole authority to determine just cause for discharge. The arbitrator shall be governed in his decision by plant rules and regulations and shall not add to nor subtract from these rules and regulations. The arbitrator shall have the power to award normal pay for the period missed, minus any monies earned. The Company shall pay the expenses of the arbitrator. The arbitrator will make his decision known within fifteen (15) days of the closing of the hearing.

COMPANY POLICY ON UNIONS

Included in the policy manual should be a statement regarding unions, the following is an example:

Company Policy on Unions

Your company has adopted the same policy as many of the great progressive corporations. We prefer to deal with our people directly rather than through a third party. This is a union-free organization; it always has been, and it is certainly our desire that it always be that way. This does not mean that from time to time we do not have problems; however, we have always been able to work these out among ourselves without the intervention of outsiders.

No organization is free from day-to-day problems, but we believe that we have policies and practices to help resolve these problems. Unions have never gotten anyone his job, neither have they caused anyone to keep his job. Only all of us, working together to make this a viable, healthy organization, are able to do that.

We encourage you to bring your problems to your supervisor, or anyone else you feel can help you, and we, in turn, promise to listen and give the best possible response that we can.

In today's world, there are many pressures. We want to keep our organization free from artificially created tensions that can be brought on by the intervention of outsiders, such as unions. We feel that a union would be of no advantage to any of us. It would hurt the business on which we depend for our livelihood. We accept our responsibility to provide the best working conditions, pay, and benefits that we can afford. It is not necessary for you to pay union dues to enjoy the pay and benefits provided in this booklet.

Chapter Nine

Discipline

Contrary to our belief as union organizers that union-free companies' discipline was arbitrary, capricious, and quick, we know from fifteen years of work with management that many companies lack *any* disciplinary program. Stories of employees with seventeen years' service being terminated without notice or supervisors summarily terminating employees after an argument abounded. The opposite is true. Management in union-free companies does not have a problem with overdiscipline, but with underdiscipline; where supervisors, viewing discipline as Armageddon, do nothing about progressive discipline, or drop an atomic bomb on a fly. These supervisors talk about "the straw that broke the camel's back" or "after all I've done for them, look what they've done to me."

95/5 RULE

Management should remember the 95/5 rule of employee relations in discipline: In a plant, hospital, or any organization, 5 percent of the people create 95 percent of the problems—absenteeism, lateness, scrap, rework, safety, carelessness, bad attitude, poor performance, lack of dedication, abuse of patients, bad telephone manners, and all other disciplinary issues management must deal with.

If the 95/5 rule is valid and if less than 1 percent of employees in most companies are terminated, doesn't a higher termination rate indicate a proper disciplinary system? Not necessarily. We are *not* recommending massive terminations; we *are* recommending fairness—progressive discipline with due process.

The positive side of the 95/5 rule is that 95 percent of the people in any organization are good, sound, solid workers, ranging from acceptable to superstars. They give the company a fair day's work for a fair day's pay. The upper 95 percent may turn to a union if management fails to deal fairly and quickly with the 5 percent. Good workers see the union as protection against management's failure to deal with the 5 percent who are causing problems—not giving normal job effort. The work still gets done—either by the supervisor or in most cases by the other workers—but they resent it. Movement to another machine, excessive overtime caused by absenteeism, and rework are all problems the 95 percent are affected by because of the lack of a sound, solid disciplinary program.

Failure to take disciplinary action is often the result of apprehension about the good workers' reaction. "If we discipline this employee," management says, "the other workers would be so outraged they would turn to a union to protect themselves and the disciplined employee." However, nothing could be further from the truth. When management finally disciplines an employee, in most cases the workers' reaction is not, "Oh, my God! They didn't." or "The company is really running a concentration camp." The vast majority feel: "It's about time!"

Supervisors many times compound the problem saying: "Oh, hell! It's easier to do it myself." It is easier to do it once, perhaps, but too often employees expect supervisors to do it again and again. Supervisors who let that happen like working better than supervising.

Webster's New Collegiate Dictionary defines discipline as:

1. Training that corrects, molds, strengthens, and perfects.

2. Punishment or chastisement.

3. Control gained by enforcing obedience or order, as in a school or army, hence orderly conduct; as troops noted for discipline.

4. Rule or system of rules affecting conduct or action, especially practical rules as distinguished from dogmatic formulations.

The premise of our discipline program is that industrial discipline should correct, not punish workers. To see whether you have a good disciplinary program, take the following quiz.

		YES	NO
1.	Do you have any substandard employees on your payroll?	____	____
2.	Do you have lots of employee problems that require an excessive amount of supervisory and staff time to handle?	____	____
3.	Does your boss back you when you feel it necessary to discipline an employee?	____	____
4.	After you have fired an employee, has your boss or someone else ever forced you to reinstate him?	____	____
5.	Do you think that all supervisors in your company consistently enforce company policy?	____	____
6.	Does your company have published company rules of conduct to govern employees on company property?	____	____
7.	Are all supervisors in your company required to keep a factual record on the performance of every employee?	____	____
8.	Does your company have a formal warning procedure that lets employees know when their job performance is unsatisfactory?	____	____

If you answered yes to questions 1, 2, and 4, and no to questions 3, 5, 6, 7, and 8, your discipline program is in bad shape. To build a solid, sound disciplinary program within your organization, start with the 95/5 rule. Especially important is consideration of the marginal employee if management is going to put into its disciplinary program the ingredients for a solid cake that the union organizer can't cut. Perhaps the best statement about marginal employees and the best definition of favoritism we've seen come from a union organizer:

The Marginal Employee*

Sometimes we union people are amazed at how naive company officers are when it comes to dealing with people and unions.

To begin with, I make little headway in my efforts to organize a plant, store, or any other establishment in which the employees are happy, where they are doing a good job, and where they are treated with fair and thoughtful consideration. It can rarely be done. Let me tell you what I would do if I were the owner or manager of an establishment and I wanted to protect myself against a union.

First, I would discharge every employee that I had who was doing a poor and unsatisfactory job. We union organizers always start a drive with the disgruntled worker, the one that shirks his responsibilities, the loafer—the employee or employees that management has really meant to discharge for the past several months but for some reason hasn't. That is the kind of employee that I look for. I can't interest employees in a union who are happy, conscientious workers.

The inefficient worker, on the other hand, knows that he is a chiseler and looks for someone to blame besides himself. Very shortly, he is finding fault with his foreman, his supervisor, or his plant manager, and when he gets no consolation from within the plant, he turns to a source outside the plant, or, in other words, to a union organizer.

So, my first advice to industry would be to discharge immediately every poor and inefficient worker in the plant. Don't wait. *Do it now before it is too late.*

My next advice would be to terminate any foreman or supervisor who plays favorites with the employees under his jurisdiction. To punish one employee for an infraction of plant rules, and ignore violations of others; to require a full eight hours work from one employee and allow some of his fellow workers to get by with half-hearted work, is to invite a labor union into the plant. Foremen who play

---

*Comments of a union organizer as quoted by S. Maynard Smith, Atlanta attorney, in a speech before the Southern States Industrial Relations Conference, Birmingham, Alabama. WHAT TO DO BEFORE THE UNION COMES, Tennessee Manufacturer's Association, Nashville, Tennessee, 37201.

favorites organize more employees for me than I could ever organize through my own efforts.

BASIC STEPS IN DISCIPLINARY PROGRAMS

Three basic steps necessary to any disciplinary program are: investigation, decision making, and action.

Investigation

In addition to giving practical reasons for dealing with the bottom 5 percent of employees through investigatory processes, two equally important situations are faced by union-free organizations.

1.   Employees of union-free companies are covered by equal opportunity laws. If a union doesn't arrive on the scene over discipline cases, management may have to deal with the government. The better prepared, the more likely management will win a case at a hearing. Investigation, documented evidence is extremely important.

2.   Disciplinary termination may violate state unemployment compensation laws, requiring reinstatement of an employee. (Check your state's unemployment compensation legislation to determine exactly what must be done to meet the requirements of the law.)

Investigation normally begins with questions regarding misconduct or failure to perform basic job responsibilities: Where were you? What was the matter? What happened? Why did you do this? Why didn't you finish the assignment? Where did you leave the patient? When will the report be completed? Failure to investigate or assumption of guilt without investigation are the major mistakes made by supervisors.

For example, an orderly reassigned from one floor to another to help move a patient did not report. He had had an altercation with his supervisor before leaving his own floor, saying he was sick and tired of being moved around the hospital, that he had other patients to care for, and on top of that, it was his dinner hour and he was tired of eating a cold dinner because the cafeteria would be closed by the time he got there.

A half hour after the supervisor had ordered him to go down and help on the other floor, he still had not shown up. The supervisor fired him for insubordination, but later learned the orderly had been stuck in the elevator for forty-five minutes, a fact verified by the maintenance department. Even where bad attitude and poor cooperation are involved, employees must always be given an opportunity to explain misconduct. Get in the habit of asking who, what, why, when, where questions before taking disciplinary action.

To assist in planning procedures, a sample discipline form that supervisors can and should fill out promptly after investigation is given in Figure 9-1. This basic documentation is timely when the case comes up for review.

Management controls employee conduct by investigation in the disciplinary processes. Employees are accountable for their actions. Management can take more severe disciplinary action if employees fail or refuse to answer questions concerning their actions. Unless supervisors investigate thoroughly, the company is not meeting the burden of proof in disciplinary cases. Management bears the burden of proof; employees are assumed innocent until the company can prove them guilty.

Employees caught sleeping at work can be guilty of serious misconduct, but *why* they were sleeping must be considered. An employee leaves work early because of an emergency at home, but was it an emergency or falsification? Management may investigate and require the employee to account for his whereabouts.

Consider Case 1. A bank teller continually found excuses to leave work early, particularly on Friday afternoons. The branch manager had been lenient with minor problems at home—a sick child, and so on—but finally required accountability. On a Friday afternoon, the teller received a call, and explained he had to go home because his house had been burglarized. The manager agreed, but asked the teller to call him later that afternoon.

The manager asked on Monday why the teller had not called. The reply was he didn't remember that request. Asked for details on the breaking and entering, he said a television set, a stereo, some money, and other things had been taken. He stated he had filed a police report, and a copy was at

Figure 9-1
DATE _____
PREPARED BY _____

MANAGEMENT EDUCATION CENTER
DISCIPLINE INVESTIGATION REPORT

1. NAME OF EMPLOYEE _____

2. RULE(S) VIOLATED _____
   _____

3. FACTS (SPECIFICALLY WHAT HAPPENED AND WHAT WAS SAID)? _____
   _____
   _____
   _____
   _____
   _____

4. WHEN _____
5. WHERE _____
6. WITNESSES (IF SO, WHO?) _____
   _____

7. WHAT DID WITNESSES SAY? _____
   _____
   _____
   _____
   _____
   _____

8. WAS THERE ANY REASON FOR WITNESSES TO FALSIFY OR "EMBROIDER"
   THEIR STORY? (IF SO, EXPLAIN) _____
   _____
   _____
   _____

9. WHAT WERE THE CONSEQUENCES OF THE ALLEGED MISCONDUCT? _____
   _____
   _____
   _____
   _____
   _____

10. WAS ALLEGED MISCONDUCT DISCUSSED WITH EMPLOYEE? _____
11. WHEN _____
12. WHERE _____
13. BY WHOM _____
14. WITNESSED? _____
    _____

cont.

15. PRECISELY WHAT WAS EMPLOYEE'S RESPONSE WHEN ASKED TO EXPLAIN HIS/HER CONDUCT? _____

_____

_____

_____

_____

16. WERE THERE AGGRAVATING OR MITIGATING CIRCUMSTANCES (EXPLAIN) __

_____

_____

_____

_____

17. WERE OTHER EMPLOYEES INVOLVED? _____

18. WHO WERE THEY? _____

_____

_____

19. WHAT DID THEY DO AND SAY? _____

_____

_____

_____

20. WHAT ACTION IS BEING TAKEN IN THEIR CASES? _____

_____

_____

_____

21. WHAT PHYSICAL EVIDENCE OF THE ALLEGED MISCONDUCT IS AVAILABLE? (EVIDENCE SHOULD BE PRESERVED IF POSSIBLE) _____

_____

_____

22. ADDITIONAL COMMENTS _____

_____

_____

NOTE: ATTACH STATEMENTS OF SUPERVISORS OR WITNESSES, DIAGRAMS, PICTURES, ETC.

home. "Well, bring it in tomorrow," the manager replied. When he said he had forgotten the report on Tuesday, he was sent home to get it.

Meanwhile, the employee relations and security departments contacted the police, and established a report had not been filed. He reported to work on Wednesday and still insisted that he had filed a police report, despite being told no report was on file. Management suspended him pending further investigation. When he reported the following Monday without the report, he was discharged for poor attendance and falsification of records. The State Unemployment Board, to which he appealed, sided with the bank because of the manager's documented report. This decision was based on the employee's proven record.

Consider Case 2. A second-shift employee, habitually absent or late, was placed on final thirty-day probation and warned not to miss any more time. He still reported an hour late three times during the period, but the supervisor didn't feel this was serious enough to warrant termination.

The employee's wife called one night to report that a dog had bitten her, and the husband left work at 8 P.M. with permission to take her to the hospital. Although the shift did not end until 1 A.M., he didn't return to work until the next day. The supervisor asked how his wife was, and he said the bite wasn't serious and his wife didn't need medical coverage. A police report was requested, and he stated he had reported the dog bite orally to the sheriff's department. Because the wife didn't need medical attention, the alleged report had been oral. However, a hospital must file a written report of a dog bite to the local enforcing agency so the possibility of rabies can be checked out. The supervisor told the employee he wanted to see a copy of the report.

The plant manager decided to investigate and drove over to the hospital and the police. Although the hospital had no record of medical care, the head nurse in emergency recalled a dog bite case requiring no medical attention and said they had called the county sheriff. The nurse said they didn't bother to charge an admission fee in a case like this, otherwise a hospitalization claim could have been verified.

The plant manager talked to the sheriff's department, verifying that a dog bite report had been filed. The supervisor and the plant manager, telling the employee their investigation backed up his account, accepted this as an emergency. Management extended his probation for another thirty days because of his latenesses and his failure to contact the supervisor and told him his attendance had better improve dramatically or he would be terminated.

In both cases, the company's acceptance of burden of proof resulted in fair resolution. In Case 1, an undesirable employee was successfully terminated. In Case 2, management demonstrated to the employee they were willing to work with him on a particular problem, but also communicated clearly that the employee had to meet his obligations.

Investigation is primarily a supervisory function; personnel and the plant manager can help but the supervisor needs to record the basic information. The discipline investigation form demonstrates that basic documentation isn't all that demanding—if supervisors are willing to take time to investigate *when the problem arises. Two weeks later is too late.*

Decision Making: Verbal Warning

After investigation, management can decide, based on the facts, what discipline, if any, should be taken. Discussion follows with the employee. Tell the employee what the problem is and lay out what conduct is expected. Supervisors should talk formally with employees about the company's work expectations. Verbal warnings serve to turn an employee around and to identify failure to meet responsibilities. Verbal warnings should follow this procedure:

1.   Prepare for the discussion.

2.   Determine the time and place.

3.   Get started.

4.   Let the employee speak.

5.   Conclude the discussion.

6.   Follow up.

7.   Make a written report of the meeting.

1. *Prepare for the discussion* by addressing three fundamental points: problem, proof, and solution.

What is the *problem?* Can the supervisor state specifically what the employee has or has not done? Be specific; stay away from generalities such as attitude or cooperation. For example, in preparing for the discussion, get at the problem by stating: "Prior to leaving the work area, you must ask for my permission." This is not a personal attack on the employee, which is something to avoid. For example: "You don't care at all. You won't even *ask* permission. Anytime you want to leave you just pick up and walk away." This approach will put the employee on the defensive —and he probably won't pay much attention to anything else said.

You want him to enter into the discussion, agree or disagree, and stating the problem is more likely to bring that about than a bawling out. When the problem is stated, the response is usually shock: "Who? Me? I didn't know that. Why didn't you tell me before?" This shocked response really means that the employee is asking for *proof.*

There are two ways to try to convince an employee you know what you are talking about—dazzle him with your footwork or put the hard, cold facts on the line. Use the former; give examples of misconduct off the top of your head. For instance, the wife complains: "Harry, you don't do anything around the house. When are you going to fix that drip in the washing machine? When are you going to paint the house?" This offers a fine opening for counter argument by the husband: "I would've painted the house last week, but you insisted on our visiting your mother. I didn't want to visit the old bat!" This type of argument, like most arguments at home, are resolved by someone apologizing.

Use this approach with an employee, you will likely get this response, "See, I knew I was right!" Usually the supervisor does not apologize, the employee does not apologize, and the Berlin Wall goes up. When they meet, it's the hard stare or averted glance, and no further discussion. Avoid dazzling arguments; no one wins. Arguing over facts in black and white is difficult, and that is where investigation and preparation of proof make a positive meeting. What kind of proof? It might be: "Here is the scrap percentage you've been running," or in an office, "Here is the unfinished report I asked you to have typed by Friday, and it has fourteen typographical errors." If the facts are accepted, the employee is unlikely to start shouting.

Preparation must include determining how the employee can correct the problem—the problem's *solution.* Positive, corrective alternatives must be discussed, and if you have taken notes, discussed the problem, and gathered proof, you can share some solutions with the employee. The employee may also have some idea about solutions, however, the supervisor should have some specific plan the employee can follow.

For example, if a bank teller is out of balance, it's up to the supervisor to explain to the teller how to check for balances during the day. If an employee is having materials problems, planning prior to machine set-up is necessary to make sure needed parts for subassembly are there. Supervisors have technical knowledge, know what's going on in their departments, and are in the best position to deal with technical problems.

2. *Determine the time and place* for discussions. Conduct counseling or disciplinary sessions in private; don't chew people out in front of others. If you don't have an office, borrow one or at least get the employee to your desk where you can talk privately. Try to avoid interruptions, and by all means, leave plenty of time—make clear that you want to spend the time necessary to discuss the problem.

3. *Getting started* by setting the right tone of the meeting is important. The tone will depend on the seriousness of the offense and the length of service of the employee. To the new employee who has made the same mistake a number of times, after you've tried to correct it during normal work instruction, you may want to say, in effect, that continued mistakes could result in termination. On the other hand, if dealing with a long-service employee who has made an error without serious impact, the tone should be more conciliatory than a warning.

Employees should know the nature of the subject before the meeting. Given time to think about the issue, they may have some positive solutions. For example: "Harry, I'd like to talk to you after you finish your coffee break, concerning the errors that went into the report to the department head."

4. *Let the employee speak.* The purpose of the meeting is to solve the problem, not to hassle the employee. State the facts and listen for a few minutes. Get in the habit of using the "pregnant pause." Wait awhile after you've stated the facts. The employee will feel obligated to say something—to apologize or disagree: "You didn't understand. It wasn't really my error. Somebody else made it."

Role-playing in training makes supervisors comfortable with employee encounters. We strongly recommend seeking assistance of other supervisors, personnel, or the department head in role-playing. They act as employees and try out the supervisor's position. It's most productive if the "other side" gives you a hard time or discusses the issue. The supervisor learns to be a good listener.

5. *Conclude the discussion,* but do not let the employee leave the meeting until a solution has been agreed to. Even when the problem, the facts, and the solution have been discussed, the employee, feeling uncomfortable and embarrassed, often would rather exit stage left. A commitment to improvement is the reason for the meeting. The supervisor must

hear: "Well, I think I understand what you want," or "Yes, I'll try to be more careful," or "I understand now how serious it is to leave a patient unattended."

6. *Follow up* after the discussion. If the employee improves, don't wait—tell him. Give positive reinforcement. Following up after improvement is an excellent way of communicating that you and the employee are on the same track.

If the employee doesn't improve, try another discussion. Ask why the employee didn't get the message. The best bet is dual counseling. Bring in the department head, general foreman, or the employee relations department. Dual counseling is effective in dealing with employees, it makes employees aware that the problem is serious, and avoids the argument: "The supervisor is just picking on me," or "The supervisor doesn't like me." Dual counseling forces management to effectively prepare for discussion.

7. *Make a written record of the meeting.* A simple statement of facts is the critical aspect in motivating employees to improve and is essential if there is no improvement.

A simple but effective sample form supervisors may use to keep track of discussions with employees is shown in Figure 9-2. This Employee Performance Record isn't difficult to maintain for ten to twenty people; the record can be kept current in ten to fifteen minutes a week. When an employee performs well, jot it down. When poor performance occurs, check it out and then make a record. The instructions at the bottom of the form emphasize that it is the basis for documentation for subsequent review and/or action. The form itself may not be sufficient evidence to sustain charges, however, it is worth a lot more than the supervisor's memory in subsequent employee evaluations. This form is valuable for merit reviews. Meritorious employees will be on the plus side; marginal employees on the negative. Average employees will have few comments either good or bad. Supervisors are well advised to ask themselves: "What has that employee done that I can compliment him or her on, and record?" This form is worth its weight in gold in the event of a disciplinary hearing, and it doesn't take much time to keep up to date.

We are not advocating the foremen's little black book of 1939, where foremen kept secret records of employee's mistakes. A record of *both* good and bad performance should be kept on *all* employees. Accurate records are not only admissible at hearings, but many times they can convince hearing officers to accept a supervisor's testimony.

The form is admissible evidence before arbitrators where employees

Figure 9-2 RECORD OF EMPLOYEE'S PERFORMANCE

INSTRUCTIONS TO SUPERVISORS—Record only those things that have been discussed with your employee; record them *promptly* and *factually*. This record is your personal property and should remain *private*.

EMPLOYEE: *Mary L. Jones*   Date of Hire *3/1/80*

                                   Probationary ____

Classification *Secretary*   Status: Permanent *✓*

PLUS PERFORMANCES

4/8/80 BJW was pleased with typing job Mary did for him. So advised Mary.

5/3/80 Mary completed her 60 day probationary period. Had discussion with her & informed her of $10.00 increase. Wished her well with the company.

6/20/80 Found procedural error in report submitted by BJW. Saved 3 hours of typing. Complimented her for alertness.

MINUS PERFORMANCES

2/13/80 Absent—no call in.

2/14/80 Discussed failure to call in. Said she was too ill to talk on phone. Informed her of call in rule.

3/21/80 15 minutes late. Held up on expressway.

4/15/80 18 minutes late; alarm clock failed to go off. Advised her that her attendance record was poor & must improve.

5/10/80 Found 7 typographical errors on report. She promised to be more careful.

6/8/80 More careless work. 2 stencils returned from Mim. room who refused to run them. Mary was upset & claimed I was picking on her. Orally warned her that her performance must improve or I would have to take drastic action.

Use additional sheets if necessary for either division.

are covered by labor contracts, and before various state and federal regulatory agencies, EEOC, State Civil Rights Commission, State Unemployment Boards, and Workmen's Compensation Boards. The form demonstrates effectively that management is keeping objective (not subjective) records of all employees, regardless of age, sex, religion, or country of origin.

Check the formal instructions. Notice that only matters discussed personally with the employee, after investigation, and discussed between the supervisor and the employee are entered. The employee should have access to copies of the form.

We have discussed investigation and the first step of discipline, the verbal warning. Verbal warnings are one of the union-free supervisor's most effective tools for correcting employees who are not meeting basic job requirements. However, if verbal warnings do not succeed, hearing officers require formal disciplinary steps demonstrating every reasonable step has been taken to correct the employee. Formal discipline is the next step if verbal warnings fail.

Action: Formal Progressive Discipline

Formal discipline is necessary for employees who don't get the message. Progressive discipline follows the pattern of oral warnings, written warnings, and final warnings prior to termination, except for a major offense— an act so serious that one occurrence is legitimate cause for discharge— and this is rare. The vast majority of problems supervisors deal with are repeated minor offenses. Following is a hearing officer/arbitrator's checklist. Before discussing the rationale behind the rules, management should be aware of rules hearing officers apply. Hearing officers involved in employee discipline cases are not necessarily bound by rules of law. Judges in a court of law are bound by the law and by precedence.

Hearing officers apply the rule of reasonableness: Did management act reasonably, given reasonable conditions, and arrive at a reasonable decision? There are a few notable differences between a court of law and disciplinary hearings. Hearsay evidence may be admissible in disciplinary cases. Hearing officers often cross-examine witnesses; the burden of proof is borne by prosecutor or defense attorney in court. Reasonableness must guide supervisors in building a disciplinary case. The following examples demonstrate the difference between "shop" discipline and courts of law.

An employee covered by a union contract was making book in the shop. The personnel manager discovered he was making book after being caught twice, and notified the police of the situation. Two policemen observed the employee on the telephone calling in a bet. The employee saw them as they approached and swallowed the betting slips. The company terminated him, the police charged him with bookmaking, however, the local magistrate dismissed the case for lack of evidence. The union called for arbitration, claiming concrete evidence was lacking and the court had cleared the employee; therefore, he was entitled to return to work. The arbitrator, ruling in favor of the company, applied the reasonableness test. "As a reasonable man, I must conclude that an employee who has been caught twice before making book, and whom the company has reason to believe is making book again—he is on the telephone with small pieces of paper in his hand, sees two policemen and the personnel manager approaching, and swallows the pieces of paper—I would assume, as a reasonable man, is making book."

Consider another case. A foundry midnight shift supervisor could not find an employee at 3 A.M., went into the steel yard, and found the employee with a six-pack of beer. "Stay here; I'll be right back," he told the employee, but when he returned with a witness, both employee and the six-pack were gone. The company suspended the employee for ten days based on the reasonableness test. The case came before a hearing officer who ruled for the company on the basis of credibility of the witness. A supervisor is deemed more credible than an employee, on the basis of the "party of interest." It is not in the supervisor's interest to lie; his job is to run a safe, efficient, and orderly operation. Management can't get by without proof and fact, but in many cases of off-shifts or isolated locations, it's the supervisor's word against the employees. Other factors being equal, the supervisor's word is worth far more than the employee's word.

The purpose of discipline is to correct, not punish. A case can be made that a written warning letter or suspension without pay was given to correct an employee's behavior, but how can management contend that an employee was discharged to improve behavior?

RULES OF PROOF FOR HEARING OFFICERS

Hearing officers view discharge as "industrial capital punishment," a company discharging an employee claiming that the person is 100 percent worthless, they have tried everything, and the employee is incorrigible.

Figure 9-3 HEARING OFFICER/ARBITRATOR'S CHECKLIST

	YES	NO
1. Is the rule violated published?	_____	_____
2. Is it posted on company bulletin boards?	_____	_____
3. Did this employee ever receive a personal copy of the rule violated?	_____	_____
4. Is the rule stated in easy-to-understand wording?	_____	_____
5. Is the violated rule or order reasonably related to the orderly, efficient, and safe operation of the business?	_____	_____
6. If other employees have violated this rule or order, did they receive the same disciplinary action as this employee?	_____	_____
7. Does the company maintain factual records on all employees covering all violations of this rule or order?	_____	_____
8. Does this employee have the worst record of all employees on violation of this rule or order?	_____	_____
9. Has this employee been warned previously for violation of this rule or order?	_____	_____
10. Has this employee ever received a previous written warning of violation of this rule or order?	_____	_____
11. Has this employee ever received a final warning for the violation of this or any other published rule or order?	_____	_____
12. Was the incident that triggered the final warning or discharge carefully investigated prior to taking serious or final disciplinary action?	_____	_____
13. Is there a factual, written record showing the steps taken by the company to correct this employee's improper actions prior to serious disciplinary action?	_____	_____
14. Have similar written records been kept and similar steps taken by the company to correct the improper actions of all employees?	_____	_____
15. Does company evidence include names of witnesses, dates, time, places, and other pertinent facts on all past violations, including the last one?	_____	_____

cont.

16. Was the degree of discipline imposed on this em-
    ployee related to (a) seriousness of the proven
    offense, (b) the employee's past record, and (c)
    his length of service?   _____   _____
17. What doesn't the arbitrator ask about the em-
    ployee because he really doesn't care?   _____   _____

Before disciplining an employee, go over the checklist (figure 9-3). If all answers are yes, management will win before a hearing officer. If very many no answers are checked, the case is not fair, consistent, and justifiable, and either senior management or a hearing officer will reverse the decision. As we comment on the hearing officer's checklist, keep in mind the Employee Performance Record. Many of the hearing officer's questions can be answered positively if the company has been keeping the employment record up to date on all employees. The rules that hearing officers use as guidelines appear in Figure 9-4.

The hearing officer's first three questions are:

1. Is the rule that has been violated published?

2. Is it posted on company bulletin boards?

3. Did the employee receive a personal copy of the rule?

If management can prove that the rules are published in employee handbooks, are posted on bulletin boards throughout the facilities, and all employees received the handbook upon employment, the organization meets the test. New employees should receive the rules and regulations and sign a statement that they have received, read, and understand them. This is a sound business practice. All employees are entitled to know the rules governing conduct at your facility.

Question 4: Is the wording easy to understand? The hearing officer will ask whether employees can easily comprehend the rules. If the organization hires a large number of Hispanics or Vietnamese, the rules should be printed in their native language.

Question 5: Is the violated order reasonable in terms of safe, efficient, and orderly operation of the business? The hearing officer is asking if the rule makes sense. For example, a no-smoking rule in a steel mill would be

Figure 9-4 GENERAL COMPANY RULES

Every employee has the right to know the rules that govern employee conduct. In an organization of this size, rules have to be followed. Having them helps us to operate efficiently, ensures that your best interests will be protected, and makes our organization a safe one in which to work. They apply to all of us. They are for the benefit of all of us.

Penalties: From verbal and/or written warning to disciplinary layoff or discharge. In applying these customary penalties, consideration will be given to seniority, the employee's past record, and the severity of the offense, as well as the interval between violations.

As a guide, the following actions are not acceptable:

1. Giving false information concerning reason for being absent or tardy.

2. Carelessness in observing quality.

3. Carelessness in observing safety or housekeeping requirements.

4. Failure to report personal injuries to supervisor.

5. Removing, defacing, or changing official notices or bulletins posted in the plant.

6. Overstaying breaks or lunch periods.

7. Performance of substandard work relative to quality and quantity of production after being instructed in the proper job method

8. Stopping work to wash up before authorized to do so.

9. Indulging in horseplay or practical jokes while on Company property.

10. Unnecessarily talking to, or in any other way distracting the attention of, another employee during working hours.

cont.

11. Failure of an employee to report any damage he has caused to another employee's car parked in the Company parking lot.

12. Failure to comply with posted notices on the Company premises.

13. Being in the operating section of plant during off hours, or bringing others into the plant without prior permission.

14. Sleeping while on the job or "loafing."

15. Willfully punching or removing a time card other than your own. Making changes to your own or another's time card.

16. Gambling on Company time or property.

17. Unauthorized use of, or neglect in the case or use of, Company facilities or equipment, whether or not it results in damage or injury to equipment, production, quality, or other persons.

18. Tampering with or deliberately misusing emergency equipment, such as fire extinguishers, and so on.

19. Abusive or threatening language to fellow employees or management personnel.

20. Smoking or striking a flame in prohibited areas.

21. Offering or receiving money or other valuable considerations in exchange for a job, better working place, or any advantage in working conditions.

22. Obtaining material or other property or money from the Company by fraudulent means or misrepresentation.

23. Stealing, willfully damaging, or maliciously hiding any property belonging to other employees of the Company.

cont.

24. Falsifying Company records or reports (including personnel, physical examination, production, inventory counts, or quality control reports) or divulging Company information of a confidential nature to unauthorized persons.

25. Carrying weapons or having weapons in the plant.

26. Leaving the premises without permission of your supervisor or other person authorized to grant this permission, or failure to clock IN and OUT when leaving or returning.

27. Fighting or attempting bodily injury to another employee while on Company property.

28. Convictions in courts of law which cause employee to be regarded as undesirable.

29. Refusal to obey legitimate orders of supervision.

30. Consuming alcoholic beverages during working hours and-/or on Company property or reporting for work under the influence of alcohol.

31. Consuming drugs on Company property or reporting for work under the influence of illegal drugs.

32. Violations of any federal, state, or local law affecting the Company or your employment with the Company, including treasonable acts or statements against the United States, or attempts to, or acts of sabotage against Company property, or bringing the Company name to disrepute.

33. Excessive absenteeism or tardiness.

34. Posting of any material on the Company premises without the written approval of the Plant Manager.

35. Insubordination.

cont.

36. Unauthorized use of Company identification cards.

37. Immoral or indecent conduct.

38. Malicious gossip.

39. Accepting other employment while on leave of absence.

40. Refusing to wear hearing protection provided by the Company.

41. Refusing to wear safety shoes provided by the Company.

ridiculous, but highly reasonable in an oil refinery. Is it reasonable for a company to have a dress code? Certainly it would be for people in corporate headquarters meeting customers; a dress code for coal miners would be unreasonable unless related to safety. The days of requiring male employees to wear ties, forbidding pant suits for women, or ruling out beards are over. However, if a beard poses a safety hazard when an employee is required to wear a resuscitator or is welding, or when the employee calls on customers who expect ties, the hearing officer would probably uphold the company's requirements. Companies have trouble when their rules are arbitrary, capricious, and without basis in fact.

Questions 6 and 8: Some companies operate like ten companies— the First-Shift Company, the Second-Shift Company, the Third-Shift Company, the Maintenance Department Company, the Tool Room Company, the Stock Room Company, and so on. Supervisors tell employees, "I don't care what they do in production. This is the way I run the maintenance department," or "I don't care what the payroll department does on breaks or lunches. This is the way I run the quality control department."

Under a union contract, management must maintain the same rules and regulations for all employees, *"Do you need a union to make you do what you ought to be doing in the first place?"* For example, when employees in one department are treated one way and in another department differently, or when one shift has half an hour for lunch and the next shift has forty minutes, the policy is inconsistent. And inconsistency smacks of favoritism and discrimination, causing good people to bring in a union to make the company treat everybody fairly, justly, and equitably.

Our recommendation is for management to establish reasonable rules of conduct—in absenteeism, lateness, break time, quitting time, wash-up time, and so on—and apply the rules equitably and fairly.

Question 7: Does the company maintain factual records on all employees? If you look at the Employee Performance Form, the answer is
yes.

Question 9: Has the employee been previously warned for violation of this rule or order? Hearing officers ask: "Have you counseled the employee and tried to improve his behavior?" The Performance Record proves factually that counseling steps have been taken prior to serious or final disciplinary action.

Question 10: Has the employee ever been warned in writing of this rule or order violation? Employees are entitled to a written warning prior to serious or final disciplinary action. Figures 9-5 and 9-6 are examples of written warnings, laying out problems previously identified and discussed which the employee has failed to correct.

The following are guidelines for written warnings:

1. State material facts; for example, date, time, place, actions of individual involved.

2. Quote the Company rule violated.

3. Written warnings should outline any previous "oral warn-ings." They should be limited to the last *twelve months* and be for a comparable offense.

4. State that letter constitutes a *written reprimand.*

5. You should state the employee has a chance to improve his performance and you hope that he does so.

6. State that if the employee does not improve, he will subject himself to further disciplinary action. *Remain flexible,* don't state what it will be.

7. Give employee a copy.

8. Put a copy in employee's record.

Figure 9-5 CORRECTIVE DISCIPLINARY ACTION LETTER
TARDINESS—After Written Reprimand

Mr. James F. Smith   November 28, 1980
[Address]

Dear Mr. Smith:
The established and published company rules state that "all employees shall be at their assigned work stations, ready to perform their assigned duties, at the regular starting time." On June 12, 1980, you were given a verbal warning by me stating that unless you reported to work on time, you would be subject to further disciplinary action. I explained the numerous reasons for requiring our employees to be at work on time.

On September 14, 1980, I gave you a Written Warning Notice for failing to report to work on time in accordance with company rules. This disciplinary action was taken because you had been tardy eight (8) times in that four (4) month period. I warned you in the Written Warning Notice that failure to correct your record by reporting regularly and on time would make you subject to further disciplinary action. Since September 14, 1980, your record shows that you were late on the following days:

September 15, Wednesday	October 11, Tuesday
September 20, Monday	November 8, Monday
October 3, Monday	November 15, Monday
October 10, Monday	November 28, Thursday

On each of these dates you reported for work late and did not give me any reason that could be accepted as a reasonable excuse. Your continual tardiness has placed an added load on myself as your supervisor in scheduling work in your department. It has also placed added burden on your fellow workers who respect their responsibilities and report for work on time.

Since you have not heeded my previous warnings to correct your attendance record by reporting on time and fully meeting the responsibilities of your position, I am presenting you with a Written Warning Notice.

cont.

You are expected to correct your tardiness by reporting regularly on time. You are expected to abide with the established and published company rules or you will subject yourself to further disciplinary action up to and including termination.

Sincerely,

_____

Supervisor

Figure 9-6 REFUSAL TO PERFORM WORK ASSIGNMENT

Mr. John E. Doe   June 6, 1980
[Address]

Dear Mr. Doe:

This Written Warning Notice is given to you as a disciplinary action for your insubordination and conduct on June 5, 1980, by refusing to perform a reasonable assignment given by me as your supervisor.

Section 8 of our established and published rules states the following:

"An employee shall accept any reasonable work assignment or location assigned by their supervisor, or take reasonable directions from an individual designated as supervisor."

On June 5, 1980, I assigned you the task of making a list of all the special tooling that the Mill Department has in storage for work order 4828. You violently objected to the task, claiming that it was not your responsibility or part of your job duties.

I explained to you that your job required you to know what special tooling is available to you in working on an assigned work order and that the assigned task was well in line with your job duties. In addition, you were reminded of the insubordination rule.

I gave you an opportunity to reconsider your refusal. You still refused to perform this reasonable assignment. I then directed you to proceed with the work and stated that if you felt that your job duties did not include this kind of work, you could file a grievance in accordance with the procedure that is provided in our Company manual. In this way, the question could be resolved in an orderly manner without interrupting production of your department.

cont.

You still refused to follow my orders and I ordered you to clock out and leave the plant. Although you refused to clock out, you did leave the premises forty-five minutes later. During this forty-five-minute period, you interrupted production by conversing with six (6) of your fellow workers. I clocked you out at 3:30 P.M. after you left the premises. You will not be paid for the period from 3:30 P.M. to your normal assigned quitting time of 5:30 P.M.

This Written Warning Notice is given to you as a disciplinary action and to give you an opportunity to correct your improper conduct, and in the future to undertake reasonable work assignments that are assigned to you. You are expected to fully meet the duties and/or responsibilities of your job in the future. If you will not comply, you will be subjecting yourself to further disciplinary action.

Sincerely,

_____

Supervisor

9. A central source, for example, personnel department, should prepare all warning letters.

10. They are *signed* and *presented* (not mailed) by the first-line supervisor.

The major advantage of a written warning is that it is a serious message to the employee while being corrective; it places the employee on formal notice to improve or to expect that further discipline, up to and including discharge, will be taken. Warnings constitute documentation to hearing officers if an employee is terminated.

Question 11: Has the employee received a final warning for violation of any published rule or order? In a union shop, the hearing officer interprets this as disciplinary time off—three, ten, or more days' suspension. He requires this to prove that the employee knew continued bad conduct would warrant discharge.

In a union-free organization, disciplinary time off may not be necessary, if management has followed progressive discipline with well-detailed and documented written warnings. There may be exceptions, for example: a twenty-five- or thirty-year employee caught stealing. If the company doesn't want to discharge him, suspension without pay could be a more practical solution. Union-free organizations should issue a final, written warning in lieu of suspension in the vast majority of cases.

For the final disciplinary step, discharge, management should be more concerned about the effect on other employees than the discharged employee. Management's goal must be to convince workers that the company has been fair. Many times employees who have complained about an eight-ball worker for years change their tune when the employee is fired. Six months later, they were saying: "Poor old Harry! Look what the company did to him!" Management *must* convince workers that the company only discharges an employee after exhausting all corrective methods.

Question 12: Was the incident carefully investigated *prior to* taking serious or final disciplinary action? The words "prior to" are particularly significant. In too many cases, supervisors have judged the employee guilty prior to discussion and investigation of the incident. Supervisors know their employees well, and the bottom 5 percent very, *very* well. They have spent a lot of time on record keeping, counseling, "friendly nudges," and written warnings on the bottom 5 percent. So much of the supervisor's time has been involved that one incident becomes the "straw that broke the camel's back." One additional absence, lateness, or overstaying break, and the supervisor says: "That's it! I've had it! You're fired." This time, unfortunately, the employee has a legitimate reason. Our advice is for supervisors and managers to remove "you're fired" from their vocabularies; no member of management should have the right to fire anybody on the spot for anything. Management should have the right to say: "You're suspended. Don't report to work until you hear from me. I will let you know the extent of your discipline, if any"—emphasis on "if any." Many times, management loses a case before a hearing officer, not on the merits of the case, but on procedural issues—management hasn't followed their own written procedures. By definition, if discipline is passed out on the spot, the person's frame of mind was not calm and reasonable. The hearing officer may rule that the action exacerbated the situation—management poured fuel on the fire.

Suspension allows time for calm, collected reflection. If the supervisor made a mistake, he can say: "I've checked into the situation, and found some mitigating circumstances. You're going to be paid for the rest of your shift and nothing is going in the record. I'm sorry." A supervisor can more easily admit a mistake to an employee than to lock himself into a position where upper management reverses him. When this happens, the supervisor looks foolish.

Consider a case in point. A second-shift employee in a steel mill had an alcoholism problem, had been through various rehabilitation programs, discipline, and both the union involved and management had tried everything reasonably possible. Everyone agreed that if he reported for work under the influence again, he'd be discharged. Several months after the most recent incident, he reported for work with a liquor bottle in hand, walked up to his supervisor and asked: "Would you like a drink?" "No," said the supervisor. "What are you doing with that bottle?" At this point the employee poured the liquor all over the supervisor, who lost his temper and shouted: "That's it! You're fired!"

However, investigation showed that the employee had received a telegram that day informing him that his youngest son had been killed in combat. He headed to the nearest bar and proceeded to get drunk. Is it reasonable to fire an employee reporting under the influence on the day he learned his son had been killed? Obviously, not!

The employee was reinstated. Once an employee has been reinstated, he has quote "built a fence around himself." A discharged and reinstated employee will always declare: "They're out to get me. They tried this before." It makes it extremely difficult to fire the employee again.

Question 13: Is there a factual, written record showing steps taken by the company to correct improper actions prior to serious disciplinary action? The key words are *to correct.* The company has an obligation to provide counseling and corrective alternatives prior to discharge. For example, an alcoholic employee should receive in-house counseling directing him to Alcoholics Anonymous or other social agencies. The company need need not continue to employ workers who have alcohol or other drug abuse problems, but management has a responsibility to take reasonable steps to correct improper action prior to discharge.

An employee who has not followed standard operating procedures or has been responsible for scrap or an excessive amount of rework, is also subject to discipline.

One of management's toughest decisions is whether or not to terminate an employee; keep in mind the purpose of discipline—to correct unsatisfactory behavior.

Our recommendation is to give the employee the benefit of the doubt for all reasonable discipline prior to discharge. The company must make a substantial effort to turn the employee around, even when his past record indicates that regular, good performance is unlikely. If termination is necessary, the company bears the burden of proof and must demonstrate to hearing officers that the employee had every reasonable opportunity to improve. A major goal should be to convince other employees that the company's discipline has been fair. After a discharge, other employees will often tell their supervisor that the company's discipline has been fair and termination was warranted. When employees mention other misconduct not even known to management, a fair decision has been made. However, if a number of good employees react with silence or hostility, they are questioning management's fairness.

Fair procedure prior to termination involves discussion by the employee's immediate supervisor, department head, or general foreman, and personnel. In cases of employees with five or more years of service, a vice-president or plant manager should sign the termination notice indicating the company's deep concern with job security and proper review.

Question 14: Has the company kept similar records and taken steps to correct all employees' improper actions? This is aimed at the employee who alleges discrimination, stating, "Other employees did the same thing I did, but nothing happened to them." This is tied directly to Questions 6 and 8; the company must be able to demonstrate that all employees are treated in a similar manner. Cases have been lost at hearings, not because the company has been too tough, but because management has been inconsistent; two employees with similar misconduct, in different departments were treated differently. The personnel department should make certain of consistent application, not only of rules, but of disciplinary action taken for violation of the rules.

Question 15: Does company evidence include witnesses' names, dates, times, places, other pertinent facts, and all violations, including the last? Supervisors who keep the Employee Performance Record current can correctly answer yes. Supervisors too often leave out certain facts, forgetting to mention, for example, that an employee shoved the supervisor after being followed for two hours, shouting and swearing.

Question 16: Was the discipline imposed related to (a) the seriousness of the proven offense, (b) the employee's past record, and (c) the length of service? This rule summarizes the concept of industrial progressive discipline. For example, was the employee stealing a 98¢ pair of pliers or 800 feet of copper wire? It makes a difference. Applying the rule of reason, theft of 800 feet of copper wire is much more serious. Was he stealing the product for personal use or for resale, which is more serious? We don't suggest ignoring any kind of stealing, but the degree of discipline should be related to the seriousness of the offense. Stealing the pliers might call for a written warning; stealing 800 feet of copper wire might well result in discharge.

Drinking on the job or reporting for work intoxicated is serious. However, if a janitor and an overhead crane operator are both drunk at work, whose misconduct is more serious? Reason suggests the crane operator could seriously injure or kill other workers, but the janitor is unlikely to kill or injure anybody other than himself. The seriousness test must be applied to all offenses.

Sleeping on the job can be a very serious offense; however, prior to taking disciplinary action the intent of the employee must be determined. For example, in a year, we dealt with three sleeping offenses in one plant:

1. An employee was found asleep on a bench in the locker room by the supervisor, who asked, "What's the matter?" The employee replied, "I don't feel good." Taken to the nurse, then to the hospital, the employee had his spleen removed.

2. A fork-lift operator fell asleep on the fork-lift waiting for it to be loaded.

3. The supervisor looked for an employee for over an hour, finally went behind the kilns and found the employee asleep on an air mattress with an alarm clock.

Were all three cases the same? Obviously not. In the first case, there was no disciplinary action—the supervisor visited the hospital to make certain the employee was all right. An oral warning to the fork-lift operator was noted in his Employee Performance Record. The employee with the air mattress and alarm clock clearly intended to sleep on the job; he was discharged.

The second factor to consider is the employee's past record. Management needs to look at the offense's frequency of occurrence. Was this the first offense or the fifth? Everybody is entitled to make mistakes, but how many, how often, and within what period?

The third factor is length of service. Can a thirty-year employee steal more before discharge than a three-year employee? Can a twenty-seven-year employee report to work intoxicated more often than a seventeen-month employee? Absolutely! If you said, "Wait a minute. You just told us we've got to treat everybody the same," you misunderstood. You must treat everybody the same way if three things are true: seriousness of proven offense, the employee's past record, and length of service. If union-free companies make major mistakes in discipline, it is the failure to consider length of service before termination. Terminating an employee with ten or more years of service is a serious threat to every employee's job security. Workers will say: "If it could happen to Old Harry, it could happen to me." A union organizer telling workers to "vote for the union and we'll get good Old Harry his job back," is halfway home in organizing the plant.

We are not suggesting that management fail to discipline employees, only that these factors must be taken into consideration. Assume that security catches two employees (A and B) going out the gate with the stolen property worth $1.98. Employee A has been with the company twenty-eight years and has a clean record. Employee B has been with the company six months and also has a clean record. Lacking other facts, if the company discharged both, would disciplinary action be the same for each? Obviously not. If the company gave each a written warning letter, that would be the same disciplinary action.

If what they stole was worth $19.80, is that more serious? The rule of reason states that petty theft, grand larceny, and armed robbery are different. If the company suspended both for ten days without pay, that would be the same disciplinary action. You may feel, "Yes, but the senior employee is making more money per day." That's true, but hearing officers have said it is *de minimus,* that is, the difference is so small as to make no difference in fact.

Finally, if what they stole was worth $198.00, it is a serious disciplinary problem. If both are fired, it isn't equal discipline. Employee A will have a harder time finding another job, having to explain why he's changing jobs after twenty-eight years with the same company. Employee B probably won't even tell his next employer he ever worked for your company.

The major consideration, if both are discharged, is whether you are applying the same *economic* penalty? The twenty-eight-year employee may be unable to find gainful employment at his current income level. Hearing officers take into account the years when an employee gets the most credit in retirement systems—the last five to ten years. Most retirement systems have a formula: number of years of service times some percentage of the highest three or five last years of income. If the company discharges *both* A and B, A could be fined, assuming normal life expectancy, $90,000, and B, nothing—for the same offense. Apply the rule of reason; make the punishment fit the crime. No court would fine one person $90,000 and another nothing for the same offense.

We are not saying management should ignore rules or orders violations committed by workers with long service, but that such employees are entitled to "one last chance" prior to discharge. Supervisors ask: "What do you tell younger employees when management allows a senior employee to get by with violations? You're asking us to discriminate on the basis of seniority." Doesn't your company discriminate by giving twenty-five-year employees more vacation, first choice on vacation scheduling, pick of shifts, last out on layoff, and first return on recall? If these seniority benefits make sense, hasn't a senior employee earned one last chance prior to termination? Management explains to younger workers that they haven't earned the same rights, and that when they have twenty-five years' service, they will get the same consideration.

To summarize, the same discipline must be applied if three factors in a case apply equally to employees: seriousness of the offense, past record, and length of service. The same discipline should be applied to employees up to the point of discharge. *Do not* give one employee a suspension and another a warning letter for the same offense.

Question 17: What doesn't the hearing officer ask about the employee because he doesn't really care? He does not ask what many times management really cares about: "What kind of worker is the employee?" Management tends to allow "good workers" to come in a little late, overstay breaks and lunch hours because they do a bang-up job. Such treatment will sink your ship—other employees see it as favoritism. All workers must be treated the same, regardless of whether they are good, average, or poor in terms of work performance.

Hearing officers assume that all employees are doing a satisfactory job, or the company would have fired them. They don't care whether or not workers are good performers because they can't measure performance. They can measure the seriousness of an offense. From the record they can determine whether the accused has ever committed the offense before, and they can certainly measure length of service.

Our final thoughts on discipline are:

1. Tell the whole truth from the beginning of the investigation giving rise to disciplinary action.

2. Curb your temper in dealing with disciplinary action.

3. The quicker management's false assumptions or mistakes are corrected, the better the management team will be viewed by the work force.

Chapter Ten

Developing Management Credibility

Our major message in this book is that maintaining union-free status is a by-product of good management practices. If senior management has developed and trained effective first-line supervisors and been sensitive to employee needs in wages, hours, and benefits, there will be no successful union drive.

For employees, unionization is a lot like a heart transplant. If they think they need a union to survive, they'll get it. Employees should be made to realize that they are going to go through a painful operation that may not be necessary.

The four key factors in running a profitable business that relate to maintaining a union-free operation can be summarized as:

1. Good, effective, practical policies that deal with employees' needs.

2. Communicating policies through a variety of means—supervisors, manuals, personnel, department heads, vice-presidents, and so on.

3. 95 percent of employees will respond to fair treatment. A union, to win an election, must convince 50 percent plus one voter that the organization is unfair and a radical change is necessary.

4. Administering and communicating a disciplinary program consistently and fairly. Letting employees know what is expected of them and what action will be taken against employees who don't follow reasonable rules and guidelines. This will eliminate favoritism.

Turning to specifics, let's first discuss the organization's relations with its employees. Interaction between the supervisor and the employees is fundamental. For most employees, the supervisor is the company. If he is fair, the company is fair; if he plays games, plays favorites, or is inconsistent, it really doesn't matter what the company policy manual states: to the employees, the company is unfair.

Employees involved in a union election are deciding whether they will be better off with a union. They're also thinking: "If I vote for the union, how will my supervisor react?" A majority of employees in many successful union campaigns have felt: "If I vote for the union, that will really tick off my supervisor, that will show him!" The yes vote for the union is to get even with the supervisor and the company. The relationship supervisors develop with employees is critical to an organization's employee relations program.

REDUCING FRUSTRATION

An overlying negative theme in employee relations is frustration. Employees join unions, not by chance, but because they are irritated, upset, and angry at what is happening.

What kind of employees bring in the union? Is it the marginal worker, the poor employee, the worker who isn't giving normal effort? No, because of the 95/5 rule of employee relations. Remember 95 percent of workers are satisfactory to excellent; that 95 percent of problems—poor work, scrap, lack of cooperation, arguments, lateness, absenteeism—are caused by 5 percent.

Even if these statistics are a bit off and the percentage is 10 percent instead of 5 percent, how can a union ever win an election? Under the National Labor Relations Act, 30 percent of the employees must sign authorization cards indicating they wish union representation, and 50 percent plus one must vote for the union.

Unions are not successfully organized by a small group of disgruntled, radical hotheads, but by employees so frustrated, so turned off by management that, as a last resort, they seek an outsider to represent their interests.

This frustration is caused by four basic issues: communication, motivation, company policy, and discipline. If the company is doing a reasonable job in these areas—not perfect, simply reasonable—the majority of employees will view the company as a good place to work. The key person is the supervisor.

What makes a good supervisor, and what are key factors in selecting a supervisor? In hundreds of our seminars, we've asked supervisors to list the characteristics of a good and a poor supervisor. The following lists reflect what supervisors generally said.

Good Supervisor	*Poor Supervisor**
1. Communicates	1. Passes the buck
2. Listens	a. Up
3. Is fair and firm	b. Down
4. Trains people	2. Procrastinates
5. Gets a job done	3. Gives a quick answer
6. Cares about people	4. Yells and hollers
7. Knows the job	5. Is afraid to ask for help
8. Backs up his people	

---

*Obviously, the poor supervisor is the opposite of a good supervisor, but he is particularly poor in a crisis.

9. Motivates

10. Understands his people

11. Is consistent

12. Spends time with his people

We have asked groups of employees the same question and the list is the same. People don't need an industrial management degree to know whether or not a supervisor is dealing with them in an above-board manner.

Who should be promoted to supervisor? Some companies believe all supervisors should have college degrees, but typical college graduates want to "get ahead." Their career goal is not being a first-line supervisor; it is a stepping stone to bigger and better things. There is a place in most organizations for career foremen, who want to run their crew and have no desire to be a vice-president.

SELECTING SUPERVISORS

In working with a variety of companies for twenty years, we've asked: "If your company planned to invest $500,000 in new machinery, what would the management process involve?" The responses are:

1. Management would form a committee to investigate the operation of the machinery.

2. They would visit other companies operating the equipment to see whether or not it would produce the desired results.

3. Industrial engineers would study the plant layout to make sure how the new equipment would fit the work flow.

4. It would be put up for competitive bids.

5. In many organizations, a capital expenditure of half a million dollars or more requires approval of the board of directors.

Time involved would be anywhere from six months to a year. In other words, no organization would make such a capital investment without serious thought and detailed planning. Yet all supervisors and managers sooner or later will be asked this question and will have to make a decision: "Who do you have working for you who would make a good supervisor?"

Books have been written on the selection of supervisors, and university courses describe the characteristics and personal traits of good managers and supervisors. Companies test, and some send prospective management people to psychiatrists, trying to determine a profile indicating a high success level. We are not certain it's all that complicated, but there are some basic principles.

Historically management has tended to promote the best workers, the best technicians, tool makers, assemblers, tellers, and nurses into supervision. A new school of management theory contends that management is a skill, that a good manager can manage anything—a shoe store, hospital, automobile plant, steel mill—that technical knowledge isn't all that necessary. This theory may work at certain management levels.

For chief executive officers of major companies or organizations, it's probably true. They don't need expertise in labor relations, finance, engineering, production, and so on. Their main function is selecting and motivating specialists who *do* have expertise.

The first-level supervisor without experience, knowledge, and skill in the jobs that the employees are doing, however, will have great difficulty supervising day to day. In about half a shift, workers will discover that he is not technically competent. We aren't saying that first-level supervisors must be the most technically competent person in the crew, but they must have a degree of technical competence and confidence. Some characteristics that indicate success include:

1. A success pattern.

2. Recognition and compensation.

3. Willingness to pay the price.

4. Treatment after selection.

1. A success pattern. Discard the "round-peg-in-the-square-hole" theory developed by supervisors, managers, and executives to foist their deadwood off on each other. Consider the following scenario. Accounting calls personnel and says: "I have this bright young person here in the accounting department who is kind of a round peg in a square hole. He likes people better than numbers, has taken a Dale Carnegie course, and is getting an MBA in psychology. This person would really fit a lot better in personnel than here in accounting." The chief accountant is really saying that he can't add or subtract, and "I don't have the guts to fire this person, so I'm going to foist this deadwood off on the personnel department."

After eighteen months to two years, the personnel manager, not wanting to admit too quickly he's been had, calls the production manager and says: "I have this bright young person in personnel with a great accounting background, and he is ready for the day-to-day battle of production."

Eventually, this employee passes through nine departments and retires on the payroll with dignity, and a series of merit increases, as assistant to the vice-president for long-range planning.

Look for a success pattern, ask yourself what the employee has ever done well. If the answer is nothing, don't promote that person. If the employee was in the army, did he come out a private or a sergeant? If he played football, was he All-Conference? If a Boy Scout, was he an Eagle Scout? If she goes to church, was she president of the sodality? If she plays bridge, did she ever win a tournament? If she was on the girls' basketball team, was she the captain? We aren't suggesting that church-goers, scouts, and former army sergeants make good supervisors, we *are* saying that leadership patterns develop early in life.

Recognize that success patterns don't rule out occasional failures. Starting a gas station or an electrical repair business and going broke, for example, may not score against the potential supervisor—at least he tried. If he had a succession of failing businesses—a gas station, an electrical repair business, and a laundromat—you should be a little nervous about promoting him.

People really don't change all that much. Their basic personalities have been developed by age twelve. You could visit any seventh grade classroom and determine with 95 percent accuracy which two, three, or four children were going to be leaders in twenty to thirty years. We don't mean you could tell what they were going to be leading—the U.S. Senate, General Motors, or a bank robbing gang. You couldn't tell who would be successful in accumulating wealth, finding a cancer cure, or in making outstanding contributions in other fields. However, leadership develops early in life. There are some rare exceptions; for example, Colonel Sanders, the chicken king, made millions after age sixty-five.

2. Recognition and compensation. These are the number one goals of managers and supervisors, with recognition probably outpointing compensation.

3. Willingness to pay the price. Determine a person's willingness to pay the price of moving up the managerial ladder. Ask yourself which comes first, family or job. If it's your family, you may well be as high as you'll ever get. We're not suggesting you shouldn't drop everything and race to the hospital if your daughter breaks her arm, or that you shouldn't arrange time off to attend a family wedding. Everyone has commitments to families, friends, and relatives. On a Saturday, however, when you've promised to take the kids fishing and you're really needed at work, it's a different matter. We're not going to suggest what decision to make; not everybody wants to be a vice-president. People must make sacrifices in their personal lives to get ahead in most organizations.

Companies we have worked with are not run by unorganized managers. They are directed by hard-working, dedicated, professional individuals with a strong desire to succeed—we don't see this changing in the future. We doubt whether the president of General Motors in 1995 is currently living in a hippie colony, sporting long hair and beard, flowing robes and sandals, "trying to find himself." Chances are, the GM chief fifteen years from now is somewhere in a GM plant, working seventy to eighty hours a week.

Successful managers many times place their jobs above family; work turns them on; they are totally committed to and receive pleasure from work. They made a decision that supervisors have to make. We *do not* judge which is right or wrong. Everyone must decide what to do with their lives. Paying a price for advancement to higher management levels is not likely to change for senior managers despite comments about more leisure time, more vacation time, and more time off the job. These pronouncements are fine for public consumption, but realistically, most organizations still require dedication and great time commitment to the job.

The price of success also includes the willingness to be mobile. Anyone who has worked for an organization like IBM (which employees jokingly insist stands for, "I've Been Moved") will tell you that upward mobility requires movement from one location to another. Uprooting the family sometimes creates serious conflict between family commitments and career development. A manager may be able to turn down one or even two changes of location, but after several turndowns, that person's name may go to the bottom of the promotion list.

4. Treatment after selection. Let's turn to the situation facing management *after* the supervisor or manager has been chosen. For those of you who can implement policy and dollar decisions, or may someday ask: "What should we do once we've selected a supervisor?" To put the answer in perspective, let's first describe what you should *not do* by citing situations with which we have been involved. "Let's promote Harry to supervision," and we ask, "How much money are you going to give Harry?" Management asks: "Let's see how Harry does first." How does that play? Harry is brought in and told: "Harry, we are convinced that you are going to be a successful manager. We're not going to give you an increase now, in case we're making a mistake. By the way, Harry, you'll be losing your overtime." That really brings Harry on the management team with a rush, doesn't it.

Our recommendation is, once you've selected someone, put your money where your mouth is. Give the new supervisor an immediate minimum 15 percent increase in pay. If you promote someone and they are not worth at least a 15 percent increase, why bother with a promotion.

On the other hand, what should an organization do when a new supervisor can't make it in supervision? The advice here is to terminate the supervisor. How many of you know loyal, dedicated, hard-working demoted supervisors? They're a very bitter lot—and they know where all the skeletons are buried. They must have some leadership talent, or they wouldn't have been promoted. If they're demoted, they may use this talent and become prime movers for a union. We aren't suggesting terminating a new supervisor who requests, within a reasonable period of time, to return to his old job because he didn't like supervision. By all means, let him have his job back. Also, we don't advocate terminating recently promoted older supervisors, with twenty to thirty years with the organization. The organization has an obligation to continue his employment, give him early retirement, or make whatever arrangements are satisfactory to both employee and employer. An individual who has given a quarter of a century to the organization deserves great consideration.

Management should prepare the failing supervisor for the inevitable. Give him a month or two to get out resumes and look around for another job. Appropriate severance pay or other economic considerations may be necessary.

Many newly appointed supervisors have asked us: "When can I tell that the workers recognize me as part of management?" Flippantly we reply: "The first time you see your name on the bathroom wall, they're beginning to identify you as part of management." Seriously, however, promotion to supervision entails identity challenges that workers don't face. Supervision can be lonely. The up-from-the-ranks supervisor quite frequently has been very close to many workers, but now the give-and-take of being in the group disappears.

Supervising people you've worked with is much more difficult than supervising strangers. If you get promoted to corporal in the army you can remember issuing your first order. All your buddies thought you had become power mad. Management, if possible, should allow a ninety days' to six months' "cooling-off period" for the new supervisor. If it won't interfere with production, move him to supervising workers other than his own crew.

Recognition can be provided in a variety of ways. For example, parking spaces for supervisors, a supervisor's room where they can get away from the workers on breaks or lunch, and books and courses on how to manage.

Supervisor training should be continuous. Too many organizations hand the new supervisor a policy manual and say: "Read this and go out there and slay dragons." Training is a responsibility of management, and supervisor training should not end with the policy manual.

COMMUNICATION

The company communication system is crucial in maintaining an open relationship with employees. Lack of communication is a primary cause of employee frustration—people see things going on, but they don't understand why. Changes are made, but nobody takes the trouble to explain the reasons. Every successful union-free company we've dealt with has a formal communication system. There is no one best communication system. Much depends on organization size, type of work, and space availability. Our recommended communication system may have to be modified to fit specific situations.

Supervisor: Key in Communication

Supervisors should schedule regular employee communication meetings, preferably monthly. The Monthly Communication System:

1. Groups of six to ten, to ensure two-way communication. With fifteen to twenty-five people, two-way communication often breaks down, or two or three people dominate discussions. The smaller meeting encourages each individual to participate.

2. Meet on company time. Communication is as much a cost of doing business today as fire insurance or worker's compensation. Fit the meeting into production schedules to have as little impact as possible. In twenty-four-hour operations, meetings may have to be conducted on overtime, keeping people over a half hour at the end of a shift. Communication meetings must be run on company time.

3. Meet regularly each month. Weekly meetings may not allow adequate time to prepare. The agenda can get too long and can deteriorate into an extra-long coffee break.

Communication meetings should be divided into the formal and informal segments as follows.

I. Formal.

    a. *General information.*   The supervisor spends two to three minutes reporting on the department's *performance* that month (how orders were met, number of units handled, scrap rate, number of customer contacts, number of complaints, and quality during the period. *Health and safety* are discussed (time lost due to accidents, near-miss incidents, and other safety problems, general health, welfare, or cleanliness problems). The supervisor reports the *plans* for the coming month (what the schedule will look like, heavy or light workload, other assignments, and whether people will be moved out of the department temporarily). The supervisor clarifies and brings into focus what workers probably can see happening already; he provides three or four pieces of information.

b. *Specific information.* The specific topics the company assigns each month are almost limitless: attendance; job opportunities; safety; tuition reimbursement; housekeeping; new products, equipment, or systems; company rules and rule changes; vacations and floating holidays; security; promotions. Employees want to hear information on a variety of topics, what their supervisor thinks about programs and policies, and how he is going to apply them. The supervisor should be provided with handouts, flip charts, slides, or audio-visual aids, if necessary. The personnel or training department should design and produce the materials to ensure consistent information exchange. The supervisor may need training in public speaking and discussion group leadership.

Surveys of things people fear most—illness, death, financial programs—show that fear of speaking in front of groups ranks very high. The training department or personnel should analyze supervisors' ability to communicate to small groups. Local community college speech departments can be used to run training classes for supervisors on how to conduct meetings. Some organizations use general foremen or department heads to start meetings and gradually work supervisors into conducting the meetings. Don't rationalize that supervisors are not trained well enough to conduct a meeting and that someone else will have to do it. Part of the supervisor's basic responsibility is communications, formally and informally, with employees. Remember that having supervisors present information regularly conditions employees to rely on supervisors as information sources.

2. Informal. The second part of the meeting is open for discussion, questions, complaints, comments, and so on.

Supervisors should listen carefully to what employees are saying—and *write it down.* Note-taking makes employees feel their views are important enough to be written down, and notes help ensure supervisors will follow-up promptly on the comment or question.

Supervisors who don't have information at their finger-tips when questions are raised shouldn't respond off the top of their heads, but should promise to check, and get back with an answer. That doesn't mean waiting until the next monthly meeting, but as soon as possible.

Some companies have personnel representatives sit in on meetings. Many issues that are raised are subsequently posted on bulletin boards in question-and-answer format, carrying the information to employees in the entire operation, or the minutes of the meeting are posted. Other compa-nies hold small group meetings, with employees selected by management or by workers, which meet regularly with the manufacturing managers, administrative officers, vice-presidents, or the president.

Senior management can meet directly with the employees to find out what the problems are, but care must be exercised that employees don't use the system to bypass supervisors. While upper management may feel content when employees bypass the supervisor, management is up for questions like: "My work area is cold," "My broom needs replacing," or "I'm getting a shock off my equipment." The manager may solve these problems by promising: "I will do something about warming up your area," "I will get you a new broom," or "I will send somebody from maintenance to take care of your equipment problem."

Such managers may think—and in effect are saying to employees—that the supervisors are too stupid, too careless, or have no concern for day-to-day problems, and only I, the manager, can solve problems. Managers allow employees to develop the habit of bypassing supervisors. If managers really believe supervisors can't handle these problems, they should fire them.

Other Meetings

Other informational meetings can be scheduled during the year. These should be used to complement supervisory meetings. For example, the supervisory meeting might be held one month and a department meeting with the plant manager the alternate month. In these meetings, the manager communicates directly to employees the issues that impact the plant as a whole. The advantages are that people like to see the boss and receive information. Discussing the goals of the whole plant helps develop a feeling of teamwork and reduce the "my department," "my shift" syndrome. It makes communicating occasional bad news, such as temporary shutdown for lack of parts, much easier for the employees to accept.

The communication system may use well-prepared quarterly meetings, announced in advance, often lasting longer than a half hour. Meetings may be called to recognize employees for safety, attendance, or longevity awards; often they are also social occasions, for example, a long-term employee retiring.

The sales manager could meet once a year with production employees. This meeting would be to reduce the conflict that can develop between sales and production. The conflict usually arises over customer complaints or failure to deliver products when promised. The typical salesman dumps the blame on production. To counter this, sales could solicit testimonials from customers about product quality and customer appreciation for a particular "hot job" arriving on time. The sales manager can convey to production employees that salespeople are proud to represent them and the company.

This meeting could communicate inside information to employees about potential customers. When new orders are scheduled, production employees may try to produce the product with quality, quantity, and timeliness to ensure customer satisfaction.

Personnel should meet with employees once or twice a year to update benefits and communicate the benefit package. Most workers don't really know about or appreciate existing benefits. Personnel should explain any policy changes being considered by the company, and answer questions regarding wages, benefits, and policies.

The vice-president of operations, or the president in a small company, should discuss the state of the organization with employees once a year. In several companies prior to the annual stockholders' meeting, the company holds a job-holders' meeting. Employees are given information the stockholders are to receive, and other pertinent information. The company is telling job-holders: "You are just as important as stockholders." *Beautiful!*

This leads us back to the changing workers. They want to feel involved in the organization. It's up to management to sell the organization.

Finally, if the company has a history of employee communication meetings, it is a natural way to communicate during a union campaign. The company will have a serious credibility problem if letters are sent to employees and meetings held for the first time during a union campaign. The importance of face-to-face communication during union campaigns cannot be overemphasized. It is clearly the most effective method in countering union claims and getting the company's message across.

MOTIVATION

Many supervisors have been exposed to a variety of training programs dealing with employee motivation. College professors and behavioral psychologists are often the authors of the manuals, training programs, and texts that can explain behavioral and motivational theory to supervisors.

Among the best known is Maslow, who developed a theory called The Need Priority Model. Herzberg studied employee attitudes and helped clarify Maslow by developing a further theory, Job Content Factors and Hygiene or Maintenance Factors. A current guru of motivation, Skinner, states behaviorial change occurs "through behavior modification by positive reinforcement." Dr. Spock's *Baby and Child Care* became a bible on child-raising to many parents, most of whom interpreted the good doctor as extremely permissive in the area of discipline.

The supervisor's problem in dealing with workers day to day is how to translate a lot of academic theory to the practical world of work. We are not saying the Maslows, Herzbergs, Skinners, and Spocks are wrong; we are saying that it is often too difficult for the average supervisor to apply their theories. For example:

> The five-step classification of needs is somewhat artificial because all needs are interacting together with the whole man. Maslow's need priority model, however, does provide the supervisor with a convenient way of understanding which type of need is most likely to dominate a worker's drive in a given situation.
>
> Moreover, the need priority model does not suggest that a worker's needs can be fully satisfied by giving him some of each

of the five needs. As he receives partial satisfaction of one need, the need itself can increase or decrease . . .

or:

> A mountain climber who has climbed a high peak sees a higher one. A man satisfied by eating hamburger over a period of time may aspire to satisfy his hunger by eating sirloin steak. Workers' needs are never static. They can never be satisfied. Need satisfaction is a continuous problem for all time. The need priority model essentially tells us that satisfied needs do not help to motivate. Workers are motivated by what they are seeking. The first-line supervisor has to recognize what needs the worker is trying to satisfy in order to motivate him.*

These authors believe they are sharing insights with supervisors in interpreting behavioral or industrial psychologists' approach to dealing with workers. Many supervisors get pretty confused by this and throw up their hands, saying: "To hell with this. There's nothing *I* can use. All that motivation stuff is worthless."

Supervisors are responsible for motivating employees. We want to discuss a concept of industrial fair play. The 95 percent of employees who are satisfactory to outstanding workers expect supervisors to treat them in a fair and consistent manner. Employees don't have to work five years before they know whether they are being treated fairly or not. Where *did* they develop the concept of fairness? People learn very young. To illustrate this, consider four-year-old Mary and her friend. They can't find enough of Mary's toys to play with, so they latch on to one of brother Dennis' trucks. Six-year-old Dennis sees them playing with one of *his* toys, and responds predictably. He knocks Mary down, grabs the truck, and shouts: "That's *mine!*" Mary is no dummy, she knows where to go to stop this abuse. Sobbing, she tells Mom or Dad, "Dennis is picking on me. It's not *fair!*" By the time people are eighteen, they have a pretty good idea of what's fair, and have no trouble in recognizing fairness in the workplace.

We can apply the basic principles of fair treatment in a practical way, day to day. Beginning when an employee is hired. Who should hire em-

---

*These two quotations are taken from *Essentials of Management for First Line Supervision.* Eckles, Carmichael, Sarcheff. Wiley Hamilton Publication, 1974

ployees? There are two basic approaches. The personnel department does the hiring and the newly hired employee is given a slip and told to report to such-and-such a supervisor, or the personnel department advertises, screens, applicants, and then sends the potential employee to the immediate supervisor and the supervisor does the hiring.

Under the first approach, the supervisor has no voice in determining who works in his department. A new worker shows up, hands the supervisor a slip, and says: "Hi there, I'm your new assembler (toolmaker, nurse, . . .)." If the employee doesn't succeed, the supervisor has a perfect out. "What do you expect me to do? Look at the garbage personnel sends me. It's not my fault this employee didn't make it. It's personnel's fault."

The major advantage of the second approach is that the first-line supervisor tells the applicants whether or not they get the job. A bond develops between receiver and giver of a job. That bond should be between the first-line supervisor and employee, not between employee and the personnel department. The supervisor also makes a commitment to help the employee succeed; her reputation is on the line. *Supervisors should do their own hiring.* Personnel should monitor hiring practices for compliance with federal and state regulations.

Once the new employee is hired, the first relationship with the supervisor is during training. First impressions of the supervisor are made at this time. The employee will decide whether the supervisor really cares about him, his work progress, and welfare. What other employees will tell him about the supervisor may be important, but how he is treated by the supervisor during the training period is what really determines how he feels. Many supervisors who have been around for a few years regard training as routine, repetitive, and just plain boring, and as a result will direct a "good worker" to break in new employees. Delegating a basic supervisory responsibility is a mistake. To illustrate the effect on the new employee, the "good worker," other workers, and the supervisor, some typical shop dialogue follows.

A short break-in period for a new employee *(E)* on a machine has passed. The supervisor *(S)* stops by, looks over the shoulder of the new, insecure worker who has been wondering how he's doing, and says:

S: Hey, you're screwing that up! That's all wrong!

E: Huh? What?

S: Shut off that machine. Don't you know that you could burn it out? You don't have the proper oil pressure on that gauge.

E: Gosh! I didn't know that.

S: Well, for crying out loud. Anybody knows you've got to maintain a certain amount of pressure or this equipment will burn out. Don't you know this machine costs $25,000?

E: Gee, I didn't know . . . I'm sorry.

S: Well, you're going to have to be more careful in the future. By the way, what's your name?

E: Harry Gazordonplotz

S: Gassordon—what?

E: Gazordonplotz. I thought I did it the way the other operator told me to do it.

S: Well, we'll have to check that out.

After seeing that the employee has gotten the oil pressure adjusted properly, the supervisor stops by the "good worker," Joe (*J*), who trained him, and says:

S: Joe, that new guy was running that machine with the oil pressure down.

J: Well, I don't understand it. I told him to watch it.

S: Well, Joe, what do you think?

J: I don't know what to say . . . except, I just think he's plain dumb.

S: Well, that's the best we can find.

J: Well, if they don't get any better we're going to have a lot of problems. There's nothing I can do with somebody that slow and stupid.

Unfortunately this little dialogue occurs too often. The supervisor, using time pressure as an excuse, relies on someone else to do training. Supervisors who do not take the time to do training may make another mistake. They use second-hand information to evaluate the employee. If the second-hand information is negative, the supervisor, wanting to be a "good guy" and knowing he didn't take the time to really evaluate the employee, bends over backwards to be "fair," and allows the new employee to slide through his probationary period.

Supervisors must spend time training new employees because:

1.   The employee is entitled to one boss.

2.   The supervisor is primarily responsible for instructing how a
     job should be done.

The supervisor should demonstrate the basic functions of the job. After that, there may not be any problem in having a more seasoned employee help in training the new worker. If the supervisor has been the primary source of instruction, he can deal with problems of the new worker in an honest, fair way, including occasionally apologizing to the employee. The supervisor may accept the blame for an employee's mistake, for example: "Harry, you're running the machine without proper oil pressure; let's shut it off. I'm sorry, Harry, I must not have explained clearly that it's important to check the gauge. I probably went over that too fast. Let me go over it again." Why do that? First, it makes the employee feel at ease. Second, the new employee is unsure of himself and if his confidence is attacked, he is going to lose whatever he had. Third, the supervisor may owe the employee an apology because he *didn't* explain it fully enough.

In retraining, the employee is much more likely to accept corrections, and come to the supervisor with problems, if he feels the supervisor won't try to make him feel stupid. Most employees want to do a good job, and if treated with respect, will respond positively.

One of the most important decisions the supervisor will make about new employees is in the first fifteen to sixty days of employment: should we keep this employee as a permanent worker? Supervisors make a mistake when they let employees slide through the probationary period, despite many negative signs.

They end up with a disgruntled griper and complainer on permanent status. If probationary employees don't have the knack for work, get impatient on the telephone, don't deal well with people, and can't handle the basic parts of the job, terminate them. Give the benefit of the doubt to the *company* on probationary employees. Employees who *do not* perform satisfactorily are not going to get better; they will get worse. Do yourself and the company a favor—as soon as you identify a probationary employee as not acceptable, get rid of him. Do not wait until the end of probation.

Need to Be with Other People

Everyone knows man is a social animal. Psychologists talk about "peer group interaction," but we are not sure it's as complex as they imply. Let's use a common-sense approach. The new employee wants to become a member of the group, so the first day on the job is very important. At many retirement dinners when the honoree gets to the microphone, he starts his speech with "Forty two years ago the first person I met here was old Bill Snider. He took me over to the pickling unit and . . . "

The supervisor can help the employee start off on the right foot with introductions to a few co-workers and by discussing some areas of common interest, such as family, work experiences, and outside activities. Make certain that the new employee is directed to the lunchroom and some employees are found to share lunch with him or her.

In dealing with employees in groups, be sensitive to some basic rules. Don't chew people out in front of other people for two reasons:

1.   It embarrasses them in front of the group.

2.   The group is likely to react negatively.

A supervisor using a position of authority to demean people or bawl them out before others is resented.

If you supervise ten, twenty, or thirty employees, two to three informal groups will develop: those who lunch together; come to work together; or share common interests outside the shop. Each group will have an informal tribal leader. Generally they are respected, good workers to whom other workers may go with technical questions: "Where do you put the decimal point?" "What's the discount for Canadian currency?" "How do we get into this secure area?" Leaders often are the ones who take up a collection for a hospitalized fellow employee or assume responsibility for a group project, such as organizing a bowling league or kicking off a

Christmas collection for poor children. Supervisors must be sensitive to these informal leaders. Particularly if they have a question, rumor, or complaint. Many times they aren't just speaking for themselves, but are talking for the entire group.

In a union campaign, be sensitive to the way the informal leaders seem to be leaning. If informal leaders state to their group, "I don't think we really need the union," management's chances of winning the election have increased a hundred times.

We found out in a recent campaign that the informal leaders were the employees pushing the union, and told management a serious problem existed in getting their message to the employees. Most new employees were listening very attentively to what the leaders were saying. That was a case where the company had neglected to do pick-and-shovel work in developing fair policies and employee communication.

Caution

A mistake supervisors can make is overpromoting the tribal instinct among crews. People begin to *overidentify* with their crew; the "maintenance tribe," the "production tribe," the first-shift and second-shift tribes, and so on.

It is natural for people on a second shift, for instance, to believe they get stuck with all the dirty work, scrap, or clean-up. The supervisor makes a mistake in joining in that griping. He's telling employees he agrees things are bad, but he can't do anything about it. His role as the company's representative to the workers should be to get things done and corrected when they are not right.

Supervisors who join workers in complaining are known as "lap dog supervisors." The lap dog supervisor wants everybody to like him. His message to his employees: "Pat me on the back and tell me how wonderful I am because I want to do everything I can for you, and everybody else in the place doesn't appreciate how hard our department works, and we are just all being treated like second stringers." This supervisor is a union organizer's dream. The organizer says: "See, your supervisor even agrees how bad things are, but there's nothing that supervisor can do about it because nobody pays attention to him. You had better join the union; the company will pay attention to the union."

Not only should supervisors *not* join the gripe sessions, if they begin to hear complaints from department to department or shift to shift, they should do everything possible to defuse complaints.

People need to get together in groups. The worst punishment people can suffer is solitary confinement or the "silent treatment." Supervisors should encourage participation in a group; but that does not mean a feeling of "it's us against the rest."

The supervisor who passes the buck, who says, "They said this, they told me to tell you that, they said I can't do this," creates employee anxiety and animosity that can become impossible to change.

Recognition

The last but most important motivator is recognition. *When someone does something good, how do we let them know about it?*

Supervisors often feel that recognition is an overplayed tune and really not as important as they are told. One question we always ask older supervisors to kick off a discussion on recognition is: "If you've been married for thirty-three years, when is the last time the wife said, 'George that's enough. Now stop it, George; we're getting too old, we're not kids anymore. And I'm sick and tired of you telling me how much you love me.'" The fact is that, whether it is a married couple of thirty-three years or a brand new bride and groom, partners need positive responses. Whether you're the proud Daddy of a kid of three or a great-grandfather, you want to be remembered on Father's Day.

People need to be told that they are appreciated, and work is one of the most critical places where this must be met. Most people spend from eight to ten hours every day getting ready for work, going to work, at work, and returning home. For many, the largest part of their waking, adult life is spent in and around work; they must have recognition at work to have a good feeling about themselves.

Good managers provide recognition. They know recognition has two basic characteristics:

1. It has to be *immediate.* If not, there is a tendency to forget. The supervisor meant to tell someone about a good job on a project finished a month ago, but forgot.

2. It has to be *sincere.* It has to be natural for the supervisor; it can't be phony. The approach of the glad-hand politician won't work: "Hello there, my good friend; don't forget to vote for me. Hi! Support me and I'll get you anything you need."

An employee who didn't miss a day last year is entitled to recognition, if only: "I've reviewed the records of your attendance last year, and it was outstanding. I really appreciate the effort you made to get in every day." A step further, the supervisor might go to the plant manager and state: "I have an employee who didn't miss a day last year. Would you mind stopping by on one of your rounds to shake his hand and thank him for me?" How much does that cost? A few extra minutes.

Consider a classic example of recognition in an office. We had a special federal project to put together. We submitted the project, a request for federal monies. However, it was rejected and a new deadline was set. The entire project had to be retyped which took from Friday through Sunday. The project was finished and shipped to Washington, meeting the new deadline. The mayor was asked to drop a note of thanks to the clerical workers. When the mayor's note arrived, one woman remarked: "You know, I've been around here eleven years, and that's the first time anybody has said thank you to me for anything."

Isn't it a shame an employee would express that reaction to recognition? When considered further, however, the conclusion was reached that the shame was not with the employee, but the organization. Many people do not accept recognition very well simply because it has not been given. This employee had a poor attitude, frequently complained, and was always criticizing other people, but she was a fast typist and good production worker. She might have had a different attitude if she had been given the recognition she not only clearly wanted, but had earned. She had the feeling that nobody really cared about her. Supervisors' responsibilities include letting people know they are appreciated and doing a good job.

Managers and supervisors also want to be involved in training, don't want to be criticized in front of groups, and need recognition—many times a need greater than the people they supervise. Companies make a mistake in not providing management with training and recognition.

Recognition is the key to a union-free operation. A few of the cases we have encountered make the point.

Case 1. Fred Hill, a production worker, was bawled out and shouted at by his supervisor in front of his fellow workers. Feeling great anger and frustration when he had nowhere to grieve within the company, he talked to his next-door neighbor, a member of a union.

His neighbor set up a meeting with the local union organizer. Fred recounted his experience at the shop and received instant sympathy from the organizer. The organizer explained to Fred that unions existed because workers had to go through the very thing Fred had suffered. The organizer suggested another meeting where Fred could bring along a few of his friends. The group met two days later. The organizer was armed with a Dunn and Bradstreet report on the company, a questionnaire, and a survey sheet provided by the International Union.

After a three-hour session, the organizer had compiled the necessary information about the company. The organizer learned there were quite a few inconsistencies in management practices and favoritism was the name of the game. The organizer decided the plant was ripe for organization.

Case 2. In this case, management was insensitive to employee requests. Frustration and inability to reach management drove employees to seek outside help.

A group of employees, working in a laboratory that had nauseous fumes and was poorly ventilated, had complained for two years. Nothing had been done, although employees had requested repeatedly that the condition be corrected. Two years before at a communications meeting, an employee, Betty Parker, had informed senior management about the noxious fumes and stated that employees were going home sick at night. Management promised to look into it.

At the next communications meeting, Ken Parker, from the lab, reiterated the complaint. The plant manager toured the lab and decided there was no problem. At a meeting six months later, Nancy Elliott reported the problem unsolved. Management checked their minutes and assured her that the problem had been looked into—and there was no problem. The lab employees continued to work under the condition for another eight months.

A union organized the rest of the plant at this time, but nothing was done for the laboratory people. The union chief steward told them: "You could do what we did. We went out and got a union." At a meeting with the union, the lab people were told: "We will not only correct your environmental problem, but will improve your wages and benefits as well." The lab voted overwhelmingly for the union.

Case 3. In this case, a company only seven years old started a new plant in the South. Most of the people hired for the operation, management and employees, were selected with little planning. The result was that many workers weren't able to meet job requirements. The plant manager selected was a disaster. An introvert who didn't like or trust people, he created an atmosphere of fear in the plant. He disciplined one employee after another, never involving supervisors, who also were in fear of losing their jobs. During the first seven months, he fired seven employees and two supervisors.

One of the two supervisors fired was the only Spanish-speaking supervisor in the plant, which had 40 percent Hispanic employees. The plant manager also earned a reputation as a ladies' man and made advances to women in the plant.

A triggering incident brought an end to the reign of terror. The plant manager demoted a superintendent to second-shift supervisor. As a result, the demoted superintendent, formerly a union member, called a meeting with the employees to bring in a union. With the discontent, harassment, and lack of job security, he had little difficulty convincing them a union was necessary. When the union filed a petition with the National Labor Relations Board, the plant manager learned for the first time that he was in the midst of a union campaign.

The cases demonstrate problems that organizations bring upon themselves when they fail to listen to employee dissatisfaction.

PART THREE

THE
ELECTION
CAMPAIGN

Chapter Eleven

The Campaign from the Union's Side

In 90 percent of union campaigns, the union is invited into the organization by its employees. In Chapter 1, we discussed the "Oh, my God . . . they didn't" approach by the union organizer. The union cannot succeed without internal help from a group of employees and, in most instances, can't get beyond the front door unless there are legitimate issues that have the employees scared.

Fear and frustration are the raw materials that the union organizer molds into a winning campaign. Unions are also able to build on the feeling of many workers that the company, the owners, executives, and managers are skimming the cream, but the workers are getting the scraps.

The general approach of the organizer is to show concern, sympathy, and understanding about the problems of the employees. The organizer gradually works into their confidence and promises that their issues can be resolved. (See Appendix A.)

What does the union do when contacted by a disgruntled employee? They have to decide whether anyone else is involved. Are some of the other employees represented by a union? If so, what is their union's relationship with the other union? Some unions get along together and some don't. Having checked that possibility and having decided to cope with it, they start an intensive investigation of your company. They want to know its size and composition, and how stable it is financially. They would also try to determine whether or not the issues are real. Is there really a problem with the supervisors? If there isn't, many times the organizer explains how bad things really are by giving employees comparisons between their current working conditions and what it might be like in a union operation.

The union is also interested in previous union attempts to organize the company, for they want to know why the attempt was lost, which union was involved, and who the leaders were in the unsuccessful attempt. If the old union committee is still around they will want to involve them, especially if the old issues have not been solved. The old committee may have the key to opening a few department or shifts which the new group doesn't have.

They'll also want to know the physical layout of your operation. Is there more than one building; how many shifts are working; is there an isolated group, such as a warehouse or the laundry in a hospital. They will look at the possibility of other *intervening unions,* whether any craft unions are involved, and whether some other types of unions might be interested in the remainder of the unit.

The union will look at your *community,* to see whether it is anti-union or is it a pro-union environment. This is important to organizing, for they need to know what kind of reception their effort will get in the community.

The union is also going to be interested in the management people they'd be dealing with, and whether there is an *effective* or *ineffective management* team. They want to know whether management *applies* discipline consistently, and whether *supervisors are respected.* They need to know who runs the company; is there a corporation involved which could have other unionized plants or is it controlled by a family with big houses and big cars. To get this information, they have to work with the local employees and ask the right questions.

The organizer is trained to be a good listener. As he meets with a small group of employees he has two goals:

1. Are there sufficient issues on which to build a campaign?

2. Are there any internal leadership people who can carry the campaign?

A successful organizer keeps all of the group involved but really begins to work on the informal leaders. These factors will also enter into their decision to continue the campaign. The decision is going to be based on what are chances of winning and how much time and money is the campaign going to take.

THE UNION'S FINANCIAL POSITION

A union looks at new members as a business looks at a new product. It's a matter of arithmetic: the number of employees times number of dollars-dues per month, multiplied by twelve months, and then multiplied by five (because most unions have five-year programs), gives quite a return on investment. For example, typical union dues run anywhere from $10 to $20 a month. Using the more conservative figure, $10, the union income from an operation of 200 employees would generate $24,000 a year, and $120,000 over five years. It would cost the union about $5000 to organize that operation, including prorating costs of research, legal advice, international, local offices, and computer time.

Very few businesses today could invest $5000 (a minimum figure) and get a return of $120,000 tax free in five years. So, when dealing with a union, you are dealing with a big business that has a product to sell and knows how to sell it.

The real motivation for union organizing is power. The larger the union, the more power; the more power, the better contracts and more national impact. Presidents of the large unions are as interested in power and have the same drive and determination as any executive of a major corporation. Douglas Fraser, president of the UAW, has recently been appointed to the board of directors of Chrysler Corporation. He will fit in and be an asset to that group.

If a union decides it can't win a campaign, the organizers will go back to the employees involved and lay out the facts. "It just doesn't look like there's enough interest at this time," they'll say, "but if you want to continue the campaign and get enough cards signed, the union will certainly assist you." But they'll probably add, "Unless you come back with better than 70 percent of the cards signed, there is no need to waste your time or ours." On occasion, they'll send a "kiss-off letter," after meetings and internal organizing efforts have failed to get enough cards signed: "It's up to you to decide," it says in essence. "If you are serious about joining the union, you had better move now. If you don't, we'll see you sometime down the road when there's more substantial interest."

Once the union decides to go ahead with the campaign, the union organizer selects an internal leader. Usually, this will be someone other than the disgruntled employee who made the first contact. They will look for someone respected by employees. This person may even be someone management might consider for supervisor, and the organizer will seek the leader in the largest or most important unit, for elections are a numbers game for the union.

THE ORGANIZING COMMITTEE

The organizer forms an organizing team, consisting of the leader and two lieutenants. The leader is responsible for the largest segment of the organization, and the others divide the remainder and report to the leader.

The organizer can call on local unions in the area for assistance. By using local people, he can compare their contracts with the current status of the company policies. The local union leaders also help establish the credibility of the organizer by saying what a great job he has done for them.

The organizing committee is given a goal, a time period, and will be reviewed periodically. They are indoctrinated—educated to unionization and to anything they may encounter during the campaign. The union, to ensure that their in-plant organizers can show up management in an encounter, familiarizes them with terminology, instructs them on legislation and worker's rights. For example, they learn that the National Labor Relations Act is an act of Congress to protect interstate commerce and basically the rights of workers, and that the National Labor Relations Board (NLRB) was set up by Congress to administer the act. They will also give them a complete history of the union and how it functions, and they'll deal with the key issues, particularly as employees perceive them. They will involve them in union activities, inviting them to union meetings, council meetings, and AFL/CIO meetings, where they are introduced, given titles and a tremendous amount of recognition.

The organizer now gives them specific targets, such as a build-up to department meetings within six weeks, to be followed by a general meeting of all employees, before the demand to the company and petition is filed at the NLRB for an election. The committee is directed to contact the employees who will sign a card, usually representing *about 20 percent* of any work force. Next would be the employees who are undecided, about 60 percent of any work force. Third, they contact the anti-union people, to whom they must talk, for they can't ignore them; also, these people may have some complaints against the company. They might hate unions, but might hate the company even more.

The employees are talked to at work, before starting, at lunch or anytime they can be contacted without the supervisor interfering. In some campaigns the union sponsors social events where people can get together. There is no hard sell but just personal contact and getting to meet the organizer and the other local union people.

One of the most effective tools of the union is home visits. These are conducted by an internal union committee member and the organizer. An appointment is usually made by a phone committee at a time convenient to the employees. Their husbands, wives, or other relatives are also welcome. Any questions that the employee has are dealt with one on one. The goal in this meeting is to get an employee to sign a union authorization card and confirm their support in the election. (See Figure 11-1 for three card samples.)

UNION MEETINGS

The union will next hold a general meeting, well planned, well organized, and with lots of recognition for the union's prime movers among the employees. Unions are very skilled when it comes to meetings; meetings are their bread and butter. Internal union organizers will be provided with additional flyers to distribute to employees to persuade them to consider their union. (See Figure 11-2.)

How is a union campaign meeting with employees conducted? Let's go through a simulated meeting, probably taking place immediately after work, in any place from a bowling alley to a local hotel, or an employee's home. The union is always sensitive to the type of employees they are organizing, and know what might be an appropriate meeting place for one

Figure 11-1

A

International Brotherhood of Teamsters, Chauffeurs, Warehousemen and Helpers

Teamsters Local No. 299

2741 Trumbull Avenue   WOodward 5-8750-1-2-3-4-5

Date_____19_____Ledger Page No._____

APPLICATION FOR MEMBERSHIP

Name_____ □ Married or □ Single
           Print Name

Address_____Date of Birth_____

City_____State_____Zip_____
Where   Date
Employed_____Employed_____

Amount Paid on Application $_____Bal. Due $_____

I hereby designate Teamsters Local 299, through its authorized agents, as my representative for collective bargaining.

Local 299   Signed_____

                               Social Security No._____

AGENT

(vertical text at right side:) INTERNATIONAL BROTHERHOOD OF TEAMSTERS, CHAUFFEURS, WAREHOUSEMEN AND HELPERS — Agent___ Amt. Paid $___ Bal. Due $___ Name___ — UNION HEADQUARTERS 2741 Trumbull Ave. WO. 5-8750-1-2-3-4-5 Date___19___ — VOID AFTER

B

(UAW emblem)

AUTHORIZATION TO UAW

Date_____19_____

I,_____ authorize UAW to represent
           PRINT NAME   me in collective bargaining.

_____
ADDRESS   NO.   STREET   CITY   PHONE NO.

_____
CLASS OF WORK   HOURLY RATE   CLOCK NO.   DEPT. NO.   SHIFT

Employed by_____
                     COMPANY   ADDRESS

_____
                     SIGNATURE OF EMPLOYEE

                                                         (OVER)

C

YES, I WANT THE IAM

I, the undersigned employee of

(Company) _____

authorize the International Association of Machinists and Aerospace Workers (IAM) to act as my collective bargaining agent for wages, hours and working conditions. I agree that this card may be used either to support a demand for recognition or an NLRB election, at the discretion of the union.

NAME (print)_____ DATE_____

HOME ADDRESS_____ PHONE_____

CITY_____ STATE_____ ZIP_____

JOB TITLE_____ DEPT._____ SHIFT_____

SIGN HERE **X**

NOTE: This authorization to be SIGNED and DATED in Employee's own handwriting. YOUR RIGHT TO SIGN THIS CARD IS PROTECTED BY FEDERAL LAW.

RECEIVED BY (Initial) _____

NOTE: The authorization does <u>not</u> request an election; but gives the Union the legal right to represent the employee.

Figure 11-2A

Bank Employees

Step into

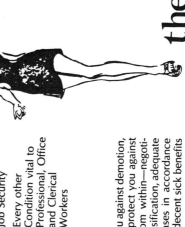

the Eighties

Your Open Door to Opportunity!

Signed contracts guarantee you:

- Better Wages
- Fully Paid Health & Welfare Plan
- Sick Leave
- Guaranteed Vacation
- Fair Hearings on Job Grievances
- Seniority Rights
- Continuous Fight to raise "White Collar" Wage to Level Paid other Trades and Professions

- Paid Holidays
- Pensions
- Overtime Pay
- Job Classification Protection
- Paid Vacations
- Job Security
- Every other Condition vital to Professional, Office and Clerical Workers

Your union contract can protect you against demotion, transfer or unjustified discharge—protect you against favoritism—provide promotion from within—negotiate salary increases, proper job classification, adequate rate ranges with automatic increases in accordance with length of service—guarantee decent sick benefits and pensions.

Office & Professional Employees International Union, AFL-CIO

339 HURON ST., TOLEDO, OHIO 43604 246-1540

How to raise your own pay!

JOIN NOW!

Figure 11-2B

group would not be appropriate for another, so the meeting place is carefully weighed.

The meeting would probably start with an employee, preferably the internal leader, introducing the union representative:

COMMITTEE
CHAIRPERSON:

I would like to thank all of you for coming to this meeting. I have asked Rick Hickson from the International Union to meet with us to answer any questions we might have concerning the union and what a union can do for us. Rick, I know a question most important on people's mind is: "What can the union do for us here?"

RICK:

First of all, I want to thank you for inviting me here today, and let me answer that question. The issue is not necessarily what a union can do for you, but more what you can do for yourself.

The function of the International is not to do things for members, but to help you achieve goals that are meaningful for you as workers and for the security and economic well-being of you and your families. The International has the skill, talent, power, and money to assist you in reaching legitimate goals. However, you are the "U" in Union. You will determine if your local union will function in a manner to bring industrial democracy to this organization.

EMPLOYEE:

How can a union do that?

RICK:

You do that through a process called collective bargaining. Let me explain how collective bargaining works. It is a process guaranteed by law to assist employees in dealing with their company. Your rights to bargaining are guaranteed by the National Labor Relations Act passed by Congress and enforced by the U.S. Supreme Court. Your company must obey the requirements of the law if it wishes to do business in this country. Collective bargaining is the best system developed to help employees solve problems that develop at work. Let me explain how you can use it.

First, you must get together and sign cards which will be used to secure a secret ballot election. *Second,* when you win the election, you have meetings to decide which issues are causing you any problems. These are submitted to the company. The company must send a senior manager to the table to answer every single item. The union doesn't require him to do this, but the *law* says he must do it. Then every issue is discussed and resolved. There is no agreement until you, the membership, have a meeting to discuss and understand the proposals and until you vote by secret ballot to accept the contract. The contract is then signed, sealed, and delivered; and no one can touch you because you have the protection of the contract.

EMPLOYEE: Why is the contract so important?

RICK: Stop and think—everything important that has ever happened to you has been covered by a contract. Think about the first car you ever bought—do you remember what it was? How did you pay for it if you didn't have the cash? You put a down payment on it and then had monthly payments. You also signed a contract to protect you and the bank. When you leased an apartment, you signed a contract setting forth terms and conditions. When you bought a home, you signed a contract. Last year when you bought a toaster or microwave oven for Christmas what did you look for on the back? A warranty contract that stated if it broke the company would repair it.

Just think—you spend 25 to 30 percent of your life at work. If you need a contract for a used car, an apartment, or toaster, how much more important is it for you to have a contract protecting your very job? Without a labor contract they could do anything tomorrow. They could close your department, change your shift, change your pay—anything they want. Once you have a union contract, you will have all the protection you will ever need.

EMPLOYEE: The company said I will be giving up my individual freedom if we vote the union in. Is that true?

RICK: The question of individual freedom is always raised by the company in a union campaign. However, the issue is not individual freedom but representation. Our union believes in a concept called the triangle of prosperity.

Figure 11-3

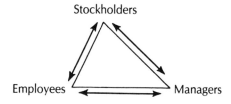

To grow and provide employment any organization needs all three ingredients of the triangle of prosperity. Stockholders have invested their money and are entitled to a return on their investment—their fair share. To guarantee their fair share, they have elected representatives called a board of directors to protect their interests.

The second thing any well-run organization needs is people to manage their organization. The management people are entitled to their fair share for the efforts they make within the organization. To guarantee that they are fairly represented, the company has a president and vice-president to deal with the board of directors.

The third thing needed to make the triangle of prosperity work is labor. And labor is entitled to its fair share for producing the product or services necessary to provide for the wages of management and a return on investment to the stockholders. The question that you as workers must answer is: who represents you as an equal partner in the triangle of prosperity? Individual workers simply do not have enough pressure to be equal partners. Collectively speaking through elected leaders, union workers can gain equal voice to have their problems resolved.

EMPLOYEE: But, our company doesn't like unions; they've told us so.

RICK: Would you be surprised to learn that your company belongs to unions? They call them associations, but they are unions. Your employer pays dues to them on a per capita basis for each employee, and these unions have local and national representatives. Why do they belong to the Chamber of Commerce, NAM, and specific trade and industrial associations? Because these organizations have worked. If collective power works for management it should also work for you.

EMPLOYEE: Can we lose anything if we join the union?

RICK: A good question. I'm sure you're all concerned about it, but the National Labor Relations Act protects your rights. As for your benefits or anything else you now have, you keep those, and you build on them. That's a matter of law.

PRO-COMPANY   But we were told we'd start without benefits,
EMPLOYEE: and we could lose some things once bargaining begins.

RICK: Well, that's a lie—a lie the company wants you to believe. No intelligent person here would have a union to *decrease* benefits. Look at the contracts we have throughout the U.S. and Canada. We have good benefits. Union people *gain* benefits. It is illegal for the company to take away benefits because you have unionized.

AGGRAVATED EMPLOYEE:
I'm really concerned about safety. Two people in our department are out right now from injuries, but nobody seems to give a damn.

RICK:
One thing we'll provide, through a contractual provision, is a safety committee composed of at least three employees to inspect the area monthly, hold meetings, and take corrective action. The union has been instrumental in creating and achieving safe working conditions. Unions through legislative action forced Congress to push OSHA—the Occupational Safety and Health Act.

AGGRAVATED EMPLOYEE:
My brother works in a union plant, and he said something about tagging equipment. How does that work?

RICK:
That's a system where the union committee has the right to tag equipment as unsafe or in need of repair, and no supervisor can force an employee to use that equipment. This is a union protection so that you don't face loss of hands, arms, eyes, or even death.

EMPLOYEE:
What does all this cost?

RICK:
I'm glad you raised that question because I'm sure a lot of people have that question on their mind.

The dues are set by the local. We recommend two hours pay per month as normal dues. This means you would be paying between $8.00 and $12.00 per month. These dues cover all expenses. There are no other charges for lawyers, court cases, arbitration, or negotiations. One-half of the dues stays here in the local for your normal business, attending conferences, and union conventions. The other half goes to the International to provide all the needed services—lobbying in the state and federal government, surveys, research, and organization.

PRO-COMPANY
EMPLOYEE: What's in it for you? Do you get a percentage?

RICK: No, my salary is a matter of public record. I do not work on commission.

PRO-COMPANY
EMPLOYEE: What is your salary?

RICK: My salary is $32,000 a year.

PRO-COMPANY
EMPLOYEE: Then why are you here?

RICK: I'm here because we learned a long time ago that the only way for employees to survive is to have collective bargaining. That is the basic reason for unions to protect you and your families.

I'm also here because your fellow employees asked the union to help solve your problems, because nobody in management would even listen to employees. Your company has a five-year program. They know where they want to be in terms of products, growth, business expansion, and new equipment for automation. The problem is: who speaks for you in that five year plan? Department heads or managers will sometimes say: "Don't worry; I will speak for you in the planning sessions," or "at executive board meetings," but don't kid yourselves. They have enough problems looking out for themselves. I've never heard of a manager at a board of directors meeting declaring: "Wait, we've got problems in our operation. Our people need more training, better equipment, better benefits." No manager in his right mind would criticize the company president, and if he did, he wouldn't be around very long. Your union has only one goal: to be effective in speaking for you—looking out for your interests. That's the reason for joining—you speak for yourselves.

PRO-COMPANY EMPLOYEE: I think unions stink and I think all you guys are parasites.

PRO-UNION EMPLOYEE: That guy is a company plant. He's anti-union, all for the company.

COMMITTEE CHAIRPERSON: We're here to let everybody have freedom to speak. This union is based on democracy. [The meeting continues.]

EMPLOYEE: How can we make the company listen to our demands.

RICK: You know, you folks should understand just how much strength you really have. For example, your company will find out this meeting was held, and I'll predict what's going to happen. The company is going to love you—once they hear about the meeting. They're going to talk to you; your supervisors will talk to you, and the president will send you letters—all because you attended this meeting. Now, you're intelligent people—you can see that if you can be that effective simply by talking about a union, think how strong you could be at the bargaining table.

PRO-UNION EMPLOYEE: Will anyone know if we sign these cards?

RICK: Only you, me and the National Labor Relations
                     Board will know.

PRO-UNION
EMPLOYEE: Who runs this election you mentioned?

RICK: The National Labor Relations Board. They are an
                     independent federal agency set up to protect
                     your rights. They will come to the plant, hand
                     you a ballot, and there will be a secret enclosed
                     voting area. You fold the ballot and put it in the
                     ballot box, and nobody will know how you
                     voted.

PRO-UNION   I heard that they can close the plant if the union
EMPLOYEE: comes in.

RICK: That's another lie. The fact is, your company is
                     in business to make a profit. I don't hear
                     anybody here saying they want to burn down
                     the building. But I do hear people saying they
                     want at least their fair share. That's what we're
                     here talking about—your fair share. We're not
                     against the president driving his big car, but I
                     think you are saying this: "I would at least like
                     my share to allow me to provide my family the
                     food, clothing, materials necessary for me to
                     survive. I'd also like to do a little more for my
                     son and daughter than say, 'No, you can't go
                     beyond high school.' I'd like to be able to send
                     my kids to places I haven't been able to go to."

PRO-COMPANY   Well, what are we going to do if the company
EMPLOYEE: won't give us these things?

RICK: You're going to be a part of the decision-making
                     process, because we will negotiate with senior
                     management. No longer will you have to talk to
                     the supervisors about your problems. You will
                     elect a person from each department who will

sit at the bargaining table with senior management. They will have to show us their books, if they say they aren't able to pay. You're going to be there in the decision-making process, as opposed to only listening and having the company dribble out little crumbs.

PRO-COMPANY EMPLOYEE: I think the question people really are asking is: what if there's a strike? What will happen to me?

RICK: Well, with our union, a strike is the last resort. We don't believe in strikes. We don't want strikes, but sometimes they happen. And they happen only as a result of your committee making such a recommendation. Even then, our international constitution provides that better than two-thirds majority must vote by secret ballot for a strike. Should you decide this is the alternative for you, the union would support and back you with strike benefits for however long it took to accomplish your goals.

PRO-COMPANY EMPLOYEE: I've heard that if we go on strike we will never make back the money we've lost during the strike.

RICK: Well, that's true—but it's only half true. I am not here to promote strikes or to suggest they're desirable. I've been on a number of strikes, and I think often they're caused by management that won't listen or by greedy employees. Having looked at your situation, I'm sure you aren't greedy. The fact is, you're *needy.* If management listens to you and to the bargaining committee, I'm certain there wouldn't be a strike. Moreover . . .

PRO-COMPANY EMPLOYEE: Wait a minute! You didn't answer the question. If we go on strike, won't we lose money?

RICK: I certainly apologize if I didn't answer the
                  question completely. Let me reiterate. The
                  company says if you go on strike for four weeks,
                  you'll need 10¢ an hour to make up your loss,
                  35¢ an hour if you strike for eight weeks, and
                  you will never make up the money you have
                  lost if your strike lasts 10 or 12 weeks or more.
                  That's only half true. You employees aren't
                  dumb; you won't cut off your nose to spite your
                  face. So what is the whole truth about strikes?
                  During a strike period, of course employees
                  have reduced incomes. The union has a strike
                  fund, as I mentioned. However, there are other
                  ways the union can help you. For example, we
                  can ask the credit union or bank to extend the
                  time period for loans, or even postpone
                  payment. The union will also pick up your
                  hospitalization costs, so you continue to have
                  protection.
                      But what about loss of money? In 1949, an
                  extensive strike in the auto industry over a
                  pension issue lasted about 114 days. The auto
                  companies agreed to provide an employee who
                  was sixty-five years old and had thirty-five years
                  of service a pension of $35 a month—and that
                  was peanuts. If you just look at that half truth,
                  you'd say: "Gee, they went on strike for
                  nothing." But what is the whole truth? There has
                  never been another strike over pensions in the
                  UAW, and the pension today for an auto
                  worker, regardless of age and with thirty years
                  of service, is a guaranteed $825 a month. In
                  addition, the last negotiations resulted in an
                  additional $45 per month for retirees to help
                  pick up the cost of living for that group. The
                  point is, once the benefit is established, it is
                  possible in subsequent negotiations to improve
                  on pensions a little bit each time. Of course, the
                  initial strike was painful, but once established the
                  principle was carried forward.

Here's another example. In the early fifties, a long strike in steel dealt with hospitalization. Remember, there were no pensions and no hospitalization before unions. Employees were out of luck if they were injured or had a family disaster. The first negotiated hospitalization after a 120-day strike was $5 per month paid by the company toward hospitalization, with employees paying the balance. Today, the cost of the medical package—including Major Medical, dental, other supplemental coverages, prescription rider, and so on—is $120 a month, paid entirely by the steel companies. Again, there hasn't been a strike over the medical package since then. The following rounds of negotiations have built up all those benefits.

Employees will not go on strike unless the issues are important enough and there is potential long-range gain. Don't be fooled by company half truths.

FEMALE EMPLOYEE:
I'm tired of the sexual harassment here. Our second-shift supervisor is constantly patting us on the behind and making advances. It's gotten so our department slogan is: "If you want to get ahead, you gotta go to bed." Will the union correct this?

RICK:
You'll find that our union has been one of the forerunners in establishing protection for women. As a matter of fact, we have contributed a lot of money toward passage of ERA. Our organization has a 40 percent ratio of women international officers and local presidents, stewards, and committee persons.

There are several ways we protect women. Initially we can put provisions in the labor agreements that women will not be discriminated against.

FEMALE EMPLOYEE:	How do you stop men from being paid more?
RICK:	The point you raise is well taken, in that managers have a sexist attitude about pay. In three offices I've recently organized, supervisors paid men higher than women, under the company's "Merit Pay Program." When we discussed this with department heads, one said: "Don't you know that the men in the workforce need more money than the women do? Most of these women are young people or their income is secondary in the family, so I try to give the men a little more money because they need it more." Now, he really believed he was not discriminating. The labor contract forced him to stop this practice by providing equal pay for work of equal value.
EMPLOYEE:	What if the union is not voted in. What happens to me?
RICK:	First, if everyone takes the time to vote, we will win. If we don't, you still will be protected by the law. If any of you feel any discrimination because you've come to this meeting, let me know and we will file an unfair labor practice against this company so fast it will make their heads spin.
COMMITTEE CHAIRPERSON:	If there are no other questions, I would like to thank Rick for coming and answering all of our questions. Anything else, Rick?
RICK:	Yes, I too would like to thank all of you for coming. It is important that you sign a card today. Voting for the union allows you to let you see if the union can solve these problems. The authorization is only good for one year, so why not give yourselves a chance to see the

results. If you're not satisfied, you can return
after a year, so you have nothing to lose.

This is a fairly typical union informational meeting. Notice that Rick
avoided arguments and questions in such a way as to make the union look
good and the employees the winner. What is he selling? Not only the
union, but also himself.

The organizer gains employees' confidence by identifying himself as
a worker. The union organizing staff will have employees the workers can
identify with, as in a Southwest campaign where the union had a Hispanic,
a good old boy from Texas, and a black. In a bank organizing campaign,
the organizing staff were primarily women who had previously worked in
offices and insurance companies, who were on loan during the organizing
drive. Many times, the organizers are young, good-looking, personable
folks with whom the employees can identify.

Union representatives adapt to any type of situation, with any group,
giving employees the answer they want. These people are intangible salespeople; their success is often in selling themselves. They shake hands,
relate personally, and identify with employees. Because they've come up
through union ranks, they have run for office, they have dealt in political
situations, or have been active in local politics. They have a tendency to
carry over their skills to develop individual rapport.

Organizers make a lot of promises. Can they do this? Absolutely! The
NLRB has ruled that unions may make specific promises about working
conditions, benefits, and *pay.*

Keep these personal factors in mind as we move to the next phase of
the campaign—the campaign from the employees' view.

Chapter Twelve

Union Campaign from the Employee's View

The article* presented in this chapter reflects accurately the feelings of the undecided voter, and 60 percent of the work force falls into this category. Obviously, this is where elections are won or lost.

Ikerd has given terrific insight to the entire campaign process. Our company was not involved in the campaign and we would not recommend many of the tactics that were used, especially the anti-union approach.

Note particularly the pro-union employees' view. Generally they are upset over a specific issue where they feel the company or a supervisor has not treated them fairly, for example, Chris Jacobsen, Sunday, September 23.

Employees who were anti-union had bad personal experiences with a union in some other company. Leo (Tuesday, September 25) had the

---

*This article was written by Russ Ikerd and published in the *Detroit News,* Dec. 16, 1979.

experience of seeing his plant close after a strike. Notice that whole shifts and departments seemed to lean one way or the other.

The anti-union material looks good to management and reinforces their bias, but it does not move the undecided voter to the management side. If anything, the anti-union propaganda turns off today's worker.

UNION DIARY
by Russ Ikerd

Union or Company—What more basic decision can a guy make?

In the quiet, pleasant city of Monroe, Michigan, the people who work at the Guardian Industries glass plant had a decision to make this fall. The men who make and pack the glass were asked to make a choice about an essential part of their lives. Would they continue to work as they always had at Guardian, or would they choose to be represented by the United Automobile Workers? The decision they had to make was either for or against unionization. When the election was held weeks later, Guardian employees rejected the union 234 to 185. But the election process was to involve everyone in the plant from the top to the bottom. This is what happened inside the plant during those weeks when Guardian men and women were trying to make up their minds. This is a diary of how people work, and think, and are caught up in a movement larger than themselves. And this is how it happened.

Saturday, September 8

"Sparky Allen, dial 329." . . . "Sparky Allen, please report to the bathroom." . . . "Sparky Allen, please report to the guard shack." . . . "Sparky Allen, to the games room." . . . "Sparky Allen, where are you?"

This went on for weeks. Sparky Allen, the elusive (an apparently reclusive) Sparky Allen was being paged incessantly between the hours of 8 A.M.–4 P.M.— our day shift. Yet, no one ever saw him or heard from him. Mr. Allen was merely a name in a game that was being played over the PA system.

Such is the nonsense that pervades the environment in which we work. It makes producing glass—a sometimes menial and always dangerous job—more enjoyable, if not easier. Nonsense keeps us loose.

Recently, however, things have been very edgy around the plant. The nonsense has been at a minimum. The reason: There's a movement to unionize the plant. In fact, there is an organizing committee in the plant from the United Auto Workers. As might be expected, the two factions—pro-Union and anti-Union—are at each other's throats. And that's no exaggeration. People's cars have been vandalized and Company property has been defaced.

This might not have anything to do with the Union movement. It might be "coincidential," as some have suggested. Just as it might be "coincidental" that a guy who was on the organizing committee (I was told) was fired recently (for reasons other than his participation in the movement, of course). Let it suffice that there have been a lot of "coincidences" since this political process began.

In today's mail, I received a form letter from our plant manager, Bill Black. The letter informed me that the UAW has attempted to organize our plant four times in the plant's nine-year existence. I have heard that the margin of defeat has been smaller each time.

Sunday, September 9

"In case you haven't noticed, Russ," Ed Reaume said, looking over his shoulder while putting the lite (piece of glass) in the box, "things have been kind of funny around here lately."

Ed was trying to explain why I had only gotten one break during a four-hour overtime stint. I was miffed not only because I hadn't gotten that second break, but because the break schedule was suspended for almost an hour, the last of my four, and I was supposed to have been the next one on break.

Who's to blame? I shouldn't really point my finger at the supervisor. After all, he has to answer to people higher up. So, I'll just blame the situation—the funny situation the Union movement has created.

Working a different shift, I couldn't help but notice the difference in attitude toward the Union. Most of the guys on my old day shift were unabashedly for the Union; while even if there does lurk a pro-Union guy on the afternoon shift, he certainly wouldn't have the audacity to say so on the line. I've been told that my new shift is predominantly anti-Union because it has a good supervisor.

But there are at least two pro-Union guys on the swing shift. One of them complains incessantly about the supervisor.

"You watch," he said, "if we break a lite he'll be right over wanting to know what happened. Who cares if we're cut and bleeding to death. He's just worried about production."

"And breaks," he said later. "We get three, and that's all."

Actually, that's all we're supposed to get. No more than three 20-minute breaks during an eight-hour shift. However, for us guys who work the line, three breaks isn't nearly enough—not after being accustomed to four, five, or even more in better times.

"And we might get them all before the day is half over," the pro-Union guy said. "Then we have to stay on the line the rest of the day. That's ridiculous. Hey, we don't even get our own gloves anymore. To hell with 'em."

The other pro-Union guy had this to say: "I think everyone's getting a little tired of the bull that's been going on around here. Right now, if the foreman don't like you, you're gone. With the Union, though, that could never happen. We would have too much power. And job classifications. We need it bad. We're material handlers, not clean-up people. We shouldn't have to do both."

Monday, September 10

Mark Weatherholt was having a tough time packing the mirror quality tonight. Mirror quality means that the glass has to be perfect—no stones, seeds, tin, or scratches, and perfectly square. The box in which he was packing the lites was set upon a rack that wouldn't stand still. In his state of despair, Mark called out for assistance. Lenny Umin, the supervisor, wanted to know why Mark, with all his years of experience, was having problems.

Mark, always the wise guy, said: "Lenny, let me put it to you this way: How many corners do you want on these lites?" A classic line, and it helped to keep us loose.

We were deluged with Company propaganda tonight. One of the pieces of literature was a reprint of an Associated Press story which appeared in the *Monroe Evening News*. Some statistics were underlined: ". . . some 28,000 auto workers laid off at Chrysler Corp . . . more than 70,000 indefinitely furloughed from the Big Three companies . . ." Underneath was written: "Vote No!" Above the story: "Don't let fancy promises change your life-style."

Another piece was a reprint of part of the "Agreement Between Guardian Industries Corp. and Local No. 174 of the UAW." It showed the pay scale at Guardian's Campbell Avenue plant in Detroit. According to the reprint, nobody there was making as much money as a starting material handler here. Written above the pay scale: "Current rumor from UAW—Campbell's average rate is higher?" Below, of course: "Vote No!"

The company even provided us with a song. It was composed by a Union member who was fined by the Union when he started a petition to get the Union out. Entitled "Good Time Charlie," it goes like this: "Good time Charlie is the Union man/Why he'll backslap you—whenever he can/-Sweet talk too—and build dreams so high/You'll wonder why he just can't fly!"

Wednesday, September 12

Received a letter from Bill Black. He wanted to talk job security: "The UAW could jeopardize your job security by creating the possibility of strikes. Thus, because of the threat of a strike, we might not be able to make deliveries to our customers, and they would probably turn to one of our many competitors. If such a situation arose, we would lose business, work schedules would have to be reduced, and some jobs might have to be eliminated. Is this the kind of *job security* the UAW would bring? Compare our outstanding record of *job security* with that of the UAW."

Then Bill went on to cite some statistics, such as the 100 UAW plants in the Detroit area have "either closed down, moved out of this area or cut back to such small numbers that practically all their employees lost their jobs during the past 25 to 30 years."

Further into the letter, Bill tells us what job security really is: *"Real job security* comes from demand for our products and demand for our products comes from quality standards and timely deliveries. No job is secure unless we are producing quality products and getting them to our customers on time at a competitive price."

Thursday, September 13

We got paid today, and that makes us happy. It was a nice check, too, considering it included a paid holiday (Labor Day) and our production bonus.

That's right, we get a production bonus here at Guardian. Once every two months. It's usually in excess of $100. The talk (circulated by anti-Union workers, no doubt) around the plant is that if the Union gets in, we can kiss our production bonus goodby. Few folks, if any, want to get less than they're getting now. That green stuff we get once a week is our lifeline.

The Company held an "open meeting" for the afternoon shift after work. I had never been to such a meeting before, so I asked some of the older guys what to expect. They said to go, listen and collect my straight-time pay afterwards. "Oh, yeah, and don't ask any questions," they cautioned. "You'll just make trouble for yourself."

The meeting was rather uneventful. It began with George Treglown, our personnel director, reading an anti-Union letter that Reed Hunter, a maintenance employee, had written. After reading the letter, George asked Reed why he had written it. Reed said that he sincerely felt that if the Union were to come to Guardian, he would lose a good deal of pride, not to mention self-accomplishment. He said that he hadn't been at Guardian that long ("since January") but that he had worked at a union shop for 25 years before that.

Whether I agreed with him or not, I had to admire Reed for standing up like that.

George then said some things. Mostly he wanted us to know that Guardian had made great strides at the Carleton plant in the past nine years without the Union, and that together we had overcome storms and rebuildings and recessions. After having said his piece, George asked if they were any questions.

The only question asked with any venom was, "How come we're not getting cost of living, George?" George answered that, although it might not seem so, we were. Tom VanRhein, our production manager, attempted to expound upon the COLA point. He went into a long spiel about the cost of living allowance being socialistic, and we didn't want that, did we? And that our wages were indeed "competitive," and that was good. And that we are all doing a helluva job making Bill Davidson, principal stockholder of Guardian Industries (as well as the Detroit Pistons), money, because, hey, "that's the bottom line. That's the American way." Tom went unchallenged. Nobody wanted to dispute what was and wasn't the American way.

Friday, September 14

The guys on the midnight shift appear to be predominantly pro-Union. There is one notable exception, however. Pete Soncrant was wearing a "Vote No" button tonight. I know Pete fairly well so I felt comfortable discussing the Union issue with him.

"Why do you wear that button, Pete?"

"Well," he said, dabbing at the beads of perspiration that inevitably dot his forehead, "if you had gotten burned once like I did, you'd wear one too."

Pete, like several others at the plant, used to work for La-Z-Boy Chair in Monroe. When La-Z-Boy packed up shop and left town, Pete was left behind on the unemployment line.

"Was it the union's fault that La-Z-Boy left town?"

He didn't say. What he did say, again, was that he had gotten burned once and he'd try his damndest not to let it happen twice.

"Also," he added, "I've got to start thinking about getting off this line."

"Yeah, Pete," someone wise-cracked. "You ain't no spring chicken anymore."

Sunday, September 16

The Union movement remains "in the shadows." They're saying so little, while the Company is saying so much. It makes for a rather unbalanced situation.

Admittedly, the organizing committee is working under adverse conditions. The Company has access to all the bulletin boards in the plant; the organizers do not. The Company has all the employees' addresses; the organizers do not. I am told that, by law, the committee will be given access to the list of employee addresses. Maybe then our mailboxes will be stuffed with pro-Union propoganda, too.

If the Union does get in, I hope to heck it slows down the line while we're packing double-strength glass. After eight hours of that, I'm exhausted.

Monday, September 17

During break, I became the target of a not-so-subtle Union pitch. It went something like this:

"Fred," T.J. asked, "exactly how many days off are those guys at GM going to get with that new contract?"

Fred answered that he thought that they were getting eight now, and that they would be getting another nine next year and nine more the year after.

"Days off?" I thought. "Are they talking vacation, sick time, personal time, or what?" I asked them.

"That's days off. Period." T.J. said. "And that doesn't include vacation time."

"Or holidays," Ulysses chipped in. "And they have 15 of those at GM."

My mind whirled. "What kinds of holidays do they have there at GM? We only get 10 here, don't we?"

"Ah, they have all kinds of strange ones . . . Martin Luther King Day . . . VD Day. . . ." Fred kidded.

I was thinking that that was a lot of time off, and T.J. was saying something about three months off, in all, when Fred added: "They're easing into a four-day work week. At the end of their third year, they'll be working what amounts to 4½ days per week. It's only a matter of time before they cut that other half day."

"They (our plant management) say that we can't compare ourselves to auto workers," Ulysses said, "yet they put that stuff on the bulletin boards about layoffs, strikes, jobs lost. . . . It's a goddamned double standard, that's what it is."

Tuesday, September 18

Here all along I've been writing off the Union's chances at Guardian, noting the organizer's slipshod campaign. But, now, I'm not so sure.

I talked with some pro-Union guys again tonight. One of them boasted: "We know pretty much how everyone's going to vote. How? Hey, we just know." I then proceeded to test them. They *do* seem to know.

"Afternoon shift (my shift) is going to hurt us, there's no doubt about that. Especially both lines and box close-up."

"We should do well in fabrication, though," another pointed out.

"Yeah, that's true. As for the midnight shift, that's almost all Union."

They would have me believe that the day and swing shifts are theirs, too. Pretty optimistic stuff, considering the UAW has already been voted down four times here.

On the other hand, the Company seems to be toning down its campaign. Already it's two days into the week and only one new piece of propaganda has appeared on the bulletin boards.

The piece was quite comical, really. It depicted a union boss as a big, fat man smoking a cigar, his chunky fingers clutching wads of cash. The caption said: "The Union Boss—He Loves Money!"

"Hey, they're scraping the bottom of the barrel," piped up a pro-Union guy.

Wednesday, September 19

Read a very interesting article about Guardian Industries, which appeared in the Business Section of the *Detroit News* on July 29. It was recommended to me by Al Doniwicha, one of the principal organizers. He considered the article a Union rallying point.

Well, I read the article—not once, but three times. And although this may sound corny, after I finished reading I felt a certain sense of pride. Yes, I felt proud

I was part of Guardian Industries. The article reaffirmed my belief that I have been working hard, but it also told me that my efforts were contributing to a successful operation.

However, I also felt that I deserve more from Guardian for my efforts. In the future, I will ask for more. Whether it will be through the upcoming Union election or when the Company conducts its annual survey of employees in the spring, I'm not sure as yet. Last spring, I was modest when answering the survey, but then I had no idea of Guardian's prominence in the glassmaking industry.

To quote from the article: "Guardian's glass operations are among the most efficient in the industry . . . Guardian needs only 200 people to operate its glass plant whereas comparable (union) plants require 400. . . ."

So, I'm working twice as hard to help Guardian be successful. I do not mind making the effort, but I do mind not being properly compensated for it. An honest day's work for an honest day's pay.

Thursday, September 20

Bob O'Brien was wearing a "Vote Yes" button. I know Bob's story well. We "trained" together for more than three months. All told, Bob has worked for Guardian Corp. for six years. All told, Bob has only six months seniority at the Carleton plant—even though he has worked here more than five years.

It's all because Bob transferred out to the California plant (in Kingsburg) the summer of 1978. For a variety of reasons, he then chose to come back to Michigan. Could Bob get his job back at the Carleton plant? Yes, but he would have to start all over again. He even had to go through the training program again. A raw deal, Bob thought, but he needed a job.

The Company in Bob's case was consistent. I give it that. There is a rule that if an employee transfers from one plant to another, he loses his plant seniority. No one at Carleton has heard of any exceptions.

Friday, September 21

At long last, the UAW has made its way into my mailbox. The three pieces of literature in the letter I received did not impress me. Only one of them tried to "sell" me on the Union. It told me who would write our contract, and why he would do a good job. Not very convincing. A second piece of literature was supposed to have been continued, but never was; that is, it was a two-page statement and I only received the first page. Very sloppy.

However, before I shake my head out of my socket, I have to consider what has been said to me all along: "The UAW didn't come to us; we went to the UAW. If you're for the Union, fine. If not, we don't want your vote. The question is, does Guardian want the Union? If so, great. If not, well, that's the way it goes."

It all seems too simple.

Saturday, September 22

Having had the last two days off, I was anxious to get back to the plant and catch up on what I had missed. Apparently, I hadn't missed much. But there were some new Company posters up on the bulletin boards—laying to rest the statement that the Company was scraping the bottom of the barrel.

One of them depicted an employee being confronted by a union boss (fat, of course). The caption read: "Sorry about your wife being sick, Sam. Rules are rules, though. You have to pay your union dues."

There was an item of greater interest on another bulletin board. It announced a company contest called "Why not put it in the bank or in your tank?" It seems the Company is inviting all production and maintenance employees—all those eligible to vote in the upcoming election—to guess how much the UAW assesses each member per year in dues. "Guess" is a rather interesting way of putting it because anyone who wants to can easily find out how much Union dues are. Regardless, all the correct "guesses" will be put in a ballot box. Whoever's name is drawn will win an equal amount of gasoline. The Company notes, "It is a lot of gallons!"

Sunday, September 23

Someone on my crew, Chris Jacobsen, had the audacity to wear a "Vote Yes" button. When I saw the button, I told him: "It takes a lot of guts to wear one of those around here."

"Well, yeah. I always used to hate the Union."

"Uh, huh. What changed your mind? You're not getting day shift like you'd been told?"

I knew that Chris had been told he'd be going on day shift. But that had been months ago.

"That and other things."

He went on to explain that he was not going to be compensated for a hand injury he had suffered some time ago—although the Company at first had said he would be.

"My two fingers will never be the same," he said, showing me his injured hand. "I used to be able to play the guitar. Not any more."

No new Company propaganda, but the Union supporters were heard from today. I was given a letter in the locker room. It was a parody of the letter Reed Hunter had written:

"Even though my house is paid for from working in union shops and inflation hurts me less than you younger guys, there is a great sense of accomplishment at Guardian. Why should we try for a cost-of-living clause that pays us $1.35 an hour when we can have a bonus that pays 30½ cents, and isn't it fun to watch and see how many ways they find to take that bonus away from us?"

The letter was signed "Gomer Hunter."

Monday, September 24

Chris Jacobsen didn't wear his "Vote Yes" button today. Instead, he wore a T-shirt with the message: "We don't hire handicaps here/We make our own." Guts, man, the guy has guts.

The Company has a new batch of propaganda up. That's not surprising, since it's the beginning of a new work-week for office employees and they, it is generally accepted, are the ones responsible for refreshing the Company's message on the bulletin boards. The new stuff, though, isn't any different from the old.

I talked to one of the guys on my crew about the Union. He didn't commit himself. He did, however, say that if the Company gave us time and a half for Sundays he would definitely vote "no." As it stands now, we get time and three-eights for two of the three Sundays we work. The difference is about $50 a month.

Tuesday, September 25

We all received a free piece of gum today. Our supervisor dispersed some Company literature that had a piece of Wrigley's Juicy Fruit gum attached to it. The message was, "Don't let the Union gum up your future."

"Hey, that's pretty good, us getting this free gum," I said to Leo. We were packing glass at a two-person station.

"I tell you what," he said, "if the Union doesn't get in, I'll buy you a whole pack of gum. What kind do you like?"

"Juicy Fruit, and you're on!"

Leo, the oldest worker on our crew by a good margin, is a staunch Union opponent. He's one of those who worked at La-Z-Boy before it shut down. I remember quite well a conversation we had a while back.

"How do you feel about the Union, Leo?"

"I tell you what," he began pulling out the ever-present cigar to help illustrate a point, "all the time I was at La-Z-Boy the union got me this much." He spread his hands about eight inches.

"The last time we went on strike everybody was looking for a vacation, some time off. They got their time off, all right. We didn't go back to work until over half a year went by. And I'll tell you something. The company made the union an offer right away, but the union turned it down. Well, after we had been off for that long the union wound up taking an offer that was less than the original offer. But you had better believe that those union officials were getting paid while we were off—the whole time."

Wednesday, September 26

A quiet day on the battlefront. Such a day reaffirms my belief that it's been a rather peaceful battle (as battles go). A few weeks ago, talk of violence, even reported acts of violence, was commonplace.

Every day when we walked into the plant we were confronted with the Company's "Vandalism Updates," listing property damage that had been reported in and around the plant since the Union movement began. No more "Vandalism Updates"; things seem much less tense.

Thursday, September 27

Brought home a "Vote Yes UAW" fingernail file and a "UAW Key to Progress" key ring. Two more items to add to my growing collection.

Also received a letter "From the Union." Actually, it was a letter from the Company pretending that I had a past-due union bill of $722.50. The Company asked, "Would you like to receive a bill like this from the Union?" Are they kidding?

Friday, September 28

The beginning of a long weekend! We get them—four days off, Friday through Monday—every 28 days. We work 21 out of 25 days, get four off, then start the cycle all over again.

Believe me, these long weekends are nice. Getting away from the whirl, grind, and clank of the machinery is something most of us appreciate a great deal.

Saturday, September 29

Went out driving and noticed a truck for sale. Interested, I stopped to check it out. After the guy—Lee was his name—told me how much he was asking, I said I'd get back to him. I explained that since there was a chance of the UAW getting in at Guardian and that, therefore, there was an outside chance of a strike, I didn't want to make such a big investment right now.

Lee seemed to understand. He was also quite curious.

"You know, I thought the Union was already in over there. You guys are making pretty good money there, aren't you?"

"Yeah, we're fairly close with other industries, or so they tell us."

"How much do you make compared to the guys at GM?"

"We're making a little less now than they are. But I guess after three years they're going to be making upwards of $11 or $12 an hour. In three years it's hard to say how much we'll be making. Course, this past July we got a $30-a-week raise."

"That's 75 cents an hour," Lee said after a quick calculation. "That's not bad. You guys got a pension program there?"

"Yeah. I don't know much about it, but some of the older guys aren't too happy with it. They're entitled to what they think is a ridiculously low amount per month per years of service."

"You guys got any stock program there? Anything else to help in retirement?"

"Some of the older guys that were working at Guardian before '76 just got some shares of stock. And they've got a thrift savings program and a few other things they call "Grow With Guardian" programs."

"When can you join the savings program?"

"The day you hire in."

"Is that right? Most union shops make you wait at least 'til you've got your 90 days in. Yeah, I used to belong to a union. I was an electrician."

"Ah, unions," Lee added as we walked away from the truck. "All they're interested in is dues. They've got to have their money. I know a lot of guys who work at Guardian. They seem pretty happy. They seem to have all the things it takes money to buy. You know, fairly well to do."

Sunday, September 30

"Hello, Tom," I called to a friend who works at Ford. "How's your house coming?"

"It's not," he replied. "Looks like we're going to have to wait until next summer to build."

"How come?"

"I got laid off."

"Oh," I paused at the nasty thought. "For how long?"

"Two months now."

I wondered what a person would do for two months without work. Heretofore that's been the least of my worries. At Guardian, nobody gets laid off. There always seems to be work to do. It may not be desirable work, but the work is there. With a union, who knows?

Monday, October 1

Went golfing. Included in the foursome were two other Guardian employees. One is decidedly pro-Union, while the other is not-so-decidedly anti-Union.

The most popular union-related topic of conversation was the two letters we all received from the Company in today's mail. One was a note of apology from George Treglown for the "Union dues bill." George said he had not sent it to be "offensive."

Neither of my Guardian golfing companions, however, thought the "bill" was "offensive." The pro-Union fellow did say the ploy was tacky.

The other letter was from Bill Black, reminding us to vote: "The Union election is just about over. You will be voting this Thursday and Friday as to whether you want to have the UAW around collecting dues or not."

The man has a way with words.

Unlike his other letters, though, this had a personal touch. It was a form letter, yes, but instead of beginning, "Dear Guardian Employee," it had my first name typed in. Then, in the first paragraph, Bill noted how long I had been working at Guardian. He added that he "appreciated" my "work, support and assistance" in that time.

Hey, like most people, I enjoy being recognized. The pro-Union fellow, however, was not as charmed as I was.

"They put down the Union people for sending out form letters, then they turn around and do the same damn thing. Big deal, so they know how long I've been working there."

Not much else was said about the Union. Seems everybody was more interested in shooting a good round of golf.

Tuesday, October 2

The Union organizers are very confident at this stage of the
battle. They continue to talk in terms of a 70 percent "Yes"
vote. Boosting their confidence level is the Company's free-
spending approach to the election. As one senior employee
said, "They're spending a helluva lot of money. I've been
around for all the other elections, but this is the maximum
they've ever spent."

It would seem so. Today, everybody received an album
with a recorded message from Bill Black. And with the album
came a chance to win another Company contest. I'm not sure
what the prizes are for in this one, but, whatever they are, they
go to the employees with lucky albums.

The album drew a tremendous response at the plant. Everybody was anxious to go home and listen to Bill Black (and
to see if they had won a prize). Joked one guy, "I'm going home
and turning on 'Bill Black and the Comets'."

The message on the album was a reiteration of the things
the Company has been saying since Day One: "We're a team;
as a team we're prospering; we have our problems; together,
without outsiders, we can attempt to solve our problems; the
UAW is a strike-happy union; the UAW means to take your
money; you really don't want the UAW."

Now, let's start doing some adding; the Company has two
contests going; the Company has churned out huge quantities
of literature for the mail and for the plant bulletin boards; the
Company has had several hundred albums made; the Company
has provided refreshments, prizes, souvenirs, and whatnot for
a jamboree (which, I am told, is a first. The Company called it
the "Ninth Annual Jamboree," but one employee said that,
while there have been Guardian family picnics every summer,
there never has been a jamboree before). In short, the Company
has spent some money.

This prompted a Union organizer to say, "Now I know
they're sweating it out. It's a shame," he added sarcastically,
"we don't have to spend that kind of money."

Wednesday, October 3

I know the election has to be tomorrow because Pete Soncrant
wore his "Vote No" T-shirt tonight.

Collected some last-minute Company and Union propaganda. I brought home two pieces from the Company and one
from the Union. Good day for the Union. Throughout the cam-

paign, the ratio has been substantially higher in the Company's favor than tonight's 2 to 1.

Thursday, October 4

One of my co-workers stopped off at the guard shack on the way to his car to drop off a material pass. It's a procedural thing: When you'd like to take some glass home, you get your supervisor to sign a material pass, which you then leave with the security guards.

After he checked in with the guards, another worker remarked, "Gettin' it while you can, hey?"

"Yeah. Tonight's the last night, I guess."

"Wait a minute," I said. "Is there a new policy taking effect soon regarding passes?"

"If the Union gets in . . ." I should have known.

Bill Black has been seen around the plant a lot lately. He being the plant manager, I guess it never occurred to me before that he should be anywhere else during a big election. The last few days however, he's been everywhere. I wonder if he's gotten any sleep recently?

For the record, I voted today. But I'm not saying how I voted. Secret ballot, you know.

Friday, October 5

I was driving past the Loose Caboose, a favorite watering hole of Guardian employees, this afternoon and saw George Treglown in the parking lot.

"Well," I said to myself, "he's either drowning his sorrows or celebrating. Either way, I'll find out soon enough."

Later, as I was walking from the parking lot to the plant, I met a Union organizer.

"Did you hear?" he said. "The Union lost by 49 votes. But we gained. Hey, we gained."

"Why? Is that the closest margin ever?"

"Yup."

"Well, are you glad it's over?" I asked. "I'll bet it's a great weight off your shoulders." (He had said before that it would be.)

"Yup. But we'll be right back at 'em next year. Hey, the Company made a lot of promises during this election. They'd better keep 'em. I'll be watching. And if they screw up . . ."

I have no doubt that he will be watching.

Once in the plant, I noticed that the unofficial election results were posted on the main bulletin board. The Union lost, 234–185.

Close? Well, as one Union fellow put it: "If 25 of those who voted 'no' had voted 'yes,' well, we'd be planning our victory party now."

Friday, October 19

"It is hearby certified that a majority of valid votes has not been cast for any labor organization at the Guardian Industries Corp. glass plant in Carleton, Michigan." Signed: Bernard Gottfried, regional director, National Labor Relations Board, Oct. 17, 1979.

Thus, everything ended up in a neat package. Not much has happened to the men who work the two lines packing glass since the vote. The guys are still on their shifts. Chris Jacobsen has not yet gone to the dayshift and Bob O'Brien still toils on the line. There's been a crackdown on certain types of free scrap wood. Perhaps that's a coincidence. We all got free turkeys from the Company this year.

And I received my pack of Juicy Fruit gum from Leo Connors.

Russ Ikerd has shown us the election process from the inside. He illustrates the conflict on the floor and the gut level reaction to the campaign by focusing on the reaction of various employees he meets. There is an ebb and flow described. He resents the company's "bottom of the barrel" approach in the Fat Union Boss propaganda and the past due union bill of $722.50, but he has pride in the company's success in an article written in *The Detroit News*. He reflects the worker's frustration over economic issues when he discusses time and one-half for Sunday equaling an additional $50.00 a month and the cost of living formula in U.A.W. contracts.

Note that the pro-union employees have a specific gripe against the company—not over money, but over promises that had been made and not kept.

In preparing for the campaign don't underestimate the ability of the workers to make rational decisions concerning their own economic interest. Don't treat the employees like fools who will believe any propaganda from the union *or* the company. Material that is honest, factual, and consistent, and presented personally in group meetings with good follow-up by the supervisor, will have a positive effect on the undecided voter.

Chapter Thirteen

The Union Campaign from Management's Side: A Positive Approach to a Negative Problem

Before we consider your primary campaign against the union, it is important to look at the causes of employee dissatisfaction that can lead to a union organization attempt.

We hope that you have developed a close relationship with your supervisors, who we assume are loyal and competent. If not, channels of communication normally used to warn you of beginning union activity may not exist.

During one of your frequent meetings with supervisors, they should be strongly advised that occurrences not directly relating to union activity can make employees insecure, fearful, and therefore, more susceptible to union approaches. These occurrences are also threatening to supervisors and management. We call these occurrences "triggering incidents."

TRIGGERING INCIDENTS

You and your supervisors must set employees' minds at rest about "triggering incidents," assuring them and demonstrating to them that you have their welfare uppermost in your concerns even though one of these incidents has happened or is about to happen. Examples of "triggering incidents" are:

1. Selling your company.   If you are selling your company, or thinking seriously about selling your company, reassure your supervisors and employees, through normal communication channels, that new management does not intend to make changes that will upset them or threaten their future security.

2. Internal changes.   Changes within your company, such as hiring a new plant manager, can cause rumors and discomfort among employees because of the "fear of the unknown." Until he has proven himself, the new manager will be viewed with suspicion. Meanwhile, the company can relax tension by laying out his background, expertise, and past record of good relations with employees. Obviously he should be a top manager or your "marketing efforts" on him won't be worth much. We presume that a progressive company wouldn't hire someone who had a poor employee relations record.

3. Hiring Relatives.   If you turn your company over to offspring or other relatives, or bring one of your relatives into the company in a key position, you will have a lot of insecure employees. We don't say you shouldn't do this, but a good communications system can do a lot to alleviate employee concern. If your relatives are known and have a reputation for incompetence or snobbery, they will get a chilly reception. You might introduce them to your employees and outline thoroughly what their positions are in the company.

4. Firing a long-term employee.   To avoid employee dissatisfaction in this situation (particularly if the employee is fired by the previously mentioned new plant manager or a new supervisor), gain employee acceptance of the firing as we suggested in discussing policy consistency, firmness in discipline, and fair and just treatment.

5. Sexual harassment.   You don't need the "sex-game" supervisor. He will make you fair game for organizers, not to mention the havoc he creates among employees. Don't wait long to take fair disciplinary action, and be sure to make it clear to employees that sexual harassment won't be tolerated in your company. Women employees may be reluctant to report sexual harassment incidents, so make your supervisors sensitive to the possibility of this sometimes very subtle problem. A woman union organizer may appear should sexual harassment be the "triggering incident" in your company.

6. *Company financial difficulties.* You may wonder why a company in financial difficulty should worry about a unionization attempt, but signs of financial strain become quickly apparent to employees. Some of these indicators might be: safety measures neglected, equipment not repaired, changes in normal business routine causing "rush orders," or "red tag orders" that put unusual pressures on employees or supervisors. Again, meet with your supervisors to explain exactly what is going on so that they can explain to employees what the changes and demands mean to workers. This is a good opportunity to develop a spirit of "pulling together" to help the company rather than developing fears among employees who don't know what is happening.

FIRST SIGNS

If, despite your best efforts, a "triggering incident" continues to upset employees, be aware of and warn your supervisors to look for *"first signs"* that a union drive may be under way.

Remember that in 90 percent of cases, employees go to the union, and in 10 percent of the cases, the union contacts employees. Initial contact with the union occurs in various ways, but almost always the drive starts with some disgruntled employee contacting the union. It's important to be sensitive to "first signs," because your chances of winning increase immensely if you can determine early that a union attempt is imminent. If you remain unaware until you get official notice, your chances decrease.

You may find out that a union is on the scene through an NLRB notice, with a petition that the union is seeking recognition. That's the worst way to find out; it means the union has been through your organization, active in the plant, and that your communications system failed to keep you posted. It also means that your supervisors haven't told you about problems arising with "triggering incidents," "first signs," or other possible signals. It could well mean that your supervisors are supporting the union. In that case, you obviously failed to communicate with your supervisors and you do not have their confidence. We will discuss communications with supervisors after covering recognition of "first signs."

"First signs" that a union drive may be developing are indicated by *any basic change in employee behavior.* What are some of the signs you should look for?

1. Unusual employee questions to supervisors. Any *technical* questions outside an employee's normal interest, such as: What is the return on the portfolio stocks in the pension program? Can pension rights or vesting be transferred if an employee leaves the company? Don't become paranoid automatically. The employee may just be on a "self-improvement" reading kick or he may be interested because a friend told him he should know more about his retirement fund. To follow up, determine whether the employee is asking for personal reasons or because an organizer is trying to find out what the company benefits are so the union can compare them to benefits under their contracts. Ask your supervisors to report any unusual questions regarding company benefits so that you can find out the reason for the questions.

2. Changes in small groups. Alert your supervisors to watch for small group changes, such as employees who have been eating together every day suddenly eating in different groups. They may be getting union authorization cards signed, or they may be planning a birthday party.

If people are wandering from one department to another, again a case where they may be soliciting card-signing, look for anything unusual, such as movement between units of people who have not wandered around before.

One area that needs particular scrutiny is the *maintenance department.* The union organizing drive starts here in many cases, because maintenance employees have *greater mobility* throughout your operation than other employees. They can chat with employees in all departments from time to time without appearing to be "out of place."

Second and third shift operations might also be monitored for unusual activity because of normal lack of supervisory control and support.

An employee who normally leaves work at 5 P.M. stays over to talk to a group in the cafeteria. The questions are how abnormal is this and why is it occurring? The supervisor can find out what is going on and why, and if problems are being discussed, what they are.

It is not unusual for union organizing to develop in a single department, a separate floor, or a particular shift. *Because internal organizing committees must attract all employees, the most convenient way, often, is to contact people on the job.* This may be why people are moving from unit to unit, and if supervisors are sensitive to this conduct, they can sound out people to find out what they are up to. If an employee from another department comes into an adjoining department, the supervisor might ask, "May I help you?" The employee is either going to explain why he is there or he will be evasive, which may be the giveaway.

Before you panic at these "first signs," find out what is going on. We are simply suggesting that *any basic change in employee patterns may signal union activity.*

This is a good time to stop and note that the union campaign took four specific stages:

1. Initial contact by employees.

2. Investigation by the union.

3. Union strategy.

4. The campaign.

There are specific steps in management's campaign against the union. *Management wins 75 percent of union elections if the following four things happen:*

1. Management hears about union activity informally and determines cause or causes of employee problems; investigates what is really taking place.

2. Management contacts employees, telling them clearly that the company does not want a union.

3. Management runs a well-planned campaign.

4. Management maintains close supervisory contact before, during, and after the election.

Normally you find out about union activity when an employee talks to a supervisor, indicating three favorable items:

1. The employee feels that communications are open.

2. He trusts his supervisor to listen and be receptive to his message.

3. He isn't sold on the union.

The supervisor should listen, using a nondirective interviewing technique. Part of that is repeating what the employee said. Here is a sample dialogue between supervisor *(S)* and employee *(E):*

E: I heard a couple of guys in the welding shop talking about a union. Or at least somebody told me they heard the guys talking.

S: Oh, really?

E: I heard there's going to be a union meeting tomorrow night.

S: Oh, is that so?

E: Yes, I heard it's going to be over at the VFW hall.

S: I guess there are a lot of meetings over there.

E: The whole production department is going to be there.

S: All of production?

E: Yeah. Bill Smith is getting them together.

S: Oh, Bill Smith.

E: Yeah. It's around that there's going to be some International Union people there to talk to the employees.

S: Really? International people?

E: Should I go to the meeting?

S: Joe, you know you're free to go to any meeting you want to, but if there are any questions at the meeting, or any problems you'd like to talk over with me, you know I'm always here to talk over anything you like. You know, rumors are always floating around, but I really appreciate your telling me about this.

Note that the supervisor kept a cool head about what he heard—and he *listened.* He also showed no reaction, pro or con, even though he might have been upset, and he didn't try to discourage the employee from attending the meeting. He was wise, because he didn't commit himself, and he knew that this employee might become his pipeline to what could happen in the future.

The supervisor should immediately report his conversation to the personnel department or the plant manager, or to whoever is available in senior management. Sometimes he may only have heard indirectly about some employees who have contacted the union, or even that grumbling employees have said they were going to the union, which may come from a third party. A supervisor may listen to anything an employee volunteers, but he cannot question the employee about union activities because that is private information and technically management is not allowed to interrogate employees about the union.

At meetings with your supervisors, you should constantly reinforce information about "triggering incidents" and "first signs." If a supervisor has a conversation with an employee, such as the one just described, this is a good time to get together with all of your supervisors and find out if they have also discerned union activity. Find out what information they have. You will keep them thinking about signs of activity, such as seeing two employees talking, which they really hadn't perceived as significant before. Thus you alert them to watch for further signs.

You should also continue to keep supervisors informed, as well as inviting them to continue to keep you informed of their observations. If you expect them to help you, you should ensure that they participate in the preparations for your campaign against union organization. Their participation is ensured, however, only if they trust you enough to lay out what they see going on. Because good supervisors generally know everything that goes on in a plant, they can usually report some of the "first signs," plus what they are hearing in their departments and who seems to be promoting the union issue. Supervisors often identify more closely with employees than with senior management, so the first meeting should not be a fault-finding, negative session. Its purpose is to inform management as to where they've gone wrong, how serious the problem is, and then to guide supervisors as to what they should do during the next few weeks.

Alternative to, or in addition to, meetings is circulating among supervisors individually to inform them and to learn what they have seen or heard. In a small company, this could be done plant-wide, and by departments in a larger operation. Supervisors in both approaches should be told to keep the information to themselves until you get back to them. As to who should represent management in either approach, personnel usually develops rapport with supervisors and is in a better position to get information from them than a line manager or senior management.

During the time you are discovering union activity from informal sources, you should try to find out what the problem is in the organization. Why is the union on the scene to begin with? What are the real issues? You may need a thick skin, because the real issue simply may be management. However, truthful communication is necessary to ascertain the facts. We know that supervisors are often reluctant to tell management *they* are the problem, so make it clear to your supervisors that they are free to tell you if management is to blame. Say to them, "If the problem is management I want to know about it. I *do* want to identify and solve the problem."

The problem often involves someone not in the particular plant operation, or somebody not associated directly with day-to-day operations—the "they" people the workers never or seldom see. In many companies, we have heard: *"They* said . . . , *they* did this . . . , *they* told me to tell you . . .*"*, and so on. In such cases, the supervisor is passing the buck over some bad news or because of unresponsive management. The supervisor doesn't want to take responsibility for the bad news, so he falls back on *"they* said." Supervisors should be careful about pointing the finger at "bad guys."

Finding out which employees are leaders for the union, and why, is very important. Your investigation may reveal that one or two leaders, or perhaps all, have reasons. They've been bypassed; legitimate complaints haven't been listened to; or they were never told why they weren't promoted when promotions were available.

Again, we want to emphasize that frequent meetings with supervisors are vital, since supervisors are apt to know what the facts are. Too often, managers have told us, when we've been called into campaigns: "It's not really a big problem. There are just a few disgruntled employees, malcontents, who are getting other people upset." That usually reflects failure to get facts the supervisors might have been able to give them—leading to dangerous delusions about their "generally good" employee relations.

Handbilling, which can occur anytime (but is usually a result of initial contact and as part of the campaign), is another way management finds out that a union drive is taking place. It is a typical union tool in the 10 percent of cases where the union contacts employees. The union organizer stands outside the plant and passes out handbills, known as "three-second flyers," intending to get a message across to employees. Mostly, the union has already accomplished what it wanted to achieve. Handbills are not tools to bring people into the union, so handbilling can be assumed to indicate a lot of activity already finished.

An exception to handbilling that indicates activity already finished is in the organizing of financial and insurance institutions, where unions have gone into financial districts and distributed flyers. This indicates serious union effort, but not a concerted employee-initiated campaign. It is what the union calls a "scattergun approach," with phone numbers or other ways of indicating interest on the part of the union. The company at this stage should not overreact to these handouts. Such overreaction may generate interest in the union.

RECOGNITION: UNION CARDS

The union sometimes contacts employers by letter or an office call. You should know that nothing in the National Labor Relations Act says an election is necessary before a union gets the right to represent employees. It simply says that any group of employees designating a labor organization as their representative has bargaining rights. The election is simply a process by which the NLRB determines whether a union represents a majority of employees, when a good-faith doubt exists. The company must take the position with the NLRB that the company has a good-faith doubt, that the majority of employees want a union. A "good-faith doubt" are key words.

If you get a letter requesting recognition, or you get cards, *do not respond.* Find knowledgeable labor law experts, and let them respond (see Figure 13-1). There must be a good-faith doubt, so if the union comes to you, *do not see them, do not take their cards.* This is a situation where "pleading ignorance" of what to do can have very serious consequences later.

If a union representative, for any reason, manages to confront you in your office or anywhere, you don't have to see him, and *don't.* You may

Figure 13-1 ANSWER LETTER TO UNION REQUEST FOR
RECOGNITION

Dear Sir:

The purpose of this letter is to acknowledge receipt of your letter dated
February 18, 19__, in which you claim that a "substantial majority of the
processing and proof clerks, typists, adjustment clerks, sensimatic operators, secretaries, analysts, commodity clerks and contract clerks" of our
bank have chosen your union as their bargaining representative and have
turned over their rights concerning their jobs, their wages and their working conditions to your union. In addition, you request recognition as the
bargaining agent.

I do not believe that a majority of our employees authorized your union
to represent them, nor do I believe that they ever will. I therefore have a
good faith doubt as to the majority status of your union in the bargaining
unit requested.

Because of this, I cannot recognize your union. Instead, I suggest that this
sort of thing be decided in the American democratic way, by a secret ballot
election conducted by the National Labor Relations Board where every
employee is free to vote according to his conscience as to what he thinks
is best for him and his family.

                                    Sincerely yours,

                                    _____

tell him, "If you have anything to say to me, put it in writing". If he offers
a batch of cards to be checked, refuse on the grounds that you don't know
who signed or why they were signed. Tell him to put it in writing, and don't
comment on the number of cards and whether there is a majority, or that
you prefer an NLRB election, or any other comments on the merits of the
situation. *Do not agree to check cards. Do not discuss number of employees involved or employees' sentiments about the union. If in doubt,
don't!* Remember, you do not have to talk to a union representative or see
a union representative. *If you can avoid it, do so.*

   As soon as any sign of union activity occurs, you should strongly and
clearly communicate to your employees that *you are not interested in a*

union and don't want a union in your organization. If a card-signing campaign is going on, tell employees that *they should not sign cards without reading them carefully.* (See Figure 13-2.) The union will often tell employees that the company is indifferent to their joining, or even that the company might be pleased to have a union. Correct *that* misinformation at the outset—and any rumors that may run counter to your true position. Some unions tell employees the cards only request an election, *when in fact their signing gives away their rights to bargain independently and constitutes a request for union membership.* If employees discover they've been lied to, they will want nothing further to do with the union. Your goal is to cut the union off at the pass—if you are successful at this point, the union campaign may stop here, and many have.

You may be pretty shaken up at this point, but you know that phase three of your management plan has started. You heard about union activity, you investigated what is going on and what the problems are, you told your employees you don't want the union, and now you must be braced to start running your campaign.

INVESTIGATION OF UNION ACTIVITY

When you are sure that there is significant union activity in your organization (rather than unfounded rumors), you should investigate further to determine how many employees are really interested in the union. Are there really only a couple of dissatisfied employees, or a meaningful number? *What union is involved?* Since unions use various approaches to their

Figure 13-2 UNION AUTHORIZATION CARDS

If anyone should come to you and ask you to sign a Union Authorization Card, we are asking you to refuse to sign it. You have a right to join and belong to a union, and you have an equal right not to join and belong to a union. If any other employee should interfere, or try to coerce you into signing a Union Authorization Card, please report it to your supervisor and we will see that the harassment is stopped immediately.

campaigns, you should find out as much as you can about the union involved so that you can take appropriate counter measures.

One of the things you can do to lay the groundwork for a solid campaign is to find out who the union organizer is. It is important to have a good profile of the organizer, to determine what type of campaign he runs, his character, community standing, or if he's an outsider. Has he won many elections? What is his salary? Is he a "big shot" or a "routine flunky?"

You can get information on the organizer through your business or trade association, and if your company belongs to an employers' association, others may have dealt with him. If he has organized other businesses in town, check with them and ask their help because they've been "through the mill" with him and his campaign.

Too many times, during unionization at this stage, management tends to pretend it isn't happening, partly because they don't want anybody to know they have problems. They thus allow the union to move in with full muscle, and never counteract what's going on until it's too late.

Use every community communications source you can find. Don't hesitate to contact anyone who has had experience in unionization of their business or organization, particularly anyone who has dealt with the organizer representing the union with which you are dealing. If you can, get copies of contracts he has negotiated and see how good they are compared to your company programs.

Countering union organizing may well relate to the style of that organizer. Some unions do little organizing and make serious mistakes, for example, displaying a bad temper in an organizing meeting (perhaps as a result of aggravating questions on the part of some of your people). In one case, one organizer dealing with a photographic processing plant composed of 90 percent women held organizing meetings in a local bar to which many of the women would not go. In another case, the organizer was dating one of the women on the internal organizing committee, and management found out that he was happily married, the father of two children, and was active in Little League baseball—facts that he had failed to communicate to his plant committee. These facts were leaked to the shop floor, and the organizer disappeared. The union won't hesitate to dig up facts about your organization. Don't hesitate to dig up facts about the union or its business representative.

Other things you need to know about the union: What is the local's financial position and what is the international's? How much do they have to spend on the organizing drive? You can simply contact the Department of Labor in Washington for this information. You will find the form for this request in Figure 13-3.

Figure 13-3 SAMPLE PURCHASE ORDER TO PUBLIC DISCLOSURE
DEPARTMENT

Company	Purchase Order
Address	No. _____
City, State, Zip	Date _____ Date Required_____
	Ship Via <u>Best Way</u> F.O.B._____
	Terms <u>Net 30 days</u>
U.S. DEPARTMENT OF LABOR	■ _____
<u>Public Disclosure Department</u>	Ship to <u>Same as above</u>
200 Constitution Avenue, N.W.	■ _____
Washington, DC 20216	■ _____

Quantity		Stock Number/Description	Price	Per
1		LM Report: copies of local by-laws, financial		
		reports and officer's salaries		
		(Type in name of Union/Regional or Local Number)		

YOU MAY CALL
FOR THIS INFORMATION: <u>Type in Company Name</u>
1/202/523-7397

For Local Information contact: <u>By Signature & Title of person</u>
<u>placing order</u>

U.S. Dept. Labor,
L-M Reporting & Disclosure Division
* *
Another address to keep on hand for copies of government documents is:

U.S. Government Printing Office   OR CALL:

Superintendent of Documents   1/202-275-3050 Customer Service
(To Order)

cont.

Washington, DC 20402   1/202-783-3238 Order Inquiry (To Get Prices)

If you do not know the price of an item, call Order Inquiry to find out. All purchase orders must be accompanied with the price of the item you are requesting and a check in the exact amount of the items ordered. $50 will establish an account with the printing office.

NLRB NOTICE OF HEARING

When the union presents its demand for recognition or a notice is received from the NLRB that a campaign is officially under way, there is some basic information shown on the formal NLRB notice (see Figure 13-4) which you should keep handy. This information includes:

1. The name of your company.

2. The location of the plant or office the union is attempting to organize.

3. The bargaining unit (who the union wishes or claims to represent in your company).

4. Number of employees claimed to be represented.

5. Local union identification.

6. The union officer or organizer (he will have signed the form).

SELECTION AND ROLE OF MANAGEMENT REPRESENTATIVE

When the union presents its demand for recognition or a notice is received from the NLRB that a campaign is officially under way, you should select someone to represent you. You have three choices:

Chapter 13 Ex. 4

FORM NLRB-502 (11-64)	UNITED STATES OF AMERICA NATIONAL LABOR RELATIONS BOARD	FORM EXEMPT UNDER 44 U.S.C. 3512

PETITION

	DO NOT WRITE IN THIS SPACE
	CASE NO.

INSTRUCTIONS.—Submit an original and four (4) copies of this Petition to the NLRB Regional Office in the Region in which the employer concerned is located.
If more space is required for any one item, attach additional sheets, numbering item accordingly.

DATE FILED

The Petitioner alleges that the following circumstances exist and requests that the National Labor Relations Board proceed under its proper authority pursuant to Section 9 of the National Labor Relations Act.

1. Purpose of this Petition *(If box RC. RM. or RD is checked and a charge under Section 8(b)(7) of the Act has been filed involving the Employer named herein, the statement following the description of the type of petition shall not be deemed made.)*

(Check one)

☐ RC—CERTIFICATION OF REPRESENTATIVE —A substantial number of employees wish to be represented for purposes of collective bargaining by Petitioner and Petitioner desires to be certified as representative of the employees.

☐ RM—REPRESENTATION (EMPLOYER PETITION)—One or more individuals or labor organizations have presented a claim to Petitioner to be recognized as the representative of employees of Petitioner.

5. Unit Involved *(In UC petition, describe PRESENT bargaining unit and attach description of proposed clarification.)*

	6a. NUMBER OF EMPLOYEES IN UNIT:
Included	PRESENT_____
	PROPOSED (BY UC/AC)
Excluded	6b. IS THIS PETITION SUPPORTED BY 30% OR MORE OF THE EMPLOYEES IN THE UNIT?*
	☐ YES ☐ NO
(If you have checked box RC in 1 above, check and complete EITHER item 7a or 7b, whichever is applicable)	*Not applicable in RM, UC, and AC

7a. ☐ Request for recognition as Bargaining Representative was made on .... and Employer

declined recognition on or about.................................. *(If no reply received, so state)*
(Month, day, year)

7b. ☐ Petitioner is currently recognized as Bargaining Representative and desires certification under the act.

8. Recognized or Certified Bargaining Agent *(If there is none, so state)*

NAME	AFFILIATION
ADDRESS	DATE OF RECOGNITION OR CERTIFICATION

9. DATE OF EXPIRATION OF CURRENT CONTRACT, IF ANY *(Show month, day, and year)*	10. IF YOU HAVE CHECKED BOX UD IN 1 ABOVE, SHOW HERE THE DATE OF EXECUTION OF AGREEMENT GRANTING UNION SHOP *(Month, day, and year)*

11a. IS THERE NOW A STRIKE OR PICKETING AT THE EMPLOYER'S ESTABLISHMENT(S) INVOLVED? YES .... NO	11b. IF SO, APPROXIMATELY HOW MANY EMPLOYEES ARE PARTICIPATING?

11c. THE EMPLOYER HAS BEEN PICKETED BY OR ON BEHALF OF ...., A LABOR
(Insert name)

ORGANIZATION, OF .... SINCE ....
(Insert address)   *(Month, day, year)*

I declare that I have read the above petition and that the statements therein are true to the best of my knowledge and belief.

....
(Petitioner and affiliation, if any)

By..   ....
(Signature of representative or person filing petition)   *(Title, if any)*

Address ....
(Street and number, city, State, and ZIP Code)   *(Telephone number)*

WILLFULLY FALSE STATEMENT ON THIS PETITION CAN BE PUNISHED BY FINE AND IMPRISONMENT (U.S. CODE, TITLE 18, SECTION 1001)

GPO 924 938

1. One of your own personnel.

2. A law firm.

3. A labor relations consulting firm.

If your union expert is one of your own people, keep the following points in mind:

1. Some large companies have an experienced labor relations staff; smaller companies sometimes have personnel or other managers who have been through previous union attempts and "know the ropes."

2. "First campaign" managers, however, may not be able to run the positive and strong campaign you need. Internal people tend to overdefend current policies and practices. Their own reputation and fairness are being challenged by the union, so they may not be able to maintain an objective approach to the campaign. They may "blow up" (like some union organizers) and swing employees to the union.

3. Managers are naturally reluctant to relay bad news to corporate headquarters because headquarters may overreact. Therefore, managers may ignore union activity because "maybe it will go away." By the time it doesn't go away, you could be well along toward a union election without the chance to react.

4. Your supervisors may not trust or confide in an internal person.

5. It is questionable whether a company manager has the time to run a union campaign along with his other responsibilities, and he may not be immediately accessible twenty-four hours a day. Your campaign chairman will spend ten to fourteen hours a day on the campaign, and unless your company is a large one with an established labor relations department, it may be best to let someone who has no other duties handle your campaign.

6. If you are certain that you have an internal person who can conduct your campaign positively and strongly—with sufficient time to devote to it—you may also want to give him the expertise and technical support of a labor relations consulting firm to advise on the campaign and a law firm to handle NLRB-related procedures.

If you don't have expertise and experience on your staff, definitely use someone who does—a law firm or labor relations consulting firm. If you choose either of these, be sure to check their past success with similar campaigns. If the firm you are considering has a history of losing, look elsewhere. If you don't investigate your law firm or labor relations consultants, you are taking a very short-sighted approach to something that may mean your very existence.

If the consultants or legal representatives say, "Let's not worry about the campaign because we can always beat the union at the bargaining table," they're not looking for a client, but for a career. They are *not* what you are looking for. Also be sure that they have enough time to concentrate on your campaign, and you should have a clear understanding about who will be doing the work. You don't want to get stuck with a junior staffer.

If your outside firm loses your campaign, fire them. You don't want them negotiating a contract for you. Before you get into the campaign, tell the firm that your purpose is to run a strong, all-out campaign; and that if they lose the election, you will hire someone else to negotiate your contract.

Your campaign against the union will be relatively short. Beat the union once and your chances of beating them again are good. If you lose, you lose *forever*. The outside firm you hire must be dedicated to your goal of winning the election.

How much will it cost to conduct your campaign? It can run as little as $4000 or as much as $36,000. Average cost is $12,000. This is one of the areas where you might be tempted to be "penny wise and pound foolish." After you have investigated various firms having successful records, get the best you possibly can.

Responsibilities and Authority

Once you have chosen your representative, internal or external, explain his *responsibilities and authority* to everyone concerned. Usually these are:

1. Acting as a clearing house for all communications.

2. Establishing campaign strategy; it cannot be run by a committee.

3. Acting as the single authority and spokesman in dealing with union representatives.

This person should always be available in person or by phone for solving problems and providing advice immediately. A crisis on the second or third shift is just as important as one on the day shift.

An example might be a situation in which the union committee challenges a supervisor by stopping production to sign cards. A second-shift supervisor hears from an employee that the union committee had told employees to refuse to work overtime. If the supervisor is able to reach the campaign director before the shift starts he is ready with answers. When two employees refuse to work overtime, he is able to take whatever disciplinary action is necessary, including possible termination. The employees stay at work, and the union's power play is stopped.

Reporting and Strategy

The campaign director must report directly to the chief executive officer on a daily reporting system without going through the company hierarchy or red tape. This may require a temporary change in reporting structures, but many decisions must be made on a minute-by-minute basis.

The director's decisions relate to everything involving union activity, including such basic issues as housekeeping, discipline, and scheduling as well as a crisis in the parking lot where an outside union organizer has violated the law by walking onto company property to handbill employees' cars. He must decide whether to call the police or deal with the situation himself. If police action might martyr the organizer, that approach may be unwise. But if the organizer is aggressive and the company will look weak by not acting because the union organizer is stopping people from leaving work or intimidating them, the police might be called. Obviously such decisions have to be made on the spot and will often need the approval of the chief operating officer.

Campaign coordination should not be run by a committee, but the chairman may set up committees for various functions to involve supervisors. They should report to the chairman for final decisions. He may ask for advice from committees, but the decisions are his.

When the time comes for the NLRB hearing, build your strategy on the time factor. The union wants a quick election. So does the NLRB (so they can "close the case"). Management will want the maximum amount of time to explain their position to the employees.

NLRB HEARING

The NLRB hearing notice will include five documents:

1. The petition.

2. A notice of appearance.

3. A notice of representation.

4. A request for commerce data.

5. A form from the board telling you your rights and describing the procedure.

Several decisions must be made at this point. First, you must decide whether you accept the fact that the union has signed up more than 30 percent of your employees (which the union alleges). You might decide to take your list of employees and their W-2 forms to the board to be checked by signature against the union cards for authenticity. However, when union organizers file their petition for a hearing, they usually have 65 percent or more employees signed up.

Management must also choose an attorney to represent the organization at the hearing. Companies, too, often send their corporate lawyer or someone in the organization who has little familiarity with labor law.

You need someone not only knowledgeable in labor law, but about the NLRB and its workings in your particular area.

Once your counsel is chosen and before you have responded to the board about your position, you should decide appropriate bargaining units for your organization. You may want to expand or limit the appropriate bargaining unit. If you designate an expanded unit, the union may not have signed enough employees from that unit to have the board order an election. On the other hand, you may want to limit your bargaining unit so that you have as few people as possible in the union, should management lose the election.

The NLRB's general rule is that they will designate the largest appropriate unit, but there are exceptions. For instance, if the union filed a petition for all the employees in a hospital, nurses or other degree professionals could exclude themselves by law. Another example would be operating engineers in a power house or outside truck drivers.

In white-collar areas where the bargaining unit determination is still developing, rulings have been conflicting. In the Wyandotte Bank case, the NLRB Regional Board in Detroit allowed six separate branches to be considered separate units, but at the National Bank of Detroit, where the union requested that only the computer department be considered a unit, the Board ruled that all clericals in the main office were in a single bargaining unit. (See NLRB decision in Appendix C.)

The board will run an election to determine whether or not the union is certified for a unit as small as 1½ people (one full time and one part-time employees).

Management must also be sensitive to board requests so that everything they want is available before or during the hearing. Assuming you are satisfied that the union has signed up 30 percent or more of your employees, we suggest submitting to the board an alphabetical list omitting departments worked in, and job descriptions. Use only first initials, not first names. You don't want to do the union's homework for them, including not designating males and females or their departments.

Management representatives will be asked to attend a preliminary NLRB hearing which is intended to expedite the election. If both parties can resolve bargaining unit issues and agree on a time and date for the election, there will be no formal hearing. If the parties can't agree, there will be a formal hearing and the board will determine the appropriate unit, and the date, time, and place of the election.

Management election rights extend to even minor factors, such as how the union spells out its name on documents. You should insist that the union spell out its full name on the grounds that the board recognizes a labor organization by its full title.

You can also designate the location of the election place in your operation. Management can designate the on-site location of the election. Holding the election where union representatives won't be walking through service or production areas prior to the election limits any contact with workers on election day.

Management's best interest lies in maximum turnout for the election. The date is important. We recommend selecting payday. Attendance is the best, and employees generally feel good about the company on payday. Avoid Mondays because of absenteeism and the "Blue Monday" syndrome. Management should maximize the polling hours, because pro-union employees will be there on time while management-prone and "undecided" employees may not. You want to give everybody ample time and opportunity to vote.

MANAGEMENT RUNS ITS CAMPAIGN

It is critical to your campaign that you *establish company credibility.* A first step is *assuring employees that they can come to their supervisor* if they want the "facts first" during the campaign. After the election date has been set (sometimes the campaign director can phone this information to you from the hearing, and it should be relayed immediately), the plant manager should call all supervisors to pass on the information about the election immediately to employees. That should be the name of the game throughout the campaign. It means employees will *hear it right, hear it first,* and *hear it from their supervisor.*

The importance of personal contact cannot be overemphasized. Stay away from "canned" campaigns, and don't rely on literature to convey your position. Your purpose is to encourage your employees to talk to their supervisors. Management will have to rely on supervisors to win the campaign, so you should be involved with them in continuous meetings and provide a training program to define the campaign and their role in it. They must be willing and eager to support the company, and constant communication with them will help to maintain their support.

Don't give your supervisors a long list of do's and don'ts. Advise them about meeting with their workers, how much literature you intend to pass out, timing of the campaign, when information will be mailed to workers at home, and who will be talking to employees in group meetings. It is important to impress upon supervisors that they are acting as "precinct captains" the same as in a political election. Supervisors should be ready with details on company policy, wages and benefit programs. Supervisors should have follow-up discussions with workers after the company has conducted an information session on specific company programs.

Tell supervisors only what they need to know about unfair labor practices, and let it go at that. In too many cases, supervisors have had so much labor law counseling that they end up saying, "I can't do *anything.*" Supervisors should be equipped with a positive attitude and they should be aware of possible pitfalls. We suggest explaining the four key things they cannot do during the campaign. You must remember T-I-P-S:

T: Threaten.   You can't threaten employees. It would be an unfair labor practice if a supervisor told an employee, "If you join the union, I'll fire you."

I: Interrogate.   It would be an unfair labor practice for a supervisor to call an employee into his office and ask, "Did you go to a union meeting?" or "Are you going to vote for the union?"

P: Promise.   It would be an unfair labor practice if a supervisor said, "If you don't join the union, I'll give you a $2.00 an hour increase."

S: Surveillance.   It would be an unfair labor practice if a supervisor drove to a local union meeting and spied or took pictures of people going in or coming out.

Otherwise, your supervisors can act within reason. They can tell the truth, cite true examples, but the burden of proof is on management. If in doubt, the supervisor should say, "It's my personal belief." They can listen —for hours if necessary. If invited for a drink, they can go. If asked questions, they can answer. To start such conversations, the supervisor may say, "Do you have any questions about the upcoming election?"

Regarding the unfair labor practice issue, a progressive organization need not run scared. You have a good record to sell, and you are allowed a rather wide latitude in what you may do during the campaign, as shown in Appendix D. You are certainly allowed to tell employees what you have done for them and that you will continue to do so. Run on your record, which is not a promise or an implication. It is simply the truth.

You can make statements about the union, and some humor is not out of place if it gets your point across. You might say: "The union is like mothers-in-law: the further away they are the easier it is to get along with them. They are great as long as they don't live under the same roof." Your campaign should stress the positive things about your company. Push your company. Don't make slamming the union the focus of your effort. You can mention, but tread lightly on, the fact that some unions have been associated with violent actions and that employees can be thrown out of the union if they are critical of union activities.

Management should quickly analyze your supervisors to determine which ones need special support and have your campaign chairman spend extra time with them. New supervisors should be provided all the information they need to be knowledgeable about company policies, programs, and direction in the campaign.

THE VOTE COUNT: MANAGEMENT'S MOST IMPORTANT TOOL

Management must know what is going on at every moment during the campaign. The best way to do that is to take frequent vote counts with supervisors. Management should know how many employees are pro-union, anti-union, or undecided at any given time. The campaign director should sit down and talk with your supervisors about every single employee in their departments—every work habit and personal characteristic they can think of.

Companies make serious errors when they don't take periodic counts with supervisors. This is particularly true when supervisors are afraid to tell management the truth about where employees stand regarding the union. It is, therefore, very important for management to gain their supervisors' confidence so that they can receive truthful, meaningful vote counts. These counts are vital guides in deciding what type of campaign to run.

To provide you with this crucial information, supervisors need to deal with three categories of employees: 20 percent pro-union, 20 percent pro-company, and 60 percent undecided. With 20 percent already on your side, you may ask, "Why would I have to say anything to a pro-company employee?" Employees who are against the union may become so involved in anti-union activities that they turn off undecided employees.

They should avoid arguments or any baiting of pro-union employees. If there is a shouting match, shoving, pushing, or fighting, management must treat pro-company and pro-union employees the same.

Management can outline to supervisors that the company's credibility is on the line, and you intend to give undecided employees the facts, not rumors or personal, vindictive arguments. It is extremely important to back up what you say to the undecided with sound information if you are to maintain company credibility. Stress to your supervisors that frequent vote counts help determine how effectively the company is maintaining its credibility.

Supervisors should be aware that every worker has someone in his or her family or a neighbor who is a union member. Supervisors should be careful about attacking the union because employees may translate such remarks into attacks on relatives and/or neighbors.

A number of firms serving management in campaigns have advised management to run hard anti-union campaigns. These campaigns can make management feel secure because they may reflect their own anti-union feelings. Employees who support the union are demeaned, possibly ostracized, and they feel badly treated. Some of the other workers may gloat for a while, but not for long. Win or lose, the company that conducts an anti-union campaign, as opposed to a pro-company campaign, ends up losing in the long run. (See Figure 13-5.)

Supervisors should be involved in role-playing to make them comfortable when they meet with employees. To establish consistency, each supervisor should be saying the same thing to his group.

UNION POWER PLAYS

A favorite union ploy is challenging the supervisor's authority. A good role-playing session should involve a challenge situation. For example, a shipping department employee *(E)* casually strolls through a production department, promoting the union to employees as he goes through the area. The department supervisor *(S)* stops him:

S: Joe, you're assigned to the shipping department. What are you doing here in assembly?

Figure 13-5A

The True Story What a Union IS... & IS NOT!

It's Important that
Everyone Understands
Exactly What a
Union Can and
Cannot Do--
by Law.

cont.

REMEMBER... A NO VOTE MEANS

- NO UNION
- NO WAGES LOST DUE TO STRIKES
- NO DUES
- NO STRIKES
- NO FINES
- NO ASSESSMENTS
- NO UNION BOSSES

VOTE NO!

Figure 13-5B

WHAT A UNION IS......

A Union **IS** an organization that makes a lot of **phony promises.**

A Union **IS** something that **you pay** a lot of money to.

A Union **IS** run by people who live off **your earnings.**

A Union **IS** more interested in Union Bosses **than you.**

A Union **IS** run by Union Bosses that have control **over you.**

A Union **IS** capable of **calling you** out on strike and making you walk a picket line.

A Union **IS** liable to turn **your friends against you.**

A Union **IS** a big business for Union Bosses.

A Union **IS** a group that needs you to replace its lost members.

A Union **IS** afraid to back up its promises by **written guarantee.**

A Union **IS** often guilty of breaking promises and mistreating members.

A Union **IS** something that involves everyone — once in, its hard to get out.

Vote NO ☒ On Election Day!

cont.

.....WHAT A UNION IS NOT

A Union **IS NOT** going to keep this plant open.

A Union **IS NOT** going to sell our products.

A Union **IS NOT** going to provide business to run this plant.

A Union **IS NOT** going to provide you with a job.

A Union **IS NOT** going to pay your paycheck.

A Union **IS NOT** going to pay for any of your benefits.

A Union **IS NOT** going to pay for your vacations and holidays.

A Union **IS NOT** interested in you—only in collecting money from you.

A Union **IS NOT** going to provide the supplies and equipment to keep your plant running.

A Union **IS NOT** responsible for carrying out the false promises it makes you.

A Union **IS NOT** interested in you or your personal problems.

—BUT YOUR COMPANY is and that's why we can and will furnish you factual proof of everything we have said above.

You see, there's a lot more to this Union thing than what the Union would have you believe. Simply by voting a union into a plant means absolutely nothing—a Union cannot itself do one single thing about your job or pay—the only thing the Union can do is to ask the Company—and if it is not reasonable to the Company and the Company says "NO" then there is nothing for the Union to do but call a strike.

E: Going to the restroom.

S: Well, did you get permission from your supervisor to leave your work area?

E: I've never had to ask my supervisor for permission to go to the restroom.

S: Yes, but why are you stopping to talk to my employees? You're interfering with their work.

E: I had a question about a part that was out in the back.

S: Joe, if you have a question about a part, you should discuss that with me, not with production workers. What part did you have a problem with?

E: I've got it corrected now. I'll see ya.

S: Just a minute, Joe. In the future, when you come into this department, if you've got something on your mind that relates to work, I expect you to report to me.

This shipping department employee was an internal union organizer, trying to demonstrate to other employees that he could do anything he wanted and go anywhere he wanted. He was probably coached by the union organizer to circulate and demonstrate the authority the internal organizing committee had gained. You need not tolerate this power play. The supervisor should handle the situation, speaking to the employee as he would normally if no union campaign were involved.

Union power plays are intended to show employees that the union can force change. If management, particularly supervisors, overreact or fail to act, the union appears to be in control of the campaign. In using the words "game" and "play" we are demonstrating that a credibility contest is going on in front of the workers.

Note that the supervisor exercised his right to question an employee who came into his department. He also gave a specific instruction about future incursions. No discipline was involved, only normal supervisory authority, and the supervisor made it plain that the employee was expected to comply with instructions in the future. If such misconduct continued, the supervisor should check with the company campaign chairman to determine what action to take.

This is an example of how role-playing can be used to prepare supervisors. The better prepared they are, the more confident they will become if confronted, and the more confident they will be when they sit down to discuss union questions with their workers. Employees will also have more confidence in the credibility of their supervisors when they see supervisors taking normal action when challenged.

During the campaign, management should reinforce supervisors' training. They must be knowledgeable about campaign issues and union tactics. The more they know about the union, its activities, and what they may expect to happen, the better off management will be in the campaign. If informed about what is going on in the campaign, they can honestly tell employees: "I don't feel we need a union here." Supervisors must feel that keeping the union out is in the best interest of the organization, themselves, and employees before they can effectively participate in the campaign.

EMPLOYEE MEETINGS

The campaign director may want to select supervisor committees to work on various campaign aspects. A committee might compare your wage scales, hours, and working conditions to those in the area. Another might get information concerning the union or unions involved, and another might talk to other employees on experiences they've had with this particular union. Committee assignments may give supervisors a greater feeling of involvement, of "being on the inside" during the campaign.

Who should talk to employees during meetings? Good choices are: the plant manager, the personnel manager, and a respected member of senior management, who may be from corporate headquarters.

One of your strategies might be an informational meeting for employees, even though the NLRB terms it a "captive audience meeting." These meetings should be carefully planned. Too often companies hold these meetings en masse, fly in a corporate mogul or senior member of management who lectures employees on his views (which may have nothing to do with employees' concerns). These should be meetings for no more than ten to fifteen people. If telling points are made—especially by someone in the audience—they can be passed on for use in other groups. The first or early small-group meeting or meetings can test the management's message and its reception.

This is the time to bring in your "Silver Fox" to meetings—the gray-haired corporate vice-president or a former plant manager who has been promoted. You can counteract the union's "Oh, my God, they didn't" strategy with one of your own. Your "Silver Fox" can sincerely say, "Oh, my God, if we only had known you were unhappy. Let's work together to solve these problems. We don't need a union to separate us." If you have the right "Silver Fox," he might strike a sympathetic chord in your employee audience, which can be followed up by the supervisors.

At this stage of the game, employees are often only asking somebody to listen who can eliminate their frustrations and at least allude to the possibility of change. Don't, though, bring in someone who doesn't understand the employees or your environment, such as someone from the North to a meeting in the South, where terminology and nomenclature are different.

Another good choice for an early meeting is a new management person. He can say, "I really didn't know what was going on, and I don't blame you for being upset. I'll pass your view along."

You want employees to perceive these meetings as opportunities for exchange of information with a management representative, particularly where communication has been shut down previously. You want the employees to know that what they say in these meetings is important to the company. Usually this will identify the issues that led employees to the union, and does not constitute unfair labor practice, while using such terms as "What are your problems?" or "What can we do to stop this campaign?" is solicitation and illegal.

Nothing in the law says you aren't allowed to listen to employees' questions or voluntary comments, or deal with irritants by normal management practices. In one campaign, employees complained about how filthy the ladies' room and other plant facilities were, to which the vice-president for operations exclaimed: "My God! That's terrible!" He suggested to the maintenance manager that the restrooms be cleaned up and readied for inspection by Monday morning. When the maintenance manager replied that his people were overtaxed and that he didn't know whether he'd have anybody available to clean up, the vice-president told him to clean up the restrooms himself and if he didn't he should get his resume ready for some other organization. The restrooms were spotless by Monday morning.

In another case, employees complained about litter and scrap left in aisles, and about boxes of rework stacked in assembly areas. Since the workers apparently had no time from regular duties to clear the litter, the company hired ten temporary workers to clean up and wax the floors over a weekend and the rework material was removed to a storage facility. Fixing lights, repairing equipment, cleanup, and any other normal management functions in themselves do not constitute an unfair labor practice.

Selecting groups is often also important. The campaign director may determine whether to hold meetings by department, or to alphabetize the entire employee list and draw small groups, with a mix of departments. This may be desirable when one department is strongly pro-union or pro-company. Mixing employees may afford you support from pro-company troops, minimize the numerical strength of the opposition, and provide undecideds with as strong a case as you and your supporters can offer.

Keeping in mind who your best choices are to conduct first meetings at which employees will have their first opportunity to hear the company's reaction to the campaign, you can save your supervisors for the follow-up exchanges with employees. If your plant manager or personnel manager conducts meetings, supervisors can be part of the audience—another chance for establishing rapport. Supervisors aren't placed in the position of hearing employees complaining about problems of which they were previously unaware.

Another aspect of meetings is the "tribal group" syndrome and informal group-leader phenomenon. These groups share common bonds and interests, and their leaders are fairly easy to identify and work with. The leader can sometimes be particularly useful in implementing communication and mobilizing support when the group members are difficult to reach or are more interested in their common problems than they are in more general problems and interests of other employees. Consider a case in point. A group of Hispanics with whom nobody in management had been able to communicate was found to have a member whom all respected and listened to, and through whom the company got its message across during a union campaign. The campaign impact and outcome may depend as much on your use of ready-made groups with influential leaders as anything else.

The age of the work force is another factor that you should take into account. Younger workers may say: "We've got nothing to lose and wouldn't it be kind of fun to get involved in collective bargaining and unions?" This may relate to your organization's hiring practice. While you must comply with the Equal Employment Opportunity Act, you may be better off with a balanced work force of younger and older, minorities, and sexes.

Women employees are particularly interested in the cost of unionization. Women often control household budgets and think more in terms of cost than men do. Many men look at union dues as insurance: "Well, I'll pay the dues and if I ever need the union, they'll be around." Organizers have had problems in operations that have large groups of women, however, because women want to know what they are getting for their dollar. and they have to think about the "premiums" they have to pay for that "insurance." "You want me to pay $120 a year in dues," they say, "but that's a lot of clothes for the kids, groceries, and extras we need around the house."

The union won't often emphasize dues and dues check-off, but it won't hurt the company, nor is it anti-union, to point out that union dues are expensive. They're a lot like taxes, with a tendency to go up while service has a tendency to go down.

Before management members meet with employees, discuss with your supervisors the material you plan to use in the meeting and the major issues you are going to cover. Ask for their suggestions on whether the issues to be discussed are of interest to employees. Once agreement is reached on subject matter, give the supervisor specific suggestions on how to follow up with individual employees who may have questions or comments following the meeting.

All during the campaign, don't forget your vote count! You have no way to judge the effectiveness of your strategy and your credibility-maintenance unless you know how the anticipated vote is going.

FORMAL OR INFORMAL CAMPAIGN

A part of your strategy deci_ .1 is whether to run a formal or informal campaign. An informal campaign is desirable where possible. Having supervisors get your message to employees, rather than bombarding them with literature and letters, maintains informality. Your strategy should focus only on issues of interest to employees. Even if you decide you've been wrong in some areas, ignore those issues employees have not raised and spend your time on those they want corrected. If you study issues being raised, you won't need to attend to others in the campaign. But *don't start answering the union*—that's negative, and you want the positive approach of marketing the good things you've been doing. Take the offensive; don't play the union's game. Force them to follow you.

As we said previously, we strongly believe it's *always* better to run a pro-company campaign, because you won't really influence anybody by talking against the union. Management who know sales techniques never attack the opposition, but in a union campaign they forget their successful techniques and some will tell employees "the real truth," all from their perspective. They say, "Unions are parasites. They don't really do anything for anybody. They cause strikes and they're basically no good." That is the worst possible tack you can take. It insults workers' intelligence and makes them suspect your motives.

How do you react to union literature? Supervisors should find out whether the employees have read it, and what they perceived it said. Don't use your own evaluation of such literature. Go by the evaluations of your supervisors and employees. If the employees haven't read a union handout, and you respond with what you think of it, they'll go back to the trash can, pick it up, and read it, thinking that something must have been stated there worth knowing, or management wouldn't have reacted. Supervisors might casually mention the company's viewpoint on the subject of the handout as it normally arises in individual employee meetings.

How do you handle the passing out of union literature, buttons, and so on? Your employees who are internal union organizers are allowed to pass out literature before and after work, on employees' time off, and on company property, but they cannot do so in work areas while people are working. Controlling such activity during the campaign will depend on your past practices in dealing with discipline. For example, safety is often a prime consideration in wearing buttons, hats, and T-shirts. If you have forbidden employees to wear them for safety reasons in the past, you can prohibit it for the same reasons now. While employees are usually allowed to wear buttons in the work area and to have stickers on their tool boxes, they are not allowed to deface company property by putting stickers or placards on walls. The union signs, therefore, *can be removed,* unless you have been permitting employees to put up other types of cute little signs. Management may not discriminate simply because the cute little sign supports the union. In any case, deal with this situation normally and don't overreact. The union would like to have you "see red" when you see one of their signs or symbols and discredit yourself in front of your employees. Remember that any move you make during the campaign should intend to motivate people *positively.*

If management has allowed sloppy procedures, such as allowing an employee to wander at will around the plant, it will be difficult to enforce discipline and proper procedures during the campaign. Consistency is the watchword—but *do* correct problems brought to your attention, even if you have not done so in the past. Demonstrate your willingness to listen and take action—carry forward on that "Oh, my God! If we had only known, we could have done something" talk from your "Silver Fox" and show good faith.

Management is not the "heavy" and should state strongly that they do not want a union. You should and must make this clear. One common union tactic is to cast management in a role favoring the union; "We're not mad at anyone, and the company isn't mad at anyone. The company would probably be happy to have a union." Management's counter should make perfectly clear *why* it is not necessary for employees to pay union dues in order to receive fair treatment from your organization.

As for those pro-union employees, treat them exactly as you treat everyone else—or you may find yourself facing charges of favoritism, harassment, and threats. If you are going to defeat the pro-union people and the union organizer, you must *not* attack them personally, but you should attack their credibility.

Unions are using another tactic to protect supporters among employees by sending a certified letter to management listing pro-union workers active in the campaign. Management is under the gun to see that these employees are not hassled or discriminated against. The NLRB will often bend over backwards to protect employees involved in union activity.

A major mistake in campaign timing is peaking too early. Elections are won or lost in the last two weeks when key points should be communicated to employees. The campaign chairman is responsible to ensure that the campaign peaks at this time. By election time, employees have been hit with a barrage of information from both sides, and they may not only be sick and tired of electioneering, but confused as well. *At this point, supervisors play their most important part.* The undecided 60 percent will ask supervisors: "Why should I believe you when you tell me to vote no in the election?" If the supervisor can say, with credibility, "You may not have always liked what I told you, but have I ever lied to you?" If the supervisor can say that, you've got a winner. This type of conversation between employee *(E)* and supervisor *(S)* should be thoroughly covered in training sessions:

E: Jim, the election is coming up and I'm really confused about what to do. The union people say one thing and the company says other things. I know we've talked about it before, but I am honestly not sure what I think about it or where I stand.

S: Well, we've all heard both sides (boy, haven't we ever, eh?), and I guess my feelings are that from my personal experience, I'd recommend that you vote no. I think the company has made a real effort to solve a lot of problems around here that they might not have known about before. I can't make any guarantees, but I feel that they really care about how employees feel.

E: Jim, I understand where you're coming from, but I just don't know who to believe any more.

S: Well, you know me, and you know some of the decisions I've come down with and had to make. Some you've liked and some you didn't like, but one thing has been consistent between you and me. I've never lied to you in the past.

E: Well, Jim, thinking back on it, I would say that's right. You've always been pretty fair with me.

S: I feel right now that we can work things out together if we just keep being fair with each other.

E: Well, I have a lot of doubts about the situation both ways.

S: I'd say all in all that this is a pretty good place to work. Even with the normal gripes we all have, I like working here and I plan to stay. Believe me, this campaign has made the company aware of small problems that they didn't realize existed. I don't believe that we need a union to force management to deal honestly with these problems. I would appreciate you voting *no*.

Also late in the campaign, unions frequently tell employees who are uncommitted: "If you can't decide one way or the other, maybe you shouldn't vote." Management should tell undecided people that *not voting is like voting for the union*. The election is decided by a simple majority of those who vote.

Midway or near the end of the campaign, the chairman may decide it is necessary to become more aggressive. To make this evaluation, your campaign director must keep his finger continually on the pulse beat by one-on-one meetings with supervisors and by circulating in departments. If the union is attempting any surprise maneuvers such as a phone-call solicitation to all employees a week before the election, he must decide whether that solicitation has to be countered. *And don't forget that all important vote count!*

Management may be able to capitalize on blunders by the union organizer or business agent. For example, in one campaign, the union organizer got upset with two employees—one pro-union—and called them "goddam liars." The incident was transmitted like wild fire throughout the organization and the organizer lost his credibility and the election.

The rumor mill doesn't always work for management. In fact, it usually doesn't. During the campaign, rumors will be rampant. Management will need a communications system to address rumors, written or verbal. Rumors can provide first clues to issues on the minds of employees.

Literature can be effective in the larger bargaining units, as long as it isn't "canned" anti-union campaign material. Management might send a few short, to-the-point informational and positive mailings to their homes. If you do use mailings, some samples are shown in Figures 13-5 and 6. Employees should be given a written summary of specific topics discussed in small-group information meetings. Summaries will provide employees with facts to talk about among themselves or, more importantly, to discuss with their supervisors.

24-HOUR RULE

At the end of the campaign, electioneering must stop 24 hours prior to election time, under NLRB rules. The 24-hour speech (see Figure 13-7) should be conducted in small groups to wrap up the campaign. Explain the voting procedure and sell all the employees on the importance of the voting. The 24-hour rule is to prevent either party from raising a surprise issue. The NLRB enforces this rule consistently on both union and management.

Figure 13-5 LOW-PROFILE LETTER

Date: _____

[Name & Address]
Dear [Employee]:

This coming Wednesday you are going to be asked to make a decision that concerns both you and [name of company]. Over the past month you have heard our position stated by myself and your supervisor urging you to remain non-union.

I feel that it is to your best interest and to the company's to maintain our union-free status.

I wish to thank you for your cooperation and your consideration of the company's position. I feel certain that after you have examined both sides that you will wish to continue our present relationship.

Sincerely,

_____
President or General Manager

Figure 13-6   Date: _____

Dear [Employee]:
[Address]

You may or may not be aware that the Steelworkers Union has filed a petition with the National Labor Relations Board. I do not feel that it is in your best interest, or mine, to have a third party come between us.

In the period between now and the election, myself, other members of management, and your supervisor will be meeting with you and your fellow employees to explain in detail the disadvantages of unionization at our plant.

cont.

I hope that you will listen to our side of the story and to the union's with an open mind. I am certain that once you are aware of all the facts you will choose to continue the relationship that we have developed in the past.

Sincerely,

_____

President or General Manager

Figure 13-7 FINAL SPEECH

For those of you who have never participated in a National Labor Relations Board Election, I would like to take this opportunity to give you a brief rundown on what will be happening tomorrow, [insert date].

The election consists of three basic phases; the pre-election conference, the voting, and the counting of the ballots.

Tomorrow at [insert time] a pre-election conference will be held between representatives of the Union, representatives of the Company, and a representative from the National Labor Relations Board. The Union and the Company will each appoint an observer who will be present at the election to ensure that the election is being held in accordance with all of the proper rules and regulations. At [insert time] tomorrow the National Labor Relations Board representative will give instructions to the observers and at the same time the NLRB representative will be checking the polling place to see to it that everything is in proper order. The Board Agent will then set up the voting booth and the ballot box.

The voting booth will be very similar to the one that you are accustomed to using in your local election. Once everything is inspected and it is agreed by both parties that everything is in order, the Union people will be escorted out of the plant. The only people present in the voting area will be the two observers, one for the Union and one for the Company, along with the NLRB representative. In the voting place will be a table, a voting booth, and a ballot box. The observers will wear badges with the word "Observer" on them and the NLRB representative will wear an agent

cont.

badge. The agent is in charge of the election. If you have any questions, talk only with him.

The voting procedure will be conducted in the following manner. Go to the voting table, standing in line if necessary. Give your name and clock number to the observers. The observers will find your name on the voting list and tell the agent your name has been found. If any questions are asked, talk only with the agent. Do not argue with the observers. After your name has been checked off, go to the agent and he will give you a ballot. Go into the vacant voting booth. Mark the ballot with one "X" only. Do not —and I repeat—*DO NOT* sign the ballot. Fold the ballot to hide the mark and leave the voting booth taking the ballot with you. Put your ballot in the ballot box yourself. Do not let anyone else touch it. After you have put the ballot in the ballot box, leave the polling place. Now you will notice that only the agent handles the blank ballots and only you handled your marked ballot. Once your marked ballot is in the ballot box it becomes mixed with all the other ballots in the box and cannot be identified. No one can determine how you have voted.

Our voting times are specified to be from [insert time] tomorrow until [insert time] tomorrow. I urge each of you to exercise your right to vote. Remember the election will be determined by the majority of the votes cast. Bear in mind also that it is important that you place your "X" only in one box so that there will be no confusion as to your choice. Should the Board Agent be unable to clearly determine how you voted, your vote would be thrown out. After the voting is completed the Board Agent will open the ballot box and count all of the ballots. The correctness will be verified by both parties along with the Board Agent. We should be able to announce the unofficial results of the election within 30 minutes after the polls close.

That takes care of the voting procedure, but I do want to make one final comment to you concerning this election. Our success here at the Company has been based on a total team effort and the ability to talk to each other without a middleman. The comments that I hear are very favorable to our continuing that same relationship. Any problems that we have had in the past have been worked out together and I know we will be able to work out any problems we may have in the years to come without a union to act as a go-between. Unions are good for one thing: unions.

cont.

I know I'm not saying anything to you that hasn't been said before. One point I would like to make here, however, is that the Company has a good record to stand on. If you compare your working conditions, working wages, and working hours to any other similar operation, union or non-union, you will find that we compare very, very favorably. I will hold our average increase up to any union average in the country. And that average holds true whether you have been here six months, or four years and six months.

Now, I understand it is being rumored among you that there are still some people who believe that should a union get in here you would keep everything you have today. They believe that you will start with what you have and build from there. Well, let me tell you, ladies and gentlemen, that should a union win this election, your contract will start with this. [Hold up blank paper.] Everything you have becomes negotiable. Let me quote to you from this publication put out by the NLRB:

> Collective bargaining as defined in the Act. Section 8(d) requires an employer and the representative of his employees to meet at reasonable times, to confer in good faith about certain matters, and to put into writing any agreement reached if requested by either party. The parties must confer in good faith with respect to wages, hours, and other terms or conditions of employment, the negotiation of an agreement, or any question arising under an agreement.

> These obligations are imposed equally on the employer and the representative of his employees. It is an unfair labor practice for either party to refuse to bargain collectively with the other. *The obligation does not, however, compel either party to agree to a proposal by the other, nor does it require either party to make a concession to the other.*

It would seem in closing there is nothing more I need to say on this matter, but I do want you to know that we in management have consistently worked to see that you don't take a back seat to anyone, and, ladies and gentlemen, you have my assurance that we will always continue to manage our programs in the future just as we have in the past.

Now, let's go out there and vote this union out of here once and for all.

Thank you.

ELECTION DAY

Just prior to the election, the NLRB representatives and members of management will thrash out final questions and details at a conference. The board will also show them the voting area, voting booths will be erected, and the ballot box will be opened for inspection and then sealed. Observers chosen by the company and the union to monitor the voting will also attend the pre-election conference and will stay in the voting area, while all nonvoters are not allowed in sight or sound of the voting area.

The union observers will probably be chosen from among employees actively involved in the organizing. We suggest that management choose someone out of the bargaining unit—someone they know is pro-company. Choose someone with a cool head, and especially someone whom employees respect. This person, however, cannot be someone in a supervisory position. (See Figure 13-8.)

The polls being opened, employees will go to the voting area, their names will be checked off, they will be handed a ballot, they will go into the voting booth, mark the ballot yes or no and come out to deposit the ballot in the ballot box. That's why we urged arranging the maximum amount of time; a large turnout usually favors the company.

When the polls close, management and union members may gather at the voting area. The NLRB agent will open the ballot box and count the ballots. Depending on whether there are any challenges, results of the election are announced.

Remember that the union needs 50 percent of those voting plus one to win, while the company takes all tie votes. If any unqualified person wishes to vote, the observers may challenge their eligibility. If the challenged ballots could determine the outcome of the election, the NLRB will set a hearing date to determine which individual ballots are to be counted.

CERTIFICATION

A *five-day* waiting period follows the election, during which the union and the company have the right to file objections to the conduct of either party that might have affected the results of the election. Following that five-day period, if nobody files objections, the board will send down a letter of

Figure 13-8 UNITED STATES OF AMERICA NATIONAL LABOR RELATIONS BOARD

INSTRUCTIONS TO ELECTION OBSERVERS

DUTIES *(General):*

1. Act as checkers and watchers.

2. Assist in identification of voters.

3. Challenge voters and ballots.

4. Otherwise assist agents of the Board.

THINGS TO DO *(Specific):*

1. Identify voter.

2. Check off the name of the person applying to vote. One check before the name by one organization. One check after the name by the other organization or the Company.

3. See that only one voter occupies a booth at any one time.

4. See that each voter deposits a ballot in the ballot box.

5. See that each voter leaves the voting room immediately after depositing his ballot.

6. Report any conflict as to the right to vote to the agent of the Board at your table.

7. Remain in the voting place until all ballots are counted in order to check on the fairness of the count, if ballots are counted at that time. If they are not counted immediately, you will be informed as to when and where ballots will be counted.

cont.

  8. Report any irregularities to the Board agent as soon as no-
     ticed.

  9. Challenge voters only for *good cause.*

 10. Wear your observer badge at all times during the conduct
     of the election.

 11. BE ON TIME. *(One-half hour before the time for the open-
     ing of the polls.)*

THINGS NOT TO DO *(Specific):*

  1. Give any help to any voter. Only an agent of the Board can
     assist the voter.

  2. Electioneer any place during the hours of the election.

  3. Argue regarding the election.

  4. Leave the polling place without the agent's consent.

  5. Use intoxicating liquors.

  6. Keep any list of those who have or have not voted.

   As an official representative of your organization, you should enter
upon this task with a fair and open mind. Conduct yourself so that no
one can find fault with your actions during the election. You are here
to see that the election is conducted in a fair and impartial manner, so
that each eligible voter has a fair and equal chance to express himself
freely and in secret.

                    NATIONAL LABOR RELATIONS BOARD

certification that the union has won or lost. If you find yourself successful, we hope that some of the good management practices we talked about earlier in this book are being followed. If you lose, we are thinking of putting out a new book next year titled: *Supervision in a Union Shop, A Handbook for Losers.*

If the union wins, you face the next step: the bargaining table and negotiation of the contract with the union. Again, we want to emphasize that you should *bring a professional in to negotiate the contract.* Do *not* let an amateur negotiate your first contract; what you negotiate in a first-time contract you will live with forever.

On the other hand, if you have won, you may relax for a while. As we said earlier, you've probably only won the first skirmish, not the war. What you have won is the right to correct those problems that surfaced during the campaign. If you ignore them your credibility and your supervisor's credibility will be lost in the next election.

SUMMARY

To summarize your campaign strategy:

1. Choose the best *successful* campaign professional you can and give him authority to run your campaign.

2. Establish company credibility with your supervisors and through them, with your employees. Keep close and constant communications. Take frequent vote counts.

3. Run a strong campaign, making it clear to your employees that you don't want the union.

4. Run a positive, pro-company campaign.

5. Use your experience to better manage your organization and prepare for your next campaign.

Appendix A

Federal Law NLRB Forms

ORGANIZING AND THE FEDERAL LAW

This section was originally prepared as course material for staff training

Important Note: The following guide is presented as background for an understanding of the law and its interpretations, as they relate to organizing. *It is not intended as a substitute for legal advice in specific situations.* Organizers should seek advice and direction through normal union channels, as to both the application of the law and union policy.

BARGAINING RIGHTS AND ORGANIZING

This section deals with getting bargaining rights, through voluntary recognition or Labor Board certification. It treats the federal labor law on organizing, employer and union unfair labor practices as they relate to organizing, and briefly the most important municipal and state laws that touch organizing.

Getting Bargaining Rights

Bargaining rights may be obtained by recognition or by NLRB certification. The simplest and quickest way to get bargaining rights is by voluntary recognition by the employer. He may recognize a union for one or more plants of his company, and he may even include in the bargaining unit employees (such as guards and supervisors) who could not be included in a Labor Board certification.

Requirements for Valid Recognition.   In order for voluntary recognition by the employer to stand up, if attacked before the NLRB by a rival union, it must meet these requirements:

There must be a valid contract in existence.   It must contain terms and conditions of employment and not merely "recognize" a union.

Such a contract must not be "premature."   In an expanding unit (usually a new plant) the Board may hold that the contract does not bar an election if substantially less than a full complement of workers is currently employed. The Board used to require that a "representative" group of workers be currently employed before it would order an election or honor a voluntary recognition. In recent rules, it has stated that 30% of the anticipated number of workers must be employed in 50% of the job classifications before it will order an election. Presumably, it would not regard voluntary recognition of a union as a bar to an election if it took place before this volume of employment had been reached in an expanding unit.

The employer must have "convincing evidence" of a majority. Such evidence could be provided in several ways—such as by a card-check or an independently conducted election—but the evidence must be clear-cut that the employer actually thought the union represented a majority of his employees.

It is not enough for a rival union merely to be on the scene in order to forestall a valid recognition, unless it has made a claim for recognition on the employer. The Board has held a contract following voluntary recognition to be a bar to an election, even when a rival union was around, under these circumstances:

-No claim had been made on the employer by the rival union;
-The employer had good evidence that the union he recognized actually represented a majority of his employees.

Obviously, however, the Board will look closely at these situations, in order to prevent "back-door" agreements which might effectively deny workers a free choice of bargaining representative.

Effect on AFL-CIO No-Raiding Pact. When a union gets bargaining rights by voluntary recognition instead of by Board certification, the AFL-CIO No-Raiding Pact does not apply for a period of one year. After the first year, the no-raid pact applies equally to voluntary recognition and Board certifications.

However, the normal Labor Board rules on contract bar and on unit questions apply in the event another union seeks to represent all or a part of an established bargaining unit.

NLRB Certification

The other method of getting bargaining rights is by Labor Board certification. This is by far the most common today. Though it takes longer to achieve, because of the election procedure, it has some advantages. The most important are these:

1. The Board will normally dismiss an election petition filed within a year of certification.

2. Where a contract is signed within a year of the issuance of certification, the Board will normally not hold an election until its expiration date (subject to contract bar rules discussed later).

3. A strike by another union against a certification is illegal.

4. A union can strike (and get other unions to strike in sympathy) against an employer refusal to honor a certification and bargain.

5. A certified bargaining agent for employees doing a certain type of work can strike if the employer assigns this work to employees belonging to another union. Without certification, such a strike might be illegal.

FEDERAL LAW ON ORGANIZING

This section sketches the basic federal law on organizing, giving its historical development and coming down through the changes in the Taft-Hartley Act of 1947 and the amendments to Taft-Hartley that relate to organizing in the Reporting and Disclosure Act of 1959 (Landrum-Griffin).

History to Wagner Act

The whole history of organizing in this country prior to 1932 (with minor and temporary exceptions) has been one of government intervention on the side of employers. For several decades in the 19th century, unions labored under the "criminal conspiracy" doctrine imported from English common law.

When this doctrine was no longer tenable, the courts produced others. One was the "illegal purposes" doctrine which held that although unions as such were not illegal, their purposes might be illegal. Under this doctrine, the purpose of setting wage rates was held to be illegal.

A companion was the "illegal means" doctrine, to the effect that although union *purposes* might be legal, the *means* for achieving them might be illegal. By this test, strikes, picketing, and boycotts were all held to be illegal.

The major employer weapon was the injunction which was used against labor organizations with devastating effect. It found its first statutory basis in the Sherman Anti-trust Act of 1890, under which employers sought injunctions against union organizations as "combinations in restraint of trade."

A second employer weapon was the "yellow-dog contract" which some employers forced their workers to sign as a condition of employment. Such a contract stipulated that the worker would not join a union as long as he worked for that employer. The first attempt to strike off this shackle was the Erdman Act, passed in 1898, applicable to the railroads only. This act made it illegal for employers to fire workers for union membership, which in effect made yellow-dog contracts unenforceable. The Supreme Court set aside the Erdman Act in 1908 on the grounds that it interfered with "freedom of contract" guaranteed by the Fifth Amendment.

A second statute which gave hope to unions—a false hope, as it turned out—was the Clayton Act of 1914 which stated that "the labor of a human being is not a commodity or article of commerce." It was mistakenly thought that this language would exempt unions from the Sherman Act, and it was widely hailed as "labor's Magna Charta." These hopes were dashed when the courts continued to issue injunctions against "restraint of trade" by unions.

Railway Labor Act (1926). The beginning of modern labor law was the Railway Labor Act of 1926. For the first time it was laid down as public policy that railroad workers had the right to organize and bargain through representatives of their own choosing, free from employer interference. This law was validated in 1930 by the Supreme Court in the Texas & New Orleans Railway case.

Norris-LaGuardia Act (1932). The principle of collective bargaining was first recognized for all workers in interstate commerce in the Norris-LaGuardia Act of 1932. This Act stated: "Whereas . . . the individual unorganized worker is commonly helpless to exercise actual liberty of contract and to protect his freedom of labor . . . it is necessary that he have full freedom of association, self-organization, and designation of representatives of his own choosing, to negotiate the terms and conditions of his employment, and that he shall be free from the interference, restraint, or coercion of employers of labor, or their agents, in the designation of such representatives or in self-organization. . . ."

In addition to this first clear statement of public policy favoring the right to organize, the Norris-LaGuardia Act severely limited the use of federal injunctions to cases involving fraud or violence. (In fact, it is commonly known as the "Anti-injunction Act.") It also rendered yellow-dog contracts unenforceable by labelling them as contrary to public policy.

This law erected barriers to legal action on behalf of employers that even the ingenuity of the courts could not evade. But it left out a vital protection for the right to organize. Unionists had always had the theoretical right to organize under the constitutional guarantees of free speech and assembly. But the employer also had the right to fire a worker for joining a union. As long as he held that right unchecked, labor organizations showed themselves unable to sustain organization on a large scale.

Section 7 (a), NRA. This famous section picked up much of the language of Section 2 of the Norris-LaGuardia Act on the right to organize and incorporated it into the "codes of fair competition." But it also contained the fatal flaw of providing no sanctions against employers who interfered with the rights enunciated for workers. The codes were declared unconstitutional in the Schechter Case in 1935.

The National Labor Relations (Wagner) Act, 1935

The growth of the labor movement as it is known today dates from the Wagner Act passed in 1935 and declared constitutional by the Supreme Court in the Jones and Laughlin Case in 1937. For the first time in American history, the employer was prohibited in specific terms from interfering with the worker's right to organize.

Right to Organize. Section 7 of the Wagner Act stated: "Employees shall have the right to self-organization, to form, join, or assist labor organizations, to bargain collectively through representatives of their own choosing, and to engage in concerted activities for the purpose of collective bargaining or other mutual aid or protection." This much was about the same as the Norris-LaGuardia Act.

Employer Unfair Labor Practices. Section 7 was called the "heart" of the Wagner Act, but it was the "muscles" provided by Section 8 which kept employers off workers' backs when they formed unions. This section established categories of "employer unfair labor practices" in organizing and bargaining, and Section 10 provided sanctions against employer violations, initially through the NLRB but ultimately enforceable in the federal courts. For the first time, the right to organize was not only enunciated but was protected by some legal teeth.

In the late thirties these restraints on employers, combined with economic distress and a genuine desire on the part of workers to organize, were effective in launching wide-scale unionization. Today they mean much less, because of watering-down of the law and particularly because of weak-kneed and employer-oriented administration of the law by the NLRB.

Representation elections. The second great innovation of the Wagner Act was its provision for representation election procedures through the NLRB. This procedure is spelled out in Section 9 of the law, supplemented by the Board's own rules and regulations and statements of procedure. No longer was it necessary for a union to strike for recognition if the employer refused to deal with it. A union claiming a majority could petition the NLRB for an election; and if it won, the employer was required to recognize and bargain with the union.

Labor-Management Relations (Taft-Hartley) Act of 1947

The philosophy of the Wagner Act was to ease the way to organization and collective bargaining and to restrict employer interference with that right. The Taft-Hartley Act specifically sought to throw roadblocks in the way of organizing and bargaining.

Its philosophy is made clear in the addition it made to Section 7, the heart of the Wagner Act. The underlined part of the following paragraph represents the Taft-Hartley addition to Wagner Act language:

> Sec. 7. Employees shall have the right to self-organization, to form, join, or assist labor organizations, to bargain collectively through representatives of their own own choosing, and to engage in *other* concerted activities for the purpose of collective bargaining or other mutual aid or protection, *and shall also have the right to refrain from any or all of such activities except to the extent that such right may be affected by an agreement requiring membership in a labor organization as a condition of employment as authorized in Section 8 (a) (3).*

Its other sections then spelled out in detail various restrictions on organizing and bargaining. These restrictions will be taken up as they arise under subsequent subject headings. The most important of these was a whole new section of "union unfair labor practices."

Labor-Management Reporting and Disclosure Act of 1959

Though commonly known as the Landrum-Griffin Act, this law was changed slightly in House-Senate conference committee from the original Landrum-Griffin Act passed in the House. It directly affects organizing in five provisions:

1. *"Hot-cargo" clauses are made illegal.* Title VII makes illegal any agreement with an employer requiring that he refrain from handling unfair or struck work. An exception is made for the garment industry.

2. *Picketing* for both organizational and recognition purposes is sharply restricted.

3. *Secondary boycotts* are further restricted.

4. *Economic strikers* are given the right to vote for a period up to one year from the commencement of a strike, at the discretion of the NLRB, if a representation election is held.

5. *Conduct of representation elections* may be delegated by the NLRB to regional directors.

Employer Violations

The Taft-Hartley Act took the old Section 8 of the Wagner Act covering employer unfair labor practices and made it into Section 8(a). It added a new Section 8 (b) on union unfair labor practices.

Categories of Employer Violations. The following actions of the employer were unlawful under the Wagner Act, and the same language was carried over in the T-H Law:

1. "Restraining, interfering, or coercing" workers in their right to organize and bargain.

2. Forming company unions or dominating unions.

3. Discriminating against workers for union membership or activity.

4. Discriminating against workers for testifying under the law.

5. Refusing to bargain collectively with a majority union.

"Free Speech" Provision

All of these were important in organizing in the late thirties. Their importance had been greatly reduced under Taft-Hartley, however, by the inclusion in that law of a new Section 8(c)—the so-called "employer free speech" section—which states:

> The expressing of any views, argument or opinion or the dissemination thereof, whether in written, printed, graphic, or visual form, shall not constitute or be evidence of an unfair labor practice under any provision of this act, if such expression contains no threat of reprisal or force or promise of benefit.

Even before the "free speech" section was written into the law in 1947, some courts were holding that employers could make statements bearing on union organizing campaigns.

Interrogation The Labor Board is still in the process of refining its views on employer free speech, but it is clear that the Eisenhower Boards gave the employer great latitude in expressing himself during organizing campaigns. For example, individual interrogation of employees during a campaign—regarded under the Wagner Act as coercive in itself—is permitted under certain circumstances.

In one case (Blue Flash Express, 1954) the employer questioned all the employees in a unit, ostensibly to see if the union had a majority. The Board said that this was all right. Its test would be whether, in view of all the circumstances, the interrogation reasonably tends to restrain or coerce employees in the exercise of rights guaranteed in the law. In a later case (Mall Tool, 1955) the Board said "an employer's technique of talking individually to his employees doesn't per se justify the voiding of an election." In this case the interviews took place at the work benches, not in the employer's office, and about half the employees were interviewed.

The old Wagner Act philosophy was that it was none of the employer's business how his employees felt about a union, and in any case that the NLRB election would tell him all he needed to know. Decisions since Taft-Hartley have drastically changed this view.

Polling of Employees   A recent case illustrates how silly the Board can get about employer polling. The Board held (Offner Electronics, 1960) that an employer cannot take a poll of the union sentiments of his employees after the Board directs an election or a consent agreement is signed. (Presumably, it would be all right beforehand!)

Employer Favoritism.   The free speech provision opened the door to the employer to express open preferences for one union as against another during an election campaign. He cannot extend special privileges to one union during an organizing campaign (Wagner Iron Works, 1955) but the incumbent union, by virtue of holding the contract, may enjoy certain privileges denied an outside union—such as access to the plant.

The employer cannot recognize one union without proof of majority, but he can do several things short of recognition to express his preference. For example, he can "predict" that the benefits will be lower if the incumbent union is displaced, or on the other hand he can say that he cannot pay the higher wage rates that will be demanded by one of the unions. Though the "threat" of reprisal in the form of a plant closing seems clear in the latter statement, it has been held by the Board to be "protected free speech."

Expressions of Opinion.   It has been held in a recent case that the employer can say that negotiations will "start from scratch" if a union gets in. The Board held this to be protected as a mere statement of fact and not a threat to withdraw benefits.

In balancing off the employer prohibitions in Sec. 8 (a) (1) against the "free speech" provision of Sec. 8 (c), the Labor Board has been giving the edge to employers.

Captive Audience.   This is the practice by an employer of calling his employees together on company time (and usually, though not always, on company premises) and giving them an anti-union speech before an election. The Board's rulings on this have been shifting in favor of the employer. They have gone through the following cycle:

1. At one time any anti-union speech by an employer to a captive audience before an election was an unfair labor practice. This was the doctrine under the Wagner Act but was changed immediately after the "free speech" provision of Taft-Hartley was enacted in 1947.

2. The next stage was the Board's view that the employer could make a captive audience speech, but the union must be given "equal time" if it did not have other opportunities to make its case "under circumstances which reasonably approach equality." This was laid down in the Bonwit Teller case in 1951 for department stores only and later extended to other industries.

3. The Board's position now is that the employer may make a captive audience speech without giving the union such an opportunity (Livingston Shirt, 1953). This is true as long as the union can solicit employees during non-working time. The Board said: "An employer's premises are the natural forum for him just as the union hall is . . . for the union."

4. A further extension of the doctrine was made in a Board ruling on an employer speech after working hours, for which attendance was "voluntary." This was held to be non-coercive, even though the pressure on union supporters not to expose themselves before an election is obvious to any organizer.

5. 24-hour Rule. All captive audience speeches are banned during the 24-hour period before an election, regardless of whether or not they are coercive. The Board feels that they have "an unwholesome and unsettling effect and tend to interfere with that sober and thoughtful choice which a free election is designed to reflect."

   Other electioneering is permissible during the 24-hour period, but it must not take place within sight or hearing of

Board agents conducting the election. Many unions voluntarily suspend organizing activities of an overt sort during this period to take no chances of upsetting the election, but this choice is not dictated by Board decisions.

Solicitation

Board rules under this heading relate to Sec. 7 guaranteeing the right to organize and Section 8 (a) prohibiting the employer from interfering with that right. For the union, a fundamental necessity in organizing is to get access to workers to get the union's message across. When an employer arbitrarily and unreasonably restricts the rights of employees to self-organization, or the right of a union to organize employees, the Board has held that Sec. 8 (a) has been violated.

Although the Board makes a point of deciding each case on the basis of its own particular circumstances, it has spun out certain guidelines which can be used in assessing the new situation. It makes distinctions between the rights of employees and the rights of non-employees (usually union organizers), and between working and non-working time.

Employees and non-employees. Employees have greater latitude than non-employees. They can solicit and distribute literature on company property, subject to certain rules described below. ("Employee" has been interpreted to mean an employee on leave and an employee of the company though from another plant or shop.) Non-employees may be denied access to parking lots and other company property when the rule is generally applied and where there is reasonable opportunity to reach employees by other means (such as house calls).

Working and non-working time. The employer may prohibit union solicitation of all kinds during working hours, on the theory that "working time is for work." However, he may not prohibit union discussion during non-working time and in non-public areas. This is so even though the non-working time is paid time, such as rest periods. The test seems to be whether or not the discussion or solicitation interferes in any way with production.

No-Distribution Rule

The Board has moved clear over to the employer's side on this matter. At one time, the employer could enforce a no-distribution rule, provided that it applied to all comers and provided the union has other "reasonable means" for reaching employees. Later the Board upheld an employer who violated his own rule but enforced it against the union. The Supreme Court upheld the Board on the grounds that the union had not asked the employer to waive the rule for it, too.

Now the Board has upheld an employer who adopted a no-distribution rule during a union organizing campaign (Star-Brite Industries, 1960). The Board says this is OK if it does not have a "discriminatory purpose" or "unfair application" and it finds neither in this case!

Discharges and Discrimination

Employers still ignore the law and discharge or otherwise discriminate (by transfers, rate-cutting and other means) against union supporters during organizing campaigns. It has become increasingly difficult to prove to the NLRB that such discharges and discrimination have been motivated by anti-unionism.

As is necessary in all cases involving charges of employer unfair labor practices, the union seeking to substantiate the charge must accumulate and present evidence of the charge to the NLRB. Affidavits concerning the charge *must be gathered immediately,* for some people get cold feet when weeks and sometimes months pass after a man has been discharged. The affidavit should be a brief but accurate statement of what the person knows about the company action.

Sanctions Against Employers

Section 10 of the law provides for the procedures to be followed if the employer (or the union) engages in unfair labor practices. Charges are filed with the NLRB and if upheld result in a cease-and-desist order ultimately enforceable in the federal courts.

Objections to Elections

Much more useful from the organizing standpoint is an objection to an election because of employer interference, provided the employer's conduct took place after the election was ordered. Objections to elections are processed much more quickly by the Board and, if sustained, result in a new election.

Technically, the Board rules for setting aside elections are not as stringent as those for finding an employer guilty of an 8 (a) charge. Even though an employer's conduct might not be unlawful under section 8 (a), the Board may find that the same conduct interfered with the free choice of a bargaining representative and order a new election.

In the General Shoe case of 1948 the Board said: "Conduct that creates an atmosphere which renders improbable a free choice will sometimes warrant invalidating an election, even though the conduct may not constitute an unfair labor practice." In the same case, the Board pointed out that the "free speech" provision, 8 (c), only applied to unfair labor practices.

Actually, this theoretical difference in the Board's mind has not meant much in practice. Its chief manifestation has been the "24-hour rule" under which captive audience speeches in the 24 hours just prior to an election constitute grounds for setting aside an election, though not unfair labor practices.

Union Unfair Labor Practices

The restrictive philosophy of the Taft-Hartley Act is well illustrated in the Section 8 (b) which it added on union unfair labor practices. (Other union conduct may result in the Board's setting aside an election, though the action itself does not constitute an unfair labor practice.)

Categories of Union Unfair Labor Practices

Briefly, this section provides that it shall be an unfair labor practice for a union or its agents (a steward has been held to be an agent) to do any of the following things:

1. To restrain or coerce—

   A. Employees in the exercises of rights guaranteed in Sec. 7 (in this case, the right not to organize or engage in collective bargaining)

   B. Employers in the selection of bargaining representatives.

2. To cause or attempt to cause an employer to discriminate against an employee or to have him discharged for anything other than a "failure to tender the periodic dues and the initiation fees uniformly required as a condition of acquiring or retaining membership."

3. To refuse to bargain collectively.

4. To engage in or encourage employees to engage in a strike or boycott under certain circumstances and for certain purposes.

5. To charge excessive initiation fees.

6. To exact pay for work not performed or not to be performed (so-called "featherbedding" prohibition aimed at Petrillo and the Musicians' Union).

7. To picket under certain circumstances.

The practices most commonly involved in organizing are those relating to "restraint and coercion" and to secondary boycotts and picketing.

Union Restraint or Coercion

Section 8 (b) (1) makes it an unfair labor practice for a union to restrain or coerce employees in their right to join or not to join a union and engage in concerted activities.

This has been held by the NLRB to prohibit:

1. Preventing persons from entering or leaving struck premises.

2. Mass picketing where it has a "coercive" effect (mass picketing as such is not mentioned in the T-H Law).

3. Extreme threats off the picket line.

4. Threatening workers with loss of job if they do not join the union (Seamprufe, 1949).

The NLRB has not been squeamish about name-calling on the picket line in most cases. But in one case persistent use of profanity and insults resulted in pickets being denied reinstatement. The furthest the Board has yet gone in this regard was in the BVD case in 1954 when it denied reinstatement to employees on the picket line who did not engage in violence but merely failed to restrain other pickets from violence. The effect of an unfair labor practice, then, can be a denial of the protection of the law for reinstatement.

Limits on Union Propaganda

For a long time, even after Taft-Hartley, the Labor Board made no effort to police or censor union propaganda in organizing campaigns. In 1953, however, in the RCA and United Aircraft cases, the Board indicated when it would step in.

> . . . as a general rule, and in the absence of coercion, it [the Board] will not undertake to censor or police union campaigns or to consider the truth or falsity of electioneering propaganda, unless the ability of the employees to evaluate such material has been so impaired by the campaign material or by campaign trickery that the uncoerced desires of the employees cannot be determined. (RCA)

The statutory basis for the Board's intervention was the provision of 8(b)(1) prohibiting unions from "coercing or restraining" employees in their rights guaranteed in Section 7. However, the Board has generally used its power to set aside elections.

In the United Aircraft case, Union A put out a fake telegram allegedly signed by the international president of Union B, making certain statements favorable to Union A. The Board set aside the election, stating:

Exaggerations, inaccuracies, partial truths, name-calling, and falsehoods, while not condoned, may be excused as legitimate propaganda, providing they are not so misleading as to prevent the exercise of a free choice by employees.

In another case, Gummed Paper Products, the Board set aside an election when a union published false wage comparisons and then, in the face of a company denial and on the eve of the election, repeated the wage comparisons and said they were based on a non-existent new contract.

The way the statute is written, unions appear to be under the same limitations as employers in the "free speech" Section 9(c), not to "threaten" employees or promise benefits. The Board has so far applied this mainly to employers, however.

The lesson from this is that union organizers must be extremely careful about statements made so close to the election that the employer has no chance to reply. If he does have a chance to reply and does not take it, the Board is unlikely to intercede even in the case of enthusiastic claims.

Sample ballots. It used to be a common practice for organizers to distribute sample ballots marked with an "X" by the name of their union. Such a practice might make it appear that the Labor Board itself wanted employees to vote as indicated.

It is permissible, however, to distribute a completely blank facsimile ballot, provided it is marked "sample" and contains no other marks.

Penalties. If union propaganda went further than the Board thinks permissible, or if a marked sample ballot is put out, the Board might set aside the election and order another.

Secondary Boycotts

Sec. 8(b)(4) of T-H prohibited unions or their agents from A) striking or refusing to use or transport goods, or B) "inducing or encouraging" employees to strike or concertedly refuse to use or transport goods when the purpose of such action was to require an employer to do any of the following:

1.   Join a union

2.   Cease using or handling any goods

3.   Recognize an uncertified union

4.   Recognize a union if another had been certified

5.   Assign work to certain employees or union members where another union has been certified for such work.

These were sweeping restrictions designed to curtail union activity aimed at employees of a secondary employer. There were still certain areas of activity, however, which the union could pursue. It could:

1.   Tell employers not to handle struck goods (since they were not "employees").

2.   Get *individuals* to refuse to handle goods, if this was not *concerted* action.

3.   Get employers to sign hot-cargo clauses to the effect that they would not deal with "unfair" or struck employers.

4.   Tell customers at a secondary employer's place of business by means of picket signs that certain items sold or used there were non-union. (As long as the union did not picket employee or delivery entrances and the wording of the sign was clearly aimed at customers or consumers.)

1959 Amendments

The restrictions in the new law make the T-H provisions seem pale. Under the new law—

Unions cannot "threaten, coerce, or restrain any person engaged in commerce," if the object is to get him to cease using a product. Even such mild boycott activity as O'Sullivan's and Kohler, aimed at employers who use these products, might run afoul of this provision.

Unions cannot appeal even to an individual employee not to work on a product.

Unions cannot have a legal hot-cargo clause with an employer, to the effect that he will not handle struck or "unfair" work. Section 8 is amended by adding the following new subsection:

> (e) It shall be an unfair labor practice for any labor organization and any employer to enter into any contract or agreement, express or implied, whereby such employer ceases or refrains from handling, using, selling, transporting or otherwise dealing in the products of any other employer, or to cease doing business with any other person, and any contract or agreement entered into heretofore or hereafter containing such an agreement shall be to such extent unenforceable and void. . . .

An exception is made for the garment industry which has many such clauses in its agreements for major garment centers, to protect itself against runaway shops and non-union competition.

Apparently no picketing at all can take place at a secondary employer's place of business, not even informational picketing whose sole purpose is to inform customers that non-union goods are being handled inside. This prohibition seems to be contained in an addition to Section 8(b)(4) which states:

> . . . for the purpose of this paragraph (4) only, nothing contained in such paragraph shall be construed to prohibit publicity, *other than picketing,* (underscoring added) for the purpose of truthfully advising the public, including consumers and members of a labor organization, that a product or products are produced by an employer with whom the labor organization has a primary dispute and are distributed by another employer, as long as such publicity does not have an effect of inducing any individual employed by any person other than the primary employer in the course of his employment to refuse to pick up, deliver, or transport any goods or not to perform any services, at the establishment of the employer engaged in such distribution. . . .

It would seem obvious from the above that informational picketing of a secondary employer where no primary dispute is involved might be prohibited. This could include picket-sign advertising that certain products were non-union. It remains to be seen if it is constitutional to restrict peaceful, truthful picketing, as the above-quoted section tries to do.

Penalties, Injunctions, and Unfair Labor Practice Charges.   Union representatives are familiar with the "law's delay" in dealing with employer unfair labor practices. Violations of the secondary boycott provisions, however, are handled with the greatest of dispatch. The General Counsel of the NLRB must give such cases top priority, and if he has "reasonable cause" to believe that a complaint should issue, he must apply for an injunction against the alleged violation. The union is then restrained while the charge is heard and an award made. There is no counterpart to these injunction provisions for any employer unfair labor practices.

Damage Suits.   Concurrently with these injunction proceedings, the employer may sue the union for damages, under Sec. 303 of the law. Such action is independent of an unfair labor practice charge.

Picketing for Recognition or Organizational Purposes

The 1959 amendments to the National Labor Relations Act add a new section which for practical purposes makes it an unfair labor practice to picket for organizational purposes or for recognition. Such picketing is an unfair labor practice (1) where another union is recognized and a question concerning representation cannot appropriately be raised at the time of the picketing; (2) where an election has been held within the preceding 12 months even though no union may have been certified; and (3) where the picketing is conducted without a petition having been filed within a reasonable period of time following the commencement of the picketing, not to exceed 30 days.

Even though it is not an unfair labor practice to engage in such picketing where such a petition has been filed, the effect of such picketing is to cause the Board to proceed to an election forthwith without regard to the usual requirements of the Act relating to the investigation of representation petitions, hearings, and the requirement that a showing of interest be provided by the petitioning union. An exception to this part of the Act permits informational picketing aimed solely at the public so long as employees of other persons do not refuse, in the course of their employment, to perform services for their employer.

While this portion of the Act does not specifically exempt unfair labor practice picketing or strikes in protest of unfair labor practices committed by an employer during an organizational campaign, it is unlikely that the Act would be held to prohibit such picketing. In the event that such unfair labor practices occur and an unfair labor practice strike is otherwise deemed advisable, advice should be obtained from the union's legal department as to the legality of such proposed action before it is commenced.

State and Municipal Laws

Interference with organizing on the part of state government takes the form of right-to-work laws and other state laws regulating organizing. In addition, there are municipal anti-leaflet ordinances and requirements for the registration of organizers.

State Right-to-Work Laws

The role of the states in labor relations took on importance with Section 14(b) of Taft-Hartley which gives the states the right to pass union security restrictions more stringent than the federal law. Eighteen states have these so-called right-to-work laws, some of them also prohibiting or circumscribing the use of the checkoff.

One effect on organizing has been to bring injunctions against strikes and picketing, on the alleged grounds that such actions have had the effect of coercing employees to join a union.

State Jurisdiction—1959 Amendments

The 1959 amendments to Taft-Hartley contained a section (Title VII, Sec. 701) giving jurisdiction over labor disputes to states where the National board declines to assert jurisdiction. Although it was not specified, it is generally agreed that the state will apply its own laws and public policy.

Since only 12 states have anything like comprehensive administrative machinery for conducting union elections, it is obvious that this provision can lead to chaotic and widely varying practices from state to state. Most "public policy" of the states lies in the direction of restraining unions and not in protecting the rights of workers to organize, strike, and picket. The prospect is not a happy one.

Effect of Norris-LaGuardia.   It remains to be seen what latitude the states will have in issuing injunctions in labor disputes "affecting interstate commerce" when the NLRB declines to act. The Norris-LaGuardia prohibits injunctions in disputes involving interstate commerce, except in cases of fraud and violence.

Municipal Ordinances

Even municipalities have tried to regulate union organizing. The chief forms of attempted regulation have been invoking anti-leaflet ordinances and requiring registration of union organizers.

Anti-leaflet Ordinances.   These are occasionally invoked to try to stop distribution of union literature. Such ordinances are almost certain to be held unconstitutional in view of several Supreme Court decisions, the oldest in 1929. Such ordinances in Milwaukee, Los Angeles, Worcester (Mass.) and Irvington (N.J.) have been held to violate free speech and freedom of the press in the First Amendment. While a case is being litigated, however, they can be effective in blocking or harassing a union organizing campaign.

Registration of Union Organizers.   These laws are cropping up principally in Southern states as harassment against organizing. Two of these have been held to be unconstitutional (Steelworkers *v.* Fuqua, Kentucky, 1957; and a case involving the Ladies Garment Workers in Baxley, Ga.). Though unlikely to stand up in court, they have helped to slow up organizing and take time and money to litigate.

★NOTICE TO EMPLOYEES

FROM THE

National Labor Relations Board

YOU HAVE THE RIGHT under Federal Law

- To self-organization
- To form, join, or assist labor organizations
- To bargain collectively through representatives of your own choosing
- To act together for the purposes of collective bargaining or other mutual aid or protection
- To refuse to do any or all of these things unless the union and employer, in a state where such agreements are permitted, enter into a lawful union security clause requiring employees to join the union.

NOTE:

The following are examples of conduct which interfere with the rights of employees and may result in the setting aside of the election.

- Threatening loss of jobs or benefits by an Employer or a Union
- Misstating important facts by a Union or an Employer where the other party does not have a fair chance to reply
- Promising or granting promotions, pay raises, or other benefits, to influence an employee's vote by a party capable of carrying out such promises
- An Employer firing employees to discourage or encourage union activity or a Union causing them to be fired to encourage union activity
- Making campaign speeches to assembled groups of employees on company time within the 24-hour period before the election
- Incitement by either an Employer or a Union of racial or religious prejudice by inflammatory appeals
- Threatening physical force or violence to employees by a Union or an Employer to influence their votes

NATIONAL LABOR RELATIONS BOARD
an agency of the
UNITED STATES GOVERNMENT

THIS IS AN OFFICIAL GOVERNMENT NOTICE AND MUST NOT BE DEFACED BY ANYONE

UNITED STATES OF AMERICA
BEFORE THE NATIONAL LABOR RELATIONS BOARD
SEVENTH REGION

NATIONAL LABOR RELATIONS BOARD

SEVENTH REGION

Room 300, Patrick V. McNamara Federal Building, Detroit, Michigan 48226
Telephone: 226-3200

RE:

I hereby designate _____
to act as my observer during the conduct of the election in the above-
captioned case.

I certify that the above-named individual is an employee of the
company and is not a supervisor within the meaning of Section 2(11) of the
Act.

_____
(Name of Company or Union)

By: _____
(Representative)

Title: _____

Section 2(Il) of the National Labor Relations Act states: "The term
'supervisor' means any individual having authority, in the interest of the
employer, to hire, transfer, suspend, lay off, recall, promote, discharge,
assign, reward, or discipline other employees, or responsibly to direct them,
or to adjust their grievance, or effectively to recommend authority is not of
a merely reoutine or clerical nature, but required the use of independent
judgement."

FORM NLRB-4812
(5-77)

NATIONAL LABOR RELATIONS BOARD

NOTICE: PARTIES INVOLVED IN A REPRESENTATION PETITION SHOULD BE AWARE OF THE FOLLOWING PROCEDURES:

Right to be represented by counsel

Any party has the right to be represented by counsel or other representative in any proceeding before the National Labor Relations Board and the courts. In the event you wish to have a representative appear on your behalf, please have your representative complete Form NLRB-4701, Notice of Appearance, and forward it to the respective regional office as soon as counsel is chosen.

Designation of representative as agent for service of documents

In the event you choose to have a representative appear on your behalf, you may also, if you so desire, use Form NLRB-4813 to designate that representative as your agent to receive exclusive service on your behalf of all formal documents and written communications in the proceeding, excepting decisions directing an election and notices of an election, and further excepting subpoenas, which are served on the person to whom they are addressed. If this form is not filed, both you and your representative will receive copies of all formal documents. If it is filed copies will be served only upon your representative, and that service will be service upon you under the statute. The designation once filed shall remain valid unless a written revocation is filed with the Regional Director.

Investigation of petition

Immediately upon receipt of the petition, the regional office conducts an impartial investigation to determine if the Board has jurisdiction, whether the petition is timely and properly filed, whether the showing of interest is adequate, and if there are any other interested parties to the proceeding or other circumstances bearing on the question concerning representation.

Withdrawal or dismissal

If it is determined that the Board does not have jurisdiction or that other criteria for proceeding to an election are not met, the petitioner is offered an opportunity to withdraw the petition. Should the petitioner refuse to withdraw, the Regional Director dismisses the petition and advises the petitioner of the reason for the dismissal and of the right to appeal to the Board.

Agreement and conduct of election

Upon the determination that the criteria are met for the Board to conduct a secret ballot election to resolve the question concerning representation, the parties are afforded the opportunity to enter into a consent election agreement. There are two forms: (1) Form NLRB-651, Agreement for Consent Election, provides that the parties accept the final determination of the Regional Director. (2) Form NLRB-652, Stipulation for Certification Upon Agreement for Consent Election, provides for the right of appeal to the Board on postelection matters. The secret ballot election will be conducted by an agent of the NLRB under the terms of the agreement and the parties shall have the right to observe and certify to the conduct of the election.

Hearing

If there are material issues which the parties cannot resolve by agreement, the Regional Director may issue a notice of hearing on the petition. At the hearing, all parties will be afforded the opportunity to state their positions and present evidence on the issues.

Scheduling of a hearing does not preclude the possibility of a consent election agreement. Approval of an agreement will serve as withdrawal of the notice of hearing.

Names and addresses of eligible voters

Upon approval of an election agreement, or upon issuance of a direction of election, the employer will be required to prepare a list of the names and addresses of eligible voters. The employer must file the eligibility list with the Regional Director within seven days after approval of the election agreement, or after the Regional Director or the Board has directed an election. The Regional Director then makes the list available to all other parties. The employer is advised early of this requirement so that there will be ample time to prepare for the eventuality that such a list becomes necessary. (This list is in addition to list of employees in the proposed unit and their job classifications to be used to verify the showing of interest by a union).

FORM NLRB-508
(4-73)

r orm Approved
O.M.B. No. 64-R0003

UNITED STATES OF AMERICA
NATIONAL LABOR RELATIONS BOARD

CHARGE AGAINST LABOR ORGANIZATION OR ITS AGENTS

INSTRUCTIONS: File an original and 3 copies of this charge and an additional copy for each organization, each local and each individual named in item 1 with the NLRB regional director for the region in which the alleged unfair labor practice occurred or is occurring.	DO NOT WRITE IN THIS SPACE
	Case No.
	Date Filed

1. LABOR ORGANIZATION OR ITS AGENTS AGAINST WHICH CHARGE IS BROUGHT

a. Name	b. Union Representative to Contact	c. Phone No.

d. Address (Street, city, State and ZIP code)

e. The above-named organization(s) or its agents has (have) engaged in and is (are) engaging in unfair labor practices within the meaning of section 8(b), subsection(s) ——————— (List Subsections) ———of the National Labor Relations Act, and these unfair labor practices are unfair labor practices affecting commerce within the meaning of the Act.

2. Basis of the Charge (Be specific as to facts, names, addresses, plants involved, dates, places, etc.)

3. Name of Employer	4. Phone No.

5. Location of Plant Involved (Street, city, State and ZIP code)	6. Employer Representative to Contact

7. Type of Establishment (Factory, mine, wholesaler, etc.)	8. Identify Principal Product or Service	9. No. of Workers Employed

10. Full Name of Party Filing Charge

11. Address of Party Filing Charge (Street, city, State and ZIP code)	12. Telephone No.

13. DECLARATION

I declare that I have read the above charge and that the statements therein are true to the best of my knowledge and belief.

By ————————————————————————   ————————————————————
        (Signature of representative or person making charge)   (Title or office, if any)

Address ——————————————————————   —————————————   ——————————
                                                          (Telephone number)   (Date)

WILLFULLY FALSE STATEMENTS ON THIS CHARGE CAN BE PUNISHED BY FINE AND IMPRISONMENT (U.S. CODE, TITLE 18, SECTION 1001)

FORM NLRB-501
(2-67)

FORM EXEMPT UNDER
44 U.S.C. 3512

UNITED STATES OF AMERICA
NATIONAL LABOR RELATIONS BOARD

CHARGE AGAINST EMPLOYER

INSTRUCTIONS: *File an original and 4 copies of this charge with NLRB regional director for the region in which the alleged unfair labor practice occurred or is occurring.*	DO NOT WRITE IN THIS SPACE
	Case No.
	Date Filed

1. EMPLOYER AGAINST WHOM CHARGE IS BROUGHT

a. Name of Employer	b. Number of Workers Employed

c. Address of Establishment (Street and number, city, State, and ZIP code)	d. Employer Representative to Contact	e. Phone No.

f. Type of Establishment (Factory, mine, wholesaler, etc.)	g. Identify Principal Product or Service

h. The above-named employer has engaged in and is engaging in unfair labor practices within the meaning of section 8(a), subsections (1) and _____ of the National Labor Relations Act,
(List subsections)

and these unfair labor practices are unfair labor practices affecting commerce within the meaning of the Act.

2. Basis of the Charge (Be specific as to facts, names, addresses, plants involved, dates, places, etc.)

By the above and other acts, the above-named employer has interfered with, restrained, and coerced employees in the exercise of the rights guaranteed in Section 7 of the Act.

3. Full Name of Party Filing Charge (If labor organization, give full name, including local name and number)

4a. Address (Street and number, city, State, and ZIP code)	4b. Telephone No.

5. Full Name of National or International Labor Organization of Which It Is an Affiliate or Constituent Unit (To be filled in when charge is filed by a labor organization)

6. DECLARATION

I declare that I have read the above charge and that the statements therein are true to the best of my knowledge and belief.

By _____   _____
(Signature of representative or person filing charge)   (Title, if any)

Address _____
(Telephone number)   (Date)

WILLFULLY FALSE STATEMENTS ON THIS CHARGE CAN BE PUNISHED BY FINE AND IMPRISONMENT (U.S. CODE, TITLE 18, SECTION 1001)

GPO 943-480

FORM NLRB - 4813
(7-72)

National Labor Relations Board

NOTICE OF DESIGNATION OF REPRESENTATIVE
AS AGENT FOR SERVICE OF DOCUMENTS

CASE NO.

TO: Regional Director,

I, the undersigned party, hereby designate my representative, whose name and address appears below and who has entered an appearance on my behalf in this proceeding, as my agent to receive exclusive service of all documents and written communications relating to this proceeding, including complaints and decisions and orders, but not including charges, amended charges, subpoenas, directions of election or notices of election, and authorize the National Labor Relations Board to serve all such documents only on said representative. This designation shall remain valid until a written revocation of it signed by me is filed with the Board.

Signature of party (please sign in ink)	Representative's name, address, zip code (print or type)	
Title		
Date	Area Code	Telephone Number

FORM NLRB - 4701
(6 -78)

National Labor Relations Board
NOTICE OF APPEARANCE

CASE NO.

TO: (Check one box only) 1/

☐ Regional Director   ☐ Executive Secretary   ☐ General Counsel
                             National Labor Relations Board   National Labor Relations Board
                             Washington, D. C. 20570   Washington, D. C. 20570

The undersigned hereby enters appearance as representative of

in the above - captioned matter.

Signature of representative (please sign in ink)	Representative's name, address, zip code (print or type)
Date	
	Area Code	Telephone Number

1/   If case is pending in Washington and Notice of Appearance is sent to the General Counsel or the Executive
     Secretary, a copy should be sent to the Regional Director of the Region in which the case was filed so that
     those records will reflect the appearance.

GPO 932 243

FORM NLRB-4541
(5-80)

NATIONAL LABOR RELATIONS BOARD

NOTICE: PARTIES INVOLVED IN AN INVESTIGATION OF AN UNFAIR LABOR PRACTICE CHARGE
          SHOULD BE AWARE OF THE FOLLOWING PROCEDURES:

Right to be represented by counsel · Any party has the right to be represented by counsel or other representative in any proceeding before the National Labor Relations Board and the courts. In the event you wish to have a representative appear on your behalf, please have your representative complete Form NLRB-4701, Notice of Appearance, and forward it to the respective regional office as soon as counsel is chosen.

Designation of representative as agent for service of documents · In the event you choose to have a representative appear on your behalf, you may also, if you so desire, use Form NLRB-4813 to designate that representative as your agent to receive exclusive service on your behalf of all formal documents and written communications in the proceeding, excepting charges and amended charges, and further excepting subpoenas which are served on the person to whom they are addressed. If this form is not filed, both you and your representative will receive copies of all formal documents, including complaints, orders, and decisions. If it is filed, copies will be served only on your representative, and that service will be considered service on you under the statute. The designation, once filed, shall remain valid unless a written revocation is filed with the Regional Director.

Impartial investigation to determine whether charge has merit · Immediately upon receipt of a charge, the regional office conducts an impartial investigation to obtain all the facts which are material and relevant to the charge. In order to determine whether the charge has merit, the Region interviews the available witnesses. Your active cooperation in making witnesses available and stating your position will be most helpful to the Region.

The Region seeks evidence from all parties. Naturally, if only the charging party cooperates in the investigation, a situation results whereby the evidence presented by the charging party may warrant the issuance of a complaint, in the absence of any explanation from the party charged with having violated the law. Where evidence of meritorious defenses is made available a number of cases are withdrawn or dismissed. Your active cooperation will result in disposing of the case at the earliest possible time, whether the case has merit or not.

If the charge lacks merit, charging party has opportunity to withdraw · If it is determined that the charge lacks merit, the charging party is offered the opportunity to withdraw it. Should the charging party refuse to withdraw the charge, the Regional Director dismisses the charge, advising the charging party of its right to appeal the dismissal to the General Counsel.

If the charge has merit, the matter may be voluntarily adjusted · If the Regional Director determines that the charge has merit, all parties are afforded an opportunity to settle the matter by voluntary adjustment. It is the policy of this office to explore and encourage voluntary adjustment before proceeding with litigation before the Board and courts, which is both costly and time consuming. The Regional Director and members of the staff are always available to discuss adjustment of the case at any stage and will be pleased to receive and act promptly upon any suggestions or comments concerning settlements.

Voluntary adjustments after issuance of complaint · If settlement is not obtained, the Regional Director will issue a complaint which is the basis for litigating the matter before the Board and courts. However, issuance of a complaint does not mean that the matter cannot still be disposed of through voluntary adjustment by the parties. On the contrary, at any stage of the proceeding the Regional Director and staff will be pleased to render any assistance in arriving at an appropriate settlement, thereby eliminating the necessity of costly and time-consuming litigation.   GPO 872 956

Appendix B

What's an Appropriate Hospital Bargaining Unit?

By

Cornelius P. Quinn

REPRINTED FROM
PRENTICE-HALL
INDUSTRIAL RELATIONS GUIDE

What's an Appropriate Hospital Bargaining Unit?

by Cornelius P. Quinn, Vice-President, Management Education Center, Inc., * *Whitmore Lake, Michigan; former negotiator for Highland Park (Michigan) General Hospital, presently represents hospitals in negotiations*

[¶ 42,138] Following Congress' extension of the National Labor Relations Act to nonprofit hospitals, the National Labor Relations Board has established guidelines for hospital bargaining units. The Board has allowed some exceptions where the parties have reached a consent agreement which is outside the established guidelines. The four categories for separate bargaining units are:

1. Registered Nurses.

2. Technical employees, including Licensed Practical Nurses.

3. Service and Maintenance employees.

4. Business Office employees.

IMPACT   A union may demand an election for any of these units separately but will not be allowed to splinter small segments from within these categories. For example, the Board has denied a unit made up only of stationary engineers. On the other hand, hospital administrations will not be permitted to demand a single unit of all employees.

Registered nurses.   The Board decisions have directed elections for a unit of all full-time and regular part-time registered nurses. The Board has ruled that the classification *Charge Nurse* is *not* supervisory. The RNs excluded from the unit are those that are classified as supervisory. The Board applies the general test for supervisor that it uses in other unit determinations:

a.   The authority to hire, discharge, promote or discipline beyond the stage of verbal reprimand.

---

*7038 Whitmore Lake Road, Whitmore Lake, Mich. 48189.

b. The authority to make effective recommendations affecting employment status and wage rates.

c. Evaluation of employees for removal from probationary status, for merit increases and for promotion.

RECOMMENDATION Review and rewrite your job descriptions to cover specifically the RNs you need to designate as supervisory. The job description should spell out their responsibilities in the areas cited above.

What to do at an NLRB hearing. Simply having a written statement is insufficient. You must be able to prove and document at the NLRB hearing that your actual practices implement the written job descriptions. You should also bring to the hearing any written policy manuals, operating procedures and flow charts that document the supervisors' functions and lines of authority. Advise witnesses who hold the disputed classifications to testify (and answer under cross-examination) as to their responsibility and the amount of time spent in each of the supervisory functions. They should be prepared to supply *documented* instances in which they exercise independent supervisory authority.

WARNING If you're not careful in preparing to prove who is supervisory and who is not supervisory, you may lose certain entire categories of employees to the union. *This test for supervisors should be applied equally in your planning for the other bargaining units.*

Technical employees, including LPNs. Technical employees are those employees whose specialized training, skills, education and job requirements establish a community of interest not shared by other service and maintenance employees. The NLRB's decision to include LPNs in the unit of technical employees rather than a part of the service and maintenance unit is a good one. It recognizes the community of interest shared by technical support employees in a medical care facility.

You could prepare now by treating this group with some distinction by considering separating their wage and salary administration, as well as certain benefits recognizing their special skills. Some examples could be certain "on-call rates" granted only to this group—or sending them to technical seminars or providing them with specialized on-the-job training, both in-house and in other medical facilities. You may require a longer probationary period and more steps in their salary progression (e.g. Junior Tech, Senior Tech, or LPN 1, 2 or 3).

Service and maintenance employees. The departments that generally have been included in a single bargaining unit are: Nursing Service (aides and orderlies), Medical Records, Housekeeping, Dietary, Laundry and Maintenance. You can also add small departments with one or two unskilled workers, such as Outpatient Department Aides, Darkroom Technicians, Blood Bank Assistants and Purchasing Stockroom Personnel. Employees in these departments have been recognized as having a general community of interest. Their wages, benefits, hours of work, ability to transfer and bid on promotions, and their supervision all stem from a single source. Generally it's the hospital administrator acting through various department heads.

LIMITATIONS   Once the bargaining unit has been fixed, management's ability to discontinue the services provided by a given department is seriously impaired. Usually it can't be done except through negotiations with the union.

PROTECT YOUR SUBCONTRACTING RIGHTS   For example, if at some point after the bargaining unit has been established you wish to subcontract the maintenance, dietary and laundry services to an outside agent, your ability to make this decision could be seriously impaired. If any of those services in the past have been contracted out or are now contracted out, you should certainly investigate thoroughly the effect of including them in a single bargaining unit.

"That's not in my job." One of the real dangers in having separate bargaining units as defined by the NLRB is that the union will "build walls" around the bargaining unit work. This is faced by every unionized company today. It's important to remember that in the medical field, the union doesn't automatically have sole and exclusive jurisdiction over your right to provide the best possible patient care

simply because it has won an election to represent certain classifications of employees.

The NLRB decisions relating to appropriate bargaining units is restricted to very technical and legal distinctions between certain classes of employees. This distinction is necessary for the orderly application of the National Labor Relations Act but does not automatically turn over to the union the hospital's responsibility to provide adequate patient service.

Patient care. Resist any language in the collective bargaining agreement and any practice that detracts from patient care. There is a constant co-mingling of work performed by people in different classifications and bargaining units. The NLRB has recognized in its decision that patient contact cannot be used as a determination for an appropriate bargaining unit. A union will attempt to limit your flexibility in assigning work to employees in different job classifications and bargaining units. Your best response is: You'll be guided primarily by what is good for the patient! A service institution cannot be viewed in the same manner as a manufacturer; patient care is different from a standard production line.

OVERLAPPING FUNCTIONS Dietary Aides or Nursing Aides may serve food trays to patients but RNs and LPNs could, as a normal part of patient care, also serve and/or feed patients. This same situation could be repeated in surgery, pediatrics, intensive care, X-ray, etc. and it's important to protect the rights of each group to perform these duties.

Business office employees. They're considered a separate unit and include Admitting, Credit and Collection, Telephone Operators and Billing Clerks in departments where cash or billing is handled—i.e. Out-patient, Pharmacy and Purchasing. In industry, production and maintenance units normally do *not* include business office employees, but in a hospital a union may petition to include a business office employee unit in an existing unit of that union. The administration should insist that it be a separate bargaining unit with its own contract.

CAUTION   Make sure you retain the right to hire qualified replacements rather than be forced to promote unskilled clerks who bid for job up-grades.

One hospital's experience. A hospital that had loose contract language in this area was forced to promote four inexperienced people to the Collection Department at a time when the department head was nearing retirement. Eighteen months after that person retired, the hospital had over a million dollars in uncollected receivables. In making phone contacts to request payment of bills, the inexperienced employees failed to get commitments for payment in many instances. That hospital's inability to hire experienced collectors greatly added to its financial crisis.

Part-time, temporary and probationary employees. The NLRB has generally included *regularly scheduled part-time employees* as part of the bargaining unit. There's no objection to including permanent part-time employees in the bargaining unit. However, their probationary period should be spelled out in hours worked rather than in days worked.

Probationary employees are normally not included in the bargaining unit and therefore aren't covered by the terms of the contract, particularly as to discharge. With the high turnover in the first year of employment, it would be desirable to spell out that the probationary period be at least 90 days worked or 720 hours worked. The union normally wants as short a probationary period as possible to have the employee covered by the contract. Your present practice will probably decide whether you have a short or long probationary period.

3–6 MONTHS PREFERRED   If your hospital is not under union contract, it's advisable to make a part of your present practice a probationary period of 3 to 6 months. This would give you a basis for continuing the practice if the hospital is organized.

Temporaries normally haven't been included as part of the bargaining unit but the union has the right to negotiate restrictions over your ability to designate an employee as temporary or permanent.

Another exclusion. The NLRB also excludes guards

and security officers from being in the same bargaining unit as other employees.

Recognition clause. The language of the recognition clause in the collective bargaining agreement is frequently taken from the bargaining unit as determined for the election. Here's some sample language:

The hospital recognizes the union as the sole and exclusive bargaining agent for all permanent employees in the classifications listed in Appendix A. [Appendix A would be the salary, classification and title for all employees included in the bargaining unit.] *All other employees of the hospital including, but not limited to, those employees who perform administrative, supervisory, clerical technical and professional functions are excluded from the bargaining unit.*

The bargaining unit should be expressed in positive terms. The list of those employees whom the union has won the right to represent should be specified in the contract. *Be sure* not to put the recognition clause in negative terms—i.e. *All employees of the hospital are in the unit excluding* (and then you list all the classifications that are excluded.) This raises a hassle with the union every time a new job's created and a decision has to be made whether or not it's included. Specific language will avoid that problem.

Summary. In bargaining with the union about the size of the unit, you should normally keep these points in mind:

1. Try to keep the unit homogeneous. All supervisory and professional positions should be excluded.

2. Try to keep probationary and temporary employees out of the unit.

3. Aim for a clear definition of the positions and classifications the union represents.

CAUTION Since NLRB coverage of medical facilities is relatively new, new guidelines keep coming down. To keep abreast of the latest developments, see P-H Labor Relations Guide.

Appendix C

NLRB Decision: Bank Bargaining Unit

UNITED STATES OF AMERICA
BEFORE THE NATIONAL LABOR RELATIONS BOARD
SEVENTH REGION

NATIONAL BANK OF DETROIT
Employer

and · · · · · · · · · · · · · · · · Case No. 7-RC-9869

LOCAL 79, SERVICE EMPLOYEES INTER-
NATIONAL UNION, AFL-CIO

Earl R. Boonstra, Esq., of Detroit,
　Michigan, appearing for the Employer.
Lee R. Franklin, Attorney, of Detroit,
　Michigan, appearing for the Petitioner.

DECISION AND ORDER

Upon a petition duly filed under Section 9(c) of the National Labor Relations Act, a hearing was held before Richard D. Hayes, Hearing Officer of the National Labor Relations Board. The Hearing Officer's rulings made at the hearing are free from prejudicial error and are hereby affirmed.

Pursuant to the provisions of Section 3(b) of the Act, the Board has delegated its powers in connection with this case to the undersigned Regional Director.

Upon the entire record in this case, the Regional Director finds:

1. The Employer is engaged in commerce within the meaning of the Act and it will effectuate the purposes of the Act to assert jurisdiction herein.

2. The labor organization involved claims to represent certain employees of the Employer.

3. No question affecting commerce exists concerning the representation of certain employees of the Employer within the meaning of Section 9(c)(1) and Section 2(6) and (7) of the Act, for the following reasons:

The parties are in disagreement as to the scope of the appropriate unit. *The Petitioner seeks a unit composed of the computer operators, key punch operators, computer tape librarians, interpreter machine operators, tabulator machine operators, and sorters employed in the Employer's Computer Service Department.* The Petitioner would further limit its unit to only those employees in the above-mentioned classifications, who work on the eighth floor at the Employer's main office in Detroit, Michigan. Petitioner alleges that there are approximately 375 employees in the unit which it seeks. Contrariwise, the Employer contends that the only appropriate unit is one comprised of all office clerical employees employed by the Employer at not only its main office in Detroit but also its outlying branch locations.

The Employer is one of the largest banks in the United States employing approximately five to six thousand persons of whom approximately twenty-five hundred, including those employees sought by the Petitioner, are classified by the Employer as office clerical employees. The Employer has approximately one hundred branch locations, all within a twenty-five mile radius of its main office.

The Computer Service Department handles two types of work: (1) checks and deposits sent into the department from the Distribution and Transit Departments; and (2) "all other work" which includes the processing of work for other departments within the bank. The employees within the Computer Service Department divide their working time almost equally between the performance of each of the above-specified functions. Work is delivered to the eighth floor by input-output clerks. It is then identified and delivered to the input-output coordinator for scheduling. There are two input-output coordinators on each of the three shifts, most of whom are former computer operators who also perform some key punch work in connection with their position.

Once the incoming work has been scheduled, it is then transferred to either the key punch or data control areas for further preliminary processing. In the key punch area, key punch operators reduce the incoming data to IBM cards on a machine which operates similarly to a standard typewriter. Key punch operators also do some distribution work and serve occasionally as typists. In the data control area, employees "batch" together the checks and deposits that are later to be run on the sorters.[1] They also do some general pickup work throughout the bank and run sorters when necessary. After the key punch and data control departments have completed their function, the incoming data is then scheduled to be run on the computers.

Computer Operators are classified as either 1, 2, or 3 according to degree of experience, with 1 the lowest grade and 3 the highest. The record indicates that the Employer hires both experienced and inexperienced computer operators, the experienced operators being hired at one of the higher classifications.

After the scheduled data has been run on the computers, clerks from input-output control pick up the work and deliver it to either the microfilm area or the data control area. These clerks also do some "bursting" and "decollating" (by machine, not by hand), since most of the computer printouts are in a continuous form and have to be separated. In the microfilm area, clerks reduce the data received to microfilm. Data Control on the other hand is responsible for the accounting function of "balancing" the data received from the computers, preparing billing for correspondent banks and customer payroll for services rendered, reconciling data received from the Computer Department and on occasion operating sorters

---

[1]A sorter is a machine into which checks and deposit slips are fed to be sorted in separate compartments in accordance with the programming of the machine. The sorter operator feeds the checks and deposits into the machine and retrieves them from the various compartments after they have been sorted.

and key punch machines. *All of these functions are performed by employees classified by the Employer as clerks.* After Data Control has completed its function, clerks from the input-output control area deliver the finished product to its appropriate destination within the bank. The Petitioner does not seek to represent any of these "clerks," but would limit its unit to those classifications previously mentioned herein.

The training involved in learning to be a key punch operator or computer operator varies from two or three days of on-the-job training for key punch operators to longer on-the-job training, either separate from or in conjunction with a formal schooling program, for computer operators. The Employer, however, has no set requirements regarding the training or skill, if any, an employee must have to fill one of these positions. *In many instances, available openings are filled by clerical employees at the bank who are interested in working in the Computer Service Department.*

With respect to sorters and tabulator machine operators, the training involved to learn these jobs is primarily on-the-job training. A sorter operator loads checks into the compartments of a sorter, presses a button and the checks are sorted by the machine. Tabulator operators operate interpreter machines and six or seven other types of tabulating equipment used in the bank. The operation of this equipment requires no formal training as the necessary skills can be acquired in a few days to a few weeks of on-the-job training.

The computer tape librarians are responsible for filing and maintaining a library of computer tapes and discs that are necessary to run the various jobs. They also do some balancing work similar to that performed by the data control clerks. The record reveals that the duties of the tape librarian are very similar to those performed by file clerks and that no special training is required for this position.

All employees of the Employer, including those sought by the Petitioner, are hired by the Employer's corporate personnel department; receive identical fringe benefits, except that insurance coverage fluctuates depending upon the salary or hourly rate paid to an employee; are subject to the same promotion policies; and are paid the same wage rate as other employees in the same job classification irrespective of the department or branch in which they work. There are both hourly rated and salaried employees in the unit sought by the Petitioner.

Supervision in the Computer Service Department emanates from the Manager of Computer Services who has under him departmental managers who manage the various departments, such as data control and key punch. Under the departmental managers there are individual supervisors on each of the three shifts.

The unit sought by the Petitioner consists of some, but not all, of the employees working on the eighth floor at the Employer's main office in the Computer Service and Transit Departments. Employees in the unit sought by the Petitioner operate computers, key punch machines, sorters, tabulating machines and other similar equipment. *Operation of this equipment is not, however, limited to those employees sought by the Petitioner. The Employer has employees in other departments and on other floors of its main office who operate the same or similar equipment as that operated by the employees sought by the Petitioner.*

Although the Computer Service Department is to some degree separated from other departments in the bank, the separation is not for purposes of segregating these employees or their particular duties from the other bank employees. It is rather to protect the machinery against dust and other outside variables which could cause its malfunction. *Indeed, the evidence indicates that computer service employees have a great deal of contact with employees from other departments.* In addition to the evidence presented by the Employer as to the amount of employee contact, one of the Petitioner's witnesses testified that employees from other departments "quite frequently" come into the Computer Service Department. The evidence also indicates that there is some interchange of employees between the Computer Service Department and other departments at the Employer's main branch office. During the period beginning March 30, 1969, and ending March 18, 1970, there were a total of 19 transfers to and from the computer services area from and to other areas of the Employer's bank. *In addition to these "permanent" transfers, there is frequent "borrowing and loaning" of employees between the various departments at the Employer's bank, including the Computer Service Department. The Computer Service Department operates 24 hours a day on a three-shift basis. It is not, however, the only department operating on this basis.*

It is clear from the record evidence that the unit sought by the Petitioner is not one comprised of "technical" employees or "craftsmen," as the Board uses these terms. See *Litton Industries of Maryland, Incorporated,* 125 NLRB 722; *American Potash & Chemical Corporation,* 107 NLRB 1418. In this connection, I note that most of the job classifications sought by the Petitioner require little, if any, formal training and can be learned by on-the-job experience within a time period varying from a few days to a few weeks. There is no indication that any of these employees exercise independent judgment in the performance of their job duties. Rather, it appears that the functions they perform are of a routine nature, recurring from day to day with little if any variation.

Nor is there any evidence that employees in the unit sought by the Petitioner have interests sufficiently distinct from the other employees in the Computer Service Department (or indeed from other office clerical employees throughout the Employer's entire operation) to warrant setting them apart for collective-bargaining purposes. The Employer's operations exhibit a high degree of integration and interdependence among the various departments. Unlike the situations in *Bank of America, National Trust and Savings Association,* 174 NLRB No. 51, and *Central Valley National Bank,* 154 NLRB 995, *the employees sought herein do not constitute a homogeneous group of skilled employees, distinct from the other bank employees.* Rather, the employees sought by the Petitioner work in daily contact with employees classified by the Employer as "clerks," none of whom the Petitioner seeks to represent. Further, employees performing similar, if not the same, duties work in other areas of the Employer's bank.

Accordingly, as the unit sought by the Petitioner constitutes but an arbitrary segment of a broader grouping of clerical employees, I shall grant the Employer's motion to dismiss the petition herein for lack of an appropriate unit. *Banco Credito Y Ahorro Ponceno,* 160 NLRB 1504; *GM Corp., GM Photographic Engineering Center,* 143 NLRB 647; *General Insurance Company of America,* 108 NLRB 80.

IT IS HEREBY ORDERED that the petition filed herein be, and it hereby is, dismissed.

(SEAL)   /s/ Jerome H. Brooks

Dated May 11, 1970	Jerome H. Brooks, Regional Director for the
at Detroit, Michigan	Seventh Region
	National Labor Relations Board
	500 Book Building
	1249 Washington Boulevard
	Detroit, Michigan 48226

Do's and Don'ts When Combating a Union Organizing Drive

WHAT A UNION CAN AND CANNOT DO DURING AN ORGANIZING DRIVE

A. The union may:

1. Attack the company, its supervisors, and all its practices.

2. Promise improved wages and benefits including specific amounts if elected.

3. Threaten that the company will take away benefits; reduce

wages, lay off employees, or close the plant if the union is
not selected.

4. Ask employees about their union views or how they intend
   to vote.

5. Give assistance to employees in supporting the union.

6. Visit employees in their homes.

7. Give free dues to those who join the union early.

8. Promise that there will not be a strike if it is selected.

B. The union may not:

1. Harm or threaten to harm employees or their property.

2. Threaten employees who do not support it with economic
   reprisal if it is selected.

C. Union organizers who are not employees.

In connection with impromptu visits by union representatives, your supervisors should be under instructions not to permit any strangers or visitors
in the plant. They have no right there and can be told to leave and/or
escorted out. The union can handbill at plant entrances on public property.

D. Employees who support or oppose the union must be treated the same, but.

1. Need not be permitted to solicit during working hours;

2. Need not be permitted to distribute literature in work areas, but must be permitted to do so in non-work areas of the plant during non-working hours.

WHAT THE COMPANY CAN AND CANNOT DO DURING AN UNION-ORGANIZING DRIVE

In two parts, we have set out a number of items which in total pretty well cover the areas supervisory employees are permitted to cover when dealing with union organizing efforts. Nothing is mentioned with respect to basic programs and policies, but rest assured that you may continue all existing programs and policies in effect without any question whatsoever (if you can *prove* it).

A. Legal aspects of what you can and cannot do

A company has the right to campaign and communicate with employees. For example, the company or its supervisors may:

1. Tell employees what its negotiating position will be if it is unionized.

2. Inform employees from time to time on the benefits they presently enjoy. (Avoid veiled promises or threats.)

3. Inform employees that the signing of a union authorization card does not mean they must vote for the union if there is an election.

4. Inform employees of the disadvantage of belonging to the union, such as the possibility of strikes, serving in a picket line, dues, fines, assessments, and one-man or clique rule.

5. Inform employees that you prefer to deal with them rather than have the union or any other outsider settle employee grievances.

6. Inform employees what you think about unions and about union policies.

7. Inform employees about any prior experience you have had with unions and whatever you know about the union officials trying to organize them.

8. Inform employees that no union can obtain more than you as an employer are able to give.

9. Inform employees how their wages and benefits compare with unionized or nonunionized concerns, where wages are lower and benefits less desirable.

10. Inform employees that the local union probably will be dominated by the international union, and that they, the members, will have little to say in its operation.

11. Inform employees of any untrue or misleading statements made by the organizer. You may give employees the correct facts.

12. Give opinions on unions and union leaders, even in derogatory terms.

13. Give legal position on labor-management matters.

14. Reply to union attacks on company policies or practices.

15. Advise employees of their legal rights, provided that employer does not encourage or finance an employee suit or proceeding.

16. Declare a fixed policy in opposition to compulsory union membership contracts.

17. Campaign against union seeking to represent the employees.

18. Insist that any solicitation of membership or discussion of union affairs be conducted outside of working time.

19. Administer discipline, layoff, grievance, etc., without regard to the union membership or nonmembership, or the employee involved.

20. Treat both union and nonunion employees alike in making assignments of preferred work, desired overtime, etc.

21. Enforce rules impartially, regardless of the employee's membership activity in a union.

22. Tell employees, if they ask, that they are free to join or not to join any organization so far as their status with the company is concerned.

B. The company or its supervisors may not:

1. Attend any union meetings, park across the street from the union hall to see which employees enter the hall, or engage in any undercover activity which would indicate that the employees are being kept under surveillance to determine who is and who is not participating in the union program.

2. Tell employees that the company will fire or punish them if they engage in union activity.

3. Lay off or discharge any employee for union activity.

4. Grant employees wage increases or special concessions in order to keep the union out.

5. Bar employee union representatives from soliciting employee memberships during *non*-working hours.

6. Ask employees about confidential union matters, meetings,

etc. (Some employees may, of their own accord, walk up and tell of such matters. It is not an unfair practice to listen, but you must not ask questions to obtain additional information.)

7. Ask employees what they think about the union or a union representative.

8. Ask employees how they intend to vote.

9. Threaten employees with economic reprisal for participating in union activities. For example, threaten to move the plant or close the business, curtail operations, reduce employee benefits.

10. Promise benefits to employees if they reject the union.

11. Give financial support or other assistance to a union or to employees, regardless of whether or not they are supporting or opposing the union.

12. Announce that you will not deal with a union.

13. Tell employees that the company will fire or punish them if they engage in union activities.

14. Ask employees whether or not they belong to a union or have signed up for a union.

15. Ask an employee, during the interview when you are hiring him, about his affiliation with a labor organization.

16. Make anti-union statements or actions that might show your preference for a nonunion person.

17. Make distinctions between union and nonunion employees when assigning overtime work or desirable work.

18. Purposely team up nonunion employees and keep them apart from those you think may belong to the labor organization.

19. Transfer workers on the basis of union affiliations or activity.

20. Choose workers to be laid off on the basis of weakening the union's strength or discouraging membership in it.

21. Discriminate against union people when disciplining employees.

22. By the nature of the work assignment, indicate that you would like to get rid of an employee because of his union activity.

23. Discipline union employees for a particular action and permit nonunion employees to go unpunished for the same action.

24. Deviate from company policy for the purpose of getting rid of a union person.

25. Take actions that adversely affect an employee's job or any pay rate because of union activity.

26. Become involved in arguments that may lead to a physical encounter with an employee over the union question.

27. Threaten a union member through a third party.

28. Threaten your workers or coerce them in an attempt to influence their vote.

29. Promise employees a reward or any future benefits if they decide "no union."

30. Tell employees overtime work (and premium pay) will be discontinued if unionized.

31. Say unionization will take away vacations, or other benefits and privileges presently enjoyed.

32. Promise employees promotions, raises, other benefits if they get out of the union or refrain from joining it.

33. Start a petition or circular against the union or encourage or take part in its circulation if started by employees.

34. Urge employees to try to induce others to oppose the union or keep out of it.

35. Visit the homes of employees to urge them to reject the union

Management Education Center
7038 Whitmore Lake Road
Whitmore Lake, Michigan 48189
(313) 769-2226